MULTIPLY

MULTIPLY

Building an Enduring Ministry

DAVID NELSON

Foreword by David C. Deuel

WIPF & STOCK · Eugene, Oregon

MULTIPLY
Building an Enduring Ministry

Copyright © 2024 David Nelson. All rights reserved. Except for brief quotations in critical publications or reviews, no part of this book may be reproduced in any manner without prior written permission from the publisher. Write: Permissions, Wipf and Stock Publishers, 199 W. 8th Ave., Suite 3, Eugene, OR 97401.

Wipf & Stock
An Imprint of Wipf and Stock Publishers
199 W. 8th Ave., Suite 3
Eugene, OR 97401

www.wipfandstock.com

PAPERBACK ISBN: 978-1-6667-8991-1
HARDCOVER ISBN: 978-1-6667-8992-8
EBOOK ISBN: 978-1-6667-8993-5

05/29/24

Crossing Cultures International
P.O. Box #610
Brandon FL 33509
https://www.cciequip.org

CCI's mission is to glorify God by equipping Christ followers with comprehensive training for effective ministry.

Scripture quotations are from The Holy Bible, English Standard Version® (ESV®), copyright ©2001 by Crossway Bibles, a publishing ministry of Good News Publishers. Used by permission. All rights reserved.

And the word of God continued to increase, and the number of the disciples multiplied greatly in Jerusalem, and a great many of the priests became obedient to the faith.

—Acts 6:7

Contents

Foreword by David C. Deuel — ix

Preface — xi

Acknowledgments — xv

Introduction — 1

Principle #1   The Power of a Godly Model — 10

Principle #2   A Close, Personal Relationship — 26

Principle #3   Effective Biblical Training — 37

Principle #4   Giving Guided Opportunities — 59

Principle #5   Entrusted Ministry — 82

Principle #6   The Centrality of the Local Church — 100

Principle #7   Engaging in God's Mission in the World — 116

Principle #8   Empowered by the Holy Spirit — 134

The Biblical Pattern for Equipping and Multiplying Leaders — 144

Conclusion — 180

Bibliography — 183

Foreword

OUR GOD IS A multiplying God. From the dawn of time and into the last days when God will consummate his plan, he multiplies elements in his creation. It is a tool he uses to work his plan. His story recorded from Genesis to Revelation is one account after another of multiplication.

Sometimes multiplying is miraculous. Take for example the supernatural increase of the children of Israel early in Exodus. The biblical account uses words and images from the Genesis creation narrative to describe the supernaturally rapid increase of the Israelites in Egyptian bondage: "But the people of Israel were fruitful and increased greatly; they multiplied and grew exceedingly strong, so that the land was filled with them" (Exod 1:7). Then there was Jesus unforgettably feeding the hungry crowd of five thousand by multiplying the loaves and the fishes.

Other times multiplication is slower and more providential. It is less spectacular and more consistent with God's patient guiding over the millennia. Multiplying is also the formula for God to accomplish his sovereign plan.

At creation, God's plan for his image connected us with him so that we reflect his glory to people around us. He may increase aspects of our lives like our years. But God can also decrease the numbers of things. Some people's lives are cut short. All increasing and decreasing is consistent with God's plan for his creation.

In the present study, God multiplies people and their churches to accomplish his redemptive plan. His salvation story is about multiplying a people for himself, those he possesses by bringing them into his family. It is about going home to the Father's house.

Almost overnight, the gospel spread and churches popped up all over the Mediterranean world and beyond. This exponential growth continues today. It is multiplication.

Christianity is the largest and fastest-growing religion.[1] This is no human accomplishment; the God of multiplication builds his church, and "the gates of hell shall not prevail against it" (Matt 16:18). Those trying to suppress the church and stop its spread discover that the harder you try to stop it, the faster it grows. It is, at once, miraculous and providential.

In this study, Dr. David Nelson, a seasoned trainer of Christian leaders across the globe, writes to remind us that the Spirit empowers multiplication and that our task is to serve the God of multiplication by conducting his mission. He will work in us and through us "without hindrance" (Acts 28:31).

DAVID C. DEUEL, PHD
Academic Dean Emeritus, The Master's Academy International
Senior Research Fellow Emeritus, International Disability Center
Catalyst for Disability Concerns, Lausanne Movement

---

1. Zurlo, *Global Christianity*.

Preface

THINK A MINUTE ABOUT the power of one apple. Inside the apple are about five seeds. Plant each of those seeds and in about five years that one seed will be five trees producing three hundred apples each (or 1,500 apples) in a season. Those 1,500 apples also have five seeds each. Plant those seeds from each apple and that will produce 7,500 trees, which will produce over two million apples—all in about ten years. This is the power of multiplication. God has invested in all his creation this ability—to multiply. This is also true in making disciples. In Acts 6:7, we read that "the word of God continued to increase, and the number of disciples multiplied greatly in Jerusalem." God has also invested in us the ability to multiply disciples. But like the apple, it takes years of investing, teaching, admonishing, and modeling to see this happen.

If you're looking for the best next thing, program, or tactic that will *quickly* transform your ministry and transform it into a megachurch or mega-ministry, *this is not a quick fix program.* Over the last thirty years, it seems that Evangelicals are looking for the next program or method to grow their ministry into a megachurch or mega-ministry. Just find where God is moving and ride the wave. Your church will grow into the thousands. Seeker sensitive. Church-planting movements. Emergent church. Disciple-making movements. Megachurches. Our propensity for large numbers instead *may* reveal an *idol* of the heart for speed and for large numbers. Matt Rhodes laments this situation. "In the intense pressure they [missionaries] feel to complete the Great Commission, missionaries often bypass the slow, unflashy work of acquiring professional skills like theological education and language fluency."[2] He continues to explain that "Missions has been inundated by a stream of 'silver-bullet' strategies. Many of these make lavish promises, ensuring well-meaning participants

---

2. Rhodes, *No Shortcut to Success*, 38.

that after reading a book or completing a short training they are now ready to lead huge movements of unchurched people to Christ."[3] His point about the lure and idol of speed is apropos: "this emphasis on speed rarely leaves time for the careful discipling of new church leaders."[4] We may really want people to trust Christ and our church reach thousands of people. Or are we in love with the power and notoriety that comes with it more than glorifying God? Only God knows.

This book is about principles—biblical principles that are time-tested and effective. How you apply them in your context is what you will need to pray and seek the Lord about. This book is about hard work—making disciples, developing relationships, following intentional principles of multiplication, and a ministry of training and teaching people in the Word.

In the book *The Patient Ferment of the Early Church: The Improbable Rise of Christianity in the Roman Empire*, author Alan Kreider notes that by the third century Christianity had spread all over the Roman Empire. "By the time of Constantine's accession, the churches not only had substantial numbers of members; they extended across huge geographical distances and demanded the attention of the imperial authorities."[5] This was not due to an aggressive evangelism program, but instead through patient trust in God's sovereign work in people's lives as they witnessed Christians who lived lives of integrity in their business dealings with those around them. The early church focused on prayer, worship, and lives of integrity. Baptismal candidates were trained by catechists who spent two to three years with these candidates to ensure that they were ready for baptism. Churches celebrated the Lord's Supper together regularly and had love feasts together where they shared meals together. Churches were composed of various ethnicities and people from across all economic specters. Roman culture was a culture of verticality, much like India, where distinctions were vivid, most illustrated by the Colosseum, where gladiatorial games were fought. People could not simply choose where they would sit but sat according to their rank—the emperor along with the seven Vestal Virgins at the bottom along with wealthy politicians, then the wealthy educated. Towards the top sat women and last of all were slaves at the very top. Christians, however, demonstrated a love for each other no matter what their social standing was, physically

---

3. Rhodes, *No Shortcut to Success*, 38.
4. Rhodes, *No Shortcut to Success*, 39.
5. Kreider, *Patient Ferment*, 8.

demonstrated by their kiss of peace to one another regardless of their level of education or economic standing. Their lifestyle, what Kreider calls their "*habitus*," of integrity, love for one another, passionate worship, training of baptismal candidates, and fellowship led to the tremendous growth of the early church.

I wonder . . . can we *patiently* trust in God's sovereign work in people's lives and live such lives of integrity and love that people will want to know the Lord Jesus we follow? In a culture that values immediacy, *patience* is not a virtue. We have all heard about the person who prayed for patience. "Lord, give me patience and give it to me *now*." Patience is not a virtue of the Western world, or for the world in general. But it was the characteristic of the early church, and this is what it takes to see a ministry of multiplication.

A ministry of multiplication is not immediate or fast-paced. Such a ministry is patient, trusting in God to sovereignly work in people's lives. It is a ministry that is intentional and deliberate, following sound biblical principles that have stood the test of time.

Math. Add. Subtract. Multiply. Divide. These are all words that may conjure up horrific memories in our minds or ill feelings in our hearts, depending upon our ability and understanding of math. Yet, the Scripture uses the word "multiply" in two specific contexts—in creation and in the early church. God endowed us with the ability physically to multiply. We have children and our children have children.

Many women who cannot bear children feel incomplete, unfulfilled, and sometimes ashamed or humiliated, as did Hannah in 1 Samuel 1. In an honor-shame culture, a person's standing is determined by the value people place on them in the community. Hannah felt ashamed and her husband's other wife provoked and humiliated her.

God also has endowed us with the ability to multiply *spiritually* by making disciples. Yet, most ministries have failed to harness this ability God has given to us through his Holy Spirit. We see the example of Jesus as a multiplier. He made disciples who made disciples who made disciples who made disciples. Jesus called them to follow him, not to lead others. We are a culture possessed with the idea of leadership, while the New Testament presents Jesus as rigorously following the will of his heavenly Father. His disciples followed him. We are followers of Christ today because a follower of Christ made us a follower of Christ.

While most ministries focus on *addition* in converts, in God's Word we see the principle of *multiplication*. Most pastors think in maintenance mode—adding enough members to provide for the budget of the church. They think about addition, not multiplication. They desire to do the work of the ministry—fulfilling their ministry from the Lord. Usually that is as far as they can see—what *they* (and their staff) *can do*. Church staff positions usually come from the outside. The paid staff and a few members do the work while the rest watch like spectators at a football game. Finding people from the outside communicates to members that only those from the outside, who are seminary graduates, are qualified for "full-time service."

The Bible, however, reveals to us principles for multiplication. What principles can we follow that will empower our churches and ministries to multiply like the early church multiplied itself? What did Jesus do that empowered his disciples to multiply and spread throughout the whole Roman Empire and eventually transform the culture?

We will examine eight principles for multiplication in this book. We will also look at the biblical pattern for equipping church leaders—the examples from Scripture—that reveals principles we can follow in the ministries God has placed us in and entrusted to us. I pray that you apply these eight principles to your life and ministry and experience the multiplying effect of making disciples who make disciples.

Dr. David Nelson
Tampa, Florida
Crossing Cultures International (CCI)

Acknowledgments

I would like to express my gratitude for the people who have greatly influenced me and the principles in this book. First and foremost, I would like to thank my Lord and Savior Jesus Christ for sending me to the nations and filling me with his Holy Spirit. I have never felt alone, no matter how remote an area I have visited. Jesus' promise in Matthew 28:20 still rings true today: "I am with you always, to the end of the age." I have seen the protection, provision, and presence of the Lord through his Holy Spirit in my life everywhere he has sent me.

I would like to thank my parents, Charles and Maybelle. My dad taught me fishing, hunting, and gardening. My mom believed in Christ when she was pregnant with me. She taught me the Bible. She prayed for me throughout my teen years. She rejoiced with concern when we moved to a remote area in the Philippines. She has been one of our prayer warriors for many years.

I would like to thank my wife, Mindy, who moved to the Philippines with me and our firstborn child in 1986. She eagerly and gracefully embraced the role as missionary and wife as we pursued starting churches that would be led by their own pastors. After we moved back to the USA, she joyfully accompanied me for ten years all across the world. She ministered to many ladies around the world, including pastors' wives, missionaries, and other women ministry leaders.

I would like to thank our vice president of corporate operations, Glenn Kurka. Glenn recruited us before we were married to the Philippines as short-term missionaries and then later invited us to return in 1986 and join the team he had assembled. He mentored me and modeled for me many godly characteristics. I am blessed that he is on the CCI team today as he oversees all the administrative duties and the structure of the CCI ministry. I would like to also thank our director of ministry relations, Amanda Boston, who has helped edit this book and has been a great encourager to me. She has arranged our ministry tours around the USA, manages our social media mediums and formats, and edits my monthly newsletters.

I would like to thank Bryan Thomas, who mentored me in the Philippines when I was right out of seminary. He showed me what it meant to love and disciple people and taught me the importance of local church-based non-formal training.

I would like to thank D. Jim O'Neill for his investment in my life in drawing the best out of me. His engaging me in dialogue and challenging me helped in my leadership development.

I would like to thank Randy Gardner, president of Bible Training Centre for Pastors, in Atlanta, Georgia. Randy visited me every six months during our last three years in the Philippines. He spent time with me then and after we returned to the USA, listening and offering godly counsel to me.

I would like to thank the board of directors of CCI, who have guided me and helped shape the CCI ministry. Thank you, Tim, Scott, Kevin, Brad, Lynn, and Bud for your encouragement and guidance. Their investment in me personally, their love for the CCI ministry, their generosity, and their friendship have been a great encouragement to me over the years.

I would like to also thank the Lord for the counsel of my close friend Norris Brown. Norris served as a board member for several years, served on the CCI team without pay, and has been a great encouragement to me as we have traveled together to many countries on mission trips, gone fishing together, attended baseball and hockey games together, and hiked many miles together.

To God be the glory; great things he has done!

Introduction

THE WORD "MULTIPLY" MAY conjure up in our minds the unending horrors of mathematical tables and formulas that leave us in a state of confusion. Yet, we experience the challenges and benefits of math daily. According to *Merriam-Webster*, "multiply" means "to increase greatly in number or amount; to become much more numerous; to cause (something) to increase greatly in number or amount; to increase in number by reproducing."[1] Thus, multiplication is more than mathematical formulas; it is *something that we experience daily*.

In the Bible, the word "multiply" is used in significant ways in both the Old and New Testaments. The words "increase" and "grow" are related to multiplication.

In the *New Bible Dictionary*, Blair defines "increase" in this way:

> A noun or verb meaning *multiplication* or growth, translating sundry Heb. and Gk. Words. Primarily the term involved the natural reproduction and germination of cattle and harvest, but always under God's direction and control (Lv. 26:4; Dt. 7:13; Ps. 67:6), as acknowledged by the tithe (Dt. 14:22; *cf.* Pr. 3:9). Hence prosperity is a sign of God's favour (Dt. 6:3), adversity of his displeasure (Je. 15:8), and man's exacting gain from possessions is condemned in the same manner as usury (Lv. 25:37; Ezk. 18:8ff.; *cf.* Ps. 62:10). . . .. In the NT the term is applied to the growth of the church in numbers (Acts 6:7; 16:5; 1 Cor. 3:6) and in depth (Eph. 4:16; Col. 2:19). It is also applied to individuals generally (Lk. 2:52; Jn. 3:30; Acts 9:22), and specifically with regard to faith (Lk. 17:5; 2 Cor. 10:15), love (1 Thes. 3:12; 4:10), knowledge (Col. 1:10), or ungodliness (2 Tim. 2:16).[2]

Brand adds:

---

1. http://www.merriam-webster.com/dictionary/multiply.
2. Blair, *New Bible Dictionary*, s.v. "increase," 505 (emphasis added).

The increase of the word of God (Acts 6:7) refers to the spread of the gospel message. *Increase* is used both for the numerical growth of the church (Acts 16:5) and for maturation (Eph. 4:16; Col. 2:19). Christian maturity is evidenced by an increase in love (1 Thess. 3:12; 4:10) and knowledge of God (Col. 1:10). Boasting in the results of one's work for God is without a basis since God gives the increase (1 Cor. 3:6, Col. 2:19).[3]

Thus, multiplication is both numerical growth and spiritual growth. While numerical growth is quantifiable, spiritual growth is difficult to measure. However, a ministry that grows numerically without spiritual growth or maturation is doomed for hardship and decline. Likewise, a ministry that grows in maturation (spiritual health) is certain to grow numerically. When a tree is healthy, has a good source of water, and has a sound root system (foundation), it will bloom, blossom, and bear much fruit. This is precisely what Jesus desires happen in his church and in our lives, but without him working in our lives and us abiding in him, we can do nothing (John 15:5).

MULTIPLY IN THE OLD TESTAMENT

The root word for "multiply" in the Old Testament is from the Hebrew word רָבָה (*rabah*). Rabah is found 246 times in 208 verses in the OT. Twenty-four times we read this word in the book of Genesis. During creation, God pronounces a blessing upon animal and human life, endowing them with the ability to reproduce, and exhorts them to fill the earth and "multiply." God says to man, "Be fruitful and *multiply* and fill the earth and subdue it and have dominion over the fish of the sea and over the birds of the heavens and over every living thing that moves on the earth." God's intention for man was to multiply and rule over all creation. According to Sailhamer,

> The importance of the blessing in v.28 cannot be overlooked. Throughout the remainder of the Book of Genesis and the Pentateuch, the "blessing" remains a central theme. The living creatures have already been blessed on the fifth day (v.22); thus the author's view of the blessing extends beyond man to that of the whole of God's living creatures. In v.28 man is also included in God's blessing. The blessing itself in these verses is primarily "posterity": "Be fruitful and increase in number; fill the earth."

---

3. Brand et al., "Increase," 816.

> Thus already the fulfillment of the blessing is tied to man's "seed" and the notion of "life"—two themes that will later dominate the narratives of the Book of Genesis.[4]

Built into the human DNA is the ability and desire for multiplication. This is obvious as we see mankind's propensity towards and abuse of sexual activity. Pornography has exploited this built-in DNA characteristic. Advertising also deliberately displays the feminine sex to capture men's attention and, thus, their money.

Multiplication also has a direct connection with ruling. According to Waltke, "This entails the notion of multiplication so as to rule (cf. 1:28). The birds and fish rule their realms through multiplication."[5] Regarding God's blessing upon mankind, Waltke states that "Humanity is given a twofold cultural mandate: to fill the earth and to rule the creation as benevolent kings (Gen. 9:2; Ps. 8:5–8; Heb. 2:5–9)."[6] Thus, God's blessing in multiplication also relates to *ruling* over God's creation.

In the creation story, God also indicates that each species would multiply "according to its kind." Thus, there would be a limitation or boundary to how plants and animals would multiply. In other words, one being would procreate within its own kind and produce a like creature. Like would produce like. A principle from this emerges indicating to us that *we produce what we are, and we do not produce what we are not*. Later, we will see that this also carries over into ministry training. In making disciples, those we disciple become like us. Theological professors beget theological professors. Educators beget educators. Church planters produce church planters. Pastors beget pastors. Evangelists produce evangelists.

Later in the books of Genesis and Exodus, God promises to Noah, Abraham, and Jacob that they would multiply and fill the earth. Genesis 17:1–2 reads, "When Abram was ninety-nine years old the Lord appeared to Abram and said to him, 'I am God Almighty; walk before me, and be blameless, that I may make my covenant between me and you, and may *multiply* you greatly.'"[7] Built within the covenant was God's desire and purpose to multiply Abraham's descendants. In Exodus 1:7, we see the fulfillment of this: "But the people of Israel were fruitful and increased greatly; they *multiplied* and grew exceedingly strong, so that the land was

---

4. Sailhamer, "Genesis," 38.
5. Waltke and Fredricks, *Genesis: a Commentary*, 63.
6. Waltke and Fredricks, *Genesis: a Commentary*, 67.

7. Unless otherwise indicated, all quotations from the Bible are from the English Standard Version (ESV).

filled with them." Thus, within creation and within the people of God, God created them with the DNA for multiplication. God's desire was for a godly heritage, where God's people raised up godly children for God's heritage and glory (cf. Mal 2:15).

Related words include מַרְבֶּה (*marbeh*) for "abundance" (Isa 33:23) or "increase" (Isa 9:6), מִרְבָּה (*mirbâ*) for "much" (Ezek 23:32, only), מַרְבִּית (*marbît*) for "increase" and "multitude," תַּרְבּוּת (*tarbût*) for "increase" and "brood" (Num 32:14, only), and תַּרְבִּית (*tarbît*) for "increment," "usury," and "interest."

According to Harris et al.,

> This [rabah] is the West Semitic form of a very common term cognate to Ugaritic *rb* and Akkadian *rahu*. This is the suffix common to so many Babylonian-Assyrian names, e.g. "Hammurabi"= "The god Ham (perhaps ʿammu) is great."... "Multiply" is read by all of the versions, but in subsequent usages a variety of translations appear, "increase" (Gen 7:17–18); "be many" (I Chr 23:17); "so much" (Gen 43:34). In single instances a great many more meanings are in evidence. In the Hiphil stem the standard and most common meaning is "multiply," but a variety of other translations are also given: "ask much" (Gen 34:12); "gather much" (Ex 16:18); "yield much" (Neh 9:37); "give more" (Num 26:54); "to heap" (Ezk 24:10)...Although generally restricted to quantitative contexts, the root *rābâ* has some use in metaphorical expressions. It is used in the following special senses: "live long" (Job 29:18); "make words great," "to brag" against God (Job 34:37), and "have many children" (I Chr 7:4).[8]

Thus, in the Old Testament, God creates the world with the ability to multiply according to one's own kind. *Multiplication is a direct result of God's proclamation of blessing upon animal and human life.* In addition, God multiplied the descendants of Abraham according to his promise and power. *Multiplication is God's initiative through the life of Abraham and is based upon the promises of God.* God is a God of abundance and has built within his creation a capacity to increase and to multiply offspring, a tithe, and his people.

---

8. Harris et al., *Theological Wordbook of the Old Testament*, 828.

INTRODUCTION

Multiply in the New Testament

The words that have the idea of multiplying in the New Testament include "increase," "grow," and "multiply." The Greek words for this include αὐξάνω (*auxanō*) and πληθύνω (*plēthunō*).

The word αὐξάνω (*auxanō*) occurs twenty-one times in the NT and is translated by the ESV as "increase," "grow," or "growth." Related to this word is αὔξησις (*auxēsis*) ("growth," two times), αὔξω (*auxō*) ("to grow," two times), συναυξάνω (*sunauxanō*) ("to grow together," one time), and ὑπεραυξάνω (*hyperauxanō*) ("to flourish," one time). In 2 Thessalonians 1:3, we read that the Thessalonians' faith had "grown abundantly." The prefix ὑπερ (*hyper*) with the verb αὐξάνω (*auxanō*) intensifies and gives emphasis to their remarkable growth. In 1 Thessalonians 1, we read that the Thessalonian believers abandoned their idols to serve the true and living God. Their testimony was broadcast throughout the whole area like a trumpet, and they became examples for the church in that region and beyond. They suffered greatly, yet became an example for all believers. In Mark 4:3ff., Jesus uses αὐξάνω (*auxanō*) in reference to the growth of the seed (i.e., the gospel) that produced thirtyfold, sixtyfold, and a hundredfold. While God's servants plant the seed, God is the one who gives *growth* (1 Cor 3:6). God not only gives seed to the sower, but he also gives grace for giving and uses the giver's gifts to encourage and bless others (2 Cor 9:10). Through the Word of God, new believers experience growth (1 Pet 2:2). Only by being closely connected to Christ can one experience growth because Christ as the Head gives growth to the body (Col 2:19). In Ephesians 4:11–16, we read that when each believer functions properly, the whole body *grows* into the image of Christ, who is the Head. *Growth, then, occurs through the Word of God proclaimed by the servants of God as they are rightly connected to Christ.*

Πληθύνω (*plēthunō*) is found twelve times in the New Testament, five times in the book of Acts (6:1, 7; 7:17; 9:31; 12:24). In Acts 6:1, because the number of disciples were "multiplying" (present-tense participle indicative of on ongoing activity), the apostles faced their first challenge: meeting the needs of Hellenistic widows. Nicoll notes that "multiply" here "denotes that the numbers *went on increasing*, and so rapidly that the Apostles found the work of relief too great for them."[9] With reference to the unmet needs of Grecian widows, Polhill comments, "The Jerusalem Christian community had witnessed considerable growth; and as is so often the case with rapid

---

9. Nicoll, *Expositor's Greek Testament: Commentary*, 164 (emphasis added).

increase, administrative problems developed."[10] However, the problem was not just an administrative problem; it was a cross-cultural problem. They faced a cross-cultural problem of caring for *Greek*-speaking Jewish widows. The Jerusalem church was composed of *Aramaic*-speaking Jews and *Greek*-speaking Jews. Greek-speaking Jews had returned to Jerusalem from the diaspora from other countries. The Septuagint was written for Greek-speaking Jews who gathered in synagogues across the Roman world. Gentile converts to Judaism, called "God-fearers," joined them in worship in the local synagogue. When cultures mix, there can be problems, but under the cross and through the Spirit, God enables us to have understanding and reconciliation. Polhill also notes,

> In Jewish society widows were particularly needy and dependent, and the Old Testament singles them out along with orphans as the primary objects of charitable deeds. The Hellenist widows may have been a particularly sizable group. Diaspora Jews often moved to Jerusalem in their twilight years to die in the holy city. When the men died, their widows were left far from their former home and family to care for them and were thus particularly in need of charity. Many of them may have been attracted to the Christian community precisely because of its concern for the material needs of its members.[11]

The apostles had the congregation choose Spirit-filled men to serve these widows. They decided to devote themselves to prayer and to "the ministry of the word" (teaching and preaching God's Word and the gospel; 6:4). According to Barrett, "Preaching is the most probable meaning of *the word of God*."[12] The word "ministry" is from the Greek noun διακονία (*diakonia*), which means service. The verbal form διακονεῖν (to serve) is found in 6:2 in reference to serving food to widows. The seven would serve *food* while the apostles would serve *God's Word*. Seven men with Greek names are brought forward and the apostles lay hands on them and pray for them, commending them to this work.

In Acts 6:7, Luke reports that the result of the apostles' decision was that "the word of God continued to *increase* [from αὐξάνω (*auxanō*)] and the number of disciples *multiplied* [from πληθύνω (*plēthunō*)] greatly in Jerusalem." Both verbs are in the imperfect tense, thus describing an ongoing action. *The Word of God was increasing, and the number of disciples*

---

10. Polhill, *Acts*, 178.
11. Polhill, *Acts*, 178.
12. Barrett, *Critical and Exegetical Commentary on Acts*, 311.

were multiplying. According to Barrett, "The meaning is clear: the word of God as the apostles continued to preach it (vv. 2, 4) *had continually increasing influence and effect*. The Word was responsible for the increasing number (ἐπληθύνετο ὁ ἀριθμός) of disciples, though these were so far confined to Jerusalem."[13] Luke notes that many priests believed in Christ as they "became obedient to the faith" (6:7).

In Acts 7:17, in Stephen's defense before the Sanhedrin, he references the growth of the Israelites in Egypt after Joseph died. They "*increased and multiplied* in Egypt." These two verbs are αὐξάνω (*auxanō*) and πληθύνω (*plēthunō*).

In Acts 9:31, after Paul's conversion and return to Tarsus, Luke summarizes this section by stating that the church (the Greek word ἐκκλησία [*ekklēsia*] is singular) all throughout Judea, Galilee, and Samaria continued to enjoy peace (imperfect verb stressing ongoing state) for a time and the church "multiplied." God gave peace to the church throughout this area and the church was built up spiritually and walked in the fear of the Lord. As a result, the church expanded.

Robertson notes, "The multiplication of the disciples kept pace with the peace, the edification, the walking in the fear of the Lord, the comfort of the Holy Spirit. The blood of the martyrs was already becoming the seed of the church. Stephen had not borne his witness in vain."[14] In this passage, Luke focuses on four aspects. First, the church enjoyed peace. There was a calm after the storm of persecution as the persecutor met Christ and his life was forever changed. Second, the church was being built up (from οἰκοδομουμένη [*oikodomoumenē*], present passive participle) through the teaching of the Word of God (cf. Acts 20:32). Jesus promised to build his church (Matt 16:18). "Building up" is used for internal, spiritual growth (cf. Eph 4:11–16). Third, they were walking in the fear of the Lord. Believers lived with respect and awe of God in their lives and reverently feared him. Finally, they walked in the exhortation or encouragement of the Holy Spirit. Their lives were guided and influenced by the Holy Spirit. This all resulted in *multiplication*. Lenski succinctly states, "The spiritual power of the church evident in its membership attracted and won men . . . *When the members walk with the fear of the Lord before their eyes and with the Spirit's encouraging voice in their hearts, the church will be strong and will also surely multiply*."[15]

13. Barrett, *Critical and Exegetical Commentary on Acts*, 316 (emphasis added).
14. Robertson, *Word Pictures in the New Testament*, Acts 9:31.
15. Lenski, *Interpretation of Acts*, 380–81 (emphasis added).

In Acts 12:24, after Herod's death due to not glorifying God, the Word of God was *increasing* (from αὐξάνω, *auxanō*) and *multiplying* (πληθύνω, *plēthunō*, in the imperfect tense signifying ongoing action in the past). Again, we have found these two words used together as in Acts 6:7 and 7:17. God causes his Word to increase and multiplies the impact of his Word. In these instances, we see that the Word of God, when proclaimed by his servants, has the power to change lives, and it *increases* and *multiplies*. Similar wording is found in Acts 16:5 and 19:20. In three instances (Acts 6:7; 9:31; and here in 12:24), Luke is summarizing his narrative section of the growth of the church. Here, even though an attempt was made by Herod to restrict the new Christian movement, God's Word prevailed, and the number of disciples *increased and multiplied*. In Acts 16:5, Luke notes that the churches "were strengthened in the faith" (Αἱ μὲν οὖν ἐκκλησίαι ἐστερεοῦντο τῇ πίστει, *ai men ekklēsiai estereounto tē pistei*) and "increased in numbers" (καὶ ἐπερίσσευον τῷ ἀριθμῷ καθ' ἡμέραν, *kai eperisseuon tō arithmō kath hēmeran*) daily after Paul, Silas, and Timothy delivered the decision from the Jerusalem council to the churches in Asia Minor where Paul and his team had preached the gospel during their first missionary journey. The word "churches" is plural, indicating local churches, and the word for "strengthen" is a passive, imperfect verb, indicating that the Holy Spirit was causing the church to strengthen. "[I]n the faith" is a reference to the content of the gospel and sound doctrine. The Word of God has the ability to strengthen a believer and to cause multiplication. In Acts 19:20, after the residents of Ephesus burned their amulets associated with magical arts, we read that "the word of the Lord continued to *increase* [αὐξάνω, *auxanō*] and prevail mightily." People responded to the gospel by repenting and believing, and the church grew rapidly. God's Word has the power through the Holy Spirit to strengthen churches and multiply believers and churches. Church multiplication is possible through the power of the Holy Spirit as the Word of God is being faithfully proclaimed and taught.

In 2 Corinthians 9:10, God *multiplies* (πληθύνω, *plēthynō*) seed for the sower. Paul writes this in connection with giving. God gives the ability to give for his work. In this passage, Paul states that God "will supply and *multiply* your seed for sowing and *increase* the harvest of your righteousness." Again, in this passage the word for "increase" is αὐξάνω (*auxanō*), to grow or to increase. God brings growth, and he multiplies the impact of his Word by multiplying the number of believers in Jesus Christ (i.e., disciples). God can multiply the impact of the gospel through our *giving* for gospel-focused ministry.

In the LXX (Septuagint), πληθύνω (*plēthunō*) is found 209 times in 189 verses. Of these occurrences, it is found thirty-two times in the book of Genesis. Seven times it is used in Genesis 1 of creation (vv. 22, 28). God blesses the animal kingdom and mankind and tells them to *multiply*. God tells Noah to *multiply* (Gen 9:1, 7). God also blesses Abraham, Isaac, and Jacob and tells them to *multiply* (Gen 17:2; 22:17; 28:3). God promises Abraham that his seed would *multiply* on earth.

Related to this is πλῆθος (*plēthos*, "crowd," thirty-one times), πίμπλημι (*pimplēmi*, "to fill," twenty-four times), ἐμπίπλημι (*empiplēmi*, "to fill," five times), παμπληθεί (*pamplēthei*, "in unison," one time), πλήμμυρα (*plēmmura*, "flood," one time), πλησμονή (*plēsmonē*, "indulgence," one time), and ἀριθμός (*arithmos*, "numbers," eighteen times). The word πλῆθος (*plēthos*) is found predominantly in Luke's writings (twenty-four times in Luke and Acts) and is usually translated "multitudes" or "numbers." The word ἀριθμός (*arithmos*) is found predominantly in Acts and in Revelation. Acts 16:5 reads, "So the churches were strengthened in the faith, and they *increased* in numbers daily."

Thus, *God is the One who increases and multiplies the impact of his Word, proclaimed by his servants in the power of his Holy Spirit. Multiplication* is directly related to *making disciples through the gospel message*. When God's servants faithfully proclaimed his Word, the number of disciples and churches *increased and multiplied*. Therefore, the DNA of the church is *to increase and multiply*, not just to continue to exist or survive, not just to preserve their culture or social identity. Multiplication through gospel proclamation in the power of the Holy Spirit is what consistently happens in the book of Acts. Thus, we can conclude that *multiplication is what God accomplishes through his servants who proclaim his Word through the power of the Holy Spirit.*

Many churches do not experience the increasing and multiplying power inherent in the gospel. Many churches exist and continue to maintain their culture, have their meetings, and endeavor to meet the needs of their membership. Some churches in the majority world are following the pattern of churches in the Western world, but some have experienced the multiplying effect of the gospel proclaimed by faithful servants. In the remainder of this book, we will outline the biblical principles that result in multiplication.

PRINCIPLE #1

The Power of a Godly Model

Follow my example, as I follow the example of Christ. (1 Cor 11:1)

A leader is one who knows the way, goes the way and shows the way.

—John C. Maxwell[1]

When I was growing up, my mother sewed clothes. Her first step was to buy a pattern, material, various spools of threads, and other needed accessories. Then she cut the pattern out and pinned the pattern to the material. Later, she cut the material around the pattern. Once finished, she began sewing the material together, piece by piece. After several days, the clothing began to take shape. Just like a pattern for clothing, God created us to follow and to learn from other people, especially excellent role models. Subconsciously, people look for other men and women to follow and imitate. People gravitate towards stronger people they want to be like.

Throughout Scripture, history, and experience, we see the power of a godly example. The most obvious example is our family. Children do what we do quicker than they do what we say. As children grow up, they learn patterns of behavior from their parents, and they invent their own patterns as well. Through events, whether good or bad, that happen to them, people create their own patterns of response and behavior. Patterns of behavior are usually imitated. You can see it in them. A child learns the pattern of anger from his or her father or mother. Children observe how their parents respond to different situations, and they begin to follow those *patterns* of behavior. Media is taking over this role of modeling.

1. "5 Leadership Thoughts," para. 4. See also Maxwell, *Life Wisdom*.

Sitcoms and movies present scenarios of how people behave and respond. Patterns of behavior are being acted out. Media has created role models for children and young people. Those who watch are learning patterns of behavior, good and bad, from the media. According to *Exploding Topics*, teens' screen time, regardless of device, has increased by two hours since 2015 to *seven hours and twenty-two minutes daily*.[2] Teenage boys spend an average of over nine hours! Imagine what values and behavior patterns teens learn from others who most likely do not adhere to biblical teachings! Children and young people are learning values from those who are acting out scenes and scenarios via media on multiple devices.

THE WORD "EXAMPLE" IN THE NEW TESTAMENT

The word for "example" and similar words are from the following Greek words: Μιμητής (*mimētēs*), Τύπος (*typos*), ὑπόδειγμα (*hypodeigma* or *deigma*), and ὑπογραμμός (*hypogrammos*).

Μιμητής, μιμέομαι, συμμιμητής (*Mimētēs, mimeomai, summimētēs*)

The Greek word *mimētēs* has the meaning of "imitator" and is used seven times in the New Testament. Related words are *mimeomai* (verb), meaning "to imitate" or "to mimic" (four times), and *summimētēs*, meaning "fellow imitator" (one time). Essentially, it has the same meaning as *following*. Listen to the New Testament writers' invitations for people to imitate godly examples.

Paul urges the Corinthian church to "be imitators" of him (1 Corinthians 4:16; 11:1). Paul explains in chapter 4 that he and the other apostles had become spectacles for the world. They had experienced poverty, hunger, thirst, persecution, and slander, and had become the "scum of the world." The Corinthians, however, were the opposite. They needed to follow Paul's *example* of *humility*. There were arrogant leaders in the church who opposed and ridiculed Paul as a weakling. He would plan to come in the power of the kingdom of God. Thiselton notes that "while the noun μιμητής and the verb μιμέομαι can indeed mean *imitator* or *to imitate*, these forms also convey a broader, less mechanical meaning, in

---

2. Duarte, "Average Screen Time," line 5.

the sense of *emulate, follow,* or *use as a model.*"³ In 1 Corinthians 11:1, Paul urges them to follow his model of humility. Again, Thiselton notes, "The pattern is that of placing the welfare of *'the other'* before that of oneself, and in this sense Paul himself takes Christ as his pattern rather than as a *model* of lifestyle in every respect."⁴

In Ephesians 5:1, Paul exhorts the church to be "imitators" of God.

"And you became *imitators* of us and of the Lord" (1 Thess 1:6).

"For you, brothers, became *imitators* of the churches of God in Christ Jesus that are in Judea. For you suffered the same things from your own countrymen as they did from the Jews" (1 Thess 2:14).

"For you yourselves know how you ought to *imitate* us, because we were not idle when we were with you" (2 Thess 3:7).

"What you have learned and received and heard and seen in me—*practice* these things, and the God of peace will be with you" (Phil 4:9).

In Hebrews 6:12, the author exhorts the church to be "*imitators* of those who through faith and patience inherit the promises."

Τύπος, ὑποτύπωσις, ἀντίτυπος, ἐντυπόω, τυπικῶς (*Typos, Hypotupōsin, Antitypos, Entypoō, Typikōs*)

In non-biblical use, τύπος (*typos*) is etymologically from *tuptō*, "to strike," "to stamp a form," or "to shape." The idea is that something has struck a blow to something else and left a mark or impression upon it. It also has the sense of "'Mould,' 'hollow form' which leaves an impress."⁵ That which makes this mark is the word *antitypos*. In the Septuagint (LXX), it is used in Exodus 25:40 of the model for the tent where God would meet with Israel.

Romans 6:17 reads, "But thanks be to God, that you who were once slaves of sin have become obedient from the heart to the *standard* [τύπος, *typos*] of teaching to which you were committed." The sense here is that *the gospel became the mold for their lives.*

In Philippians 3:17, Paul exhorts the church to *imitate* (Συμμιμηταί, *summimētai*) him: "Brothers, join in *imitating* me, and keep your eyes on those who walk according to the *example* [τύπος, *typos*] you have in us."

---

3. Thiselton, *First Epistle to the Corinthians*, 370–71.
4. Thiselton, *First Epistle to the Corinthians*, 796 (emphasis original).
5. Goppelt, "Τύπος, Ἀντίτυπος, Τυπικός, Ὑποτύπωσις," 247.

The Thessalonian believers became an example for all the believers in Macedonia and in Achaia (1 Thess 1:7). Paul demonstrated to this church while he was with them an example (τύπος, *typos*) to imitate (μιμηταὶ from *mimeomai*, verbal form for *mimētēs*).

In 1 Peter 5:3, Peter exhorts elders to be "examples to the flock" (τύπος *typoi*). In 2 Timothy 1:13, Paul exhorts Timothy to follow the "pattern" (τύπος, *typos*) of sound words he had heard from Paul.

God directs Moses to make the "tent of witness" (the tabernacle) in the wilderness "according to the pattern [τύπος, *typos*] that he had seen" (Acts 7:44).

The same idea is found in Hebrews 8:5: "See that you make everything according to the pattern [τύπος, *typos*] that was shown you on the mountain." God showed Moses the original in heaven, and Moses was to follow this original plan. In the same way, Jesus is the original pattern for us to follow. His invitation to "follow me" is still operative today, through our lives, as we invite prototypes into our lives for them to see what Jesus has done in us and how he is using us.

In John 20:25, we read that unless Thomas sees the "mark" (i.e., scars) on Jesus' hands and side, he would not believe. He would need to "place my finger into the mark [τύπος, *typos*] of the nails" or he would never believe. The idea here is of a visible mark, "a mark made as the result of a blow or pressure, *mark, trace*."[6] As the nail was pounded by a large hammer, it left an indelible mark in Jesus' hands. The spear also made such a mark on Jesus' side. These marks were *visible* marks for anyone to see. *Are we leaving marks in others' lives to emulate and follow?* The example was so powerful that it left a visible mark. What kind of marks are we leaving on those around us?

ὑπόδειγμα (*Hypodeigma*)

ὑπόδειγμα (*hypodeigma*) is "an example of behavior used for purposes of moral instruction, example, model, pattern."[7] We find this in John 13:15. Jesus had washed the disciples' feet. Following his washing of their feet, he says to them, "For I have given you an example, that you also should do just as I have done to you." His example became an opportunity for instruction on how they should relate to each other and to others.

---

6. Danker et al., *Greek-English Lexicon* (hereafter BDAG), 1019.
7. BDAG, 1037.

ὑπογραμμός (Hypogrammos)

A similar word to ὑπόδειγμα (hypodeigma) is ὑπογραμμός (hypogrammos). This word means "model," "pattern of behavior," or "pattern" and is used in 1 Peter 2:21, referring to Jesus as our model to follow in responding to persecution.

Where are the godly models for people to follow? Young people idolize sports figures and actors, most of whom are *not* godly examples. Church leaders have fallen throughout the years and have *not* been godly examples. Televangelists have been guilty of greed, amassing fortunes and extravagant houses and properties. High-profile evangelists and pastors have lived out bad examples of extravagance and greed. Prosperity gospel preachers have given the appearance of preaching the gospel in order to profit from it.

In 1 Peter 5:2, Peter exhorts elders not to serve "for shameful gain." American televangelists are not the only ones who have abused finances, avoided accountability, and lived above a modest lifestyle. Pastors in many countries have abused power and served for financial gain. These pastors are certainly not *godly* examples to imitate.

John Wooden, in his book *Wooden: A Lifetime of Observations and Reflections On and Off the Court*, states that "*Being a role model is the most powerful form of educating . . .* too often fathers neglect it because they get so caught up in making a living they forget to make a life."[8]

"FOLLOW ME AND I WILL MAKE YOU FISHERS OF MEN" (MARK 1:17)

Think for just a minute about the power of what Jesus was able to accomplish in just three years. Jesus "was able to disciple a group of men, most of whom no one else would have chosen, and taught them to DO and to BE like him in such a way that, when released, they would change the course of human history *forever*."[9] In John 1:38–39, two of John's disciples left John to follow Jesus. They asked Jesus, "Where are you staying?" They were not simply asking for his contact information or house address but wanted to spend the day with him and get to know him. Bill Hull comments, "We can only guess the content of their discussions, but we can

---

8. Quoted in "Wooden Quotes," line 7 (emphasis added).
9. Breen, *Building a Discipling Culture*, 16.

observe that, as on many occasions, they came away with their hearts aflame."[10] Hull later concludes the following: "Every Christian needs to take time to select a few people and to determine to spend time teaching them the basic fundamentals, such as Bible study, prayer, outreach, and various ministry skills. But we must be careful not only to teach the content but also to model these truths in our lives. *The example in outreach is vital; it serves as a catalyst.*"[11]

For three years, Jesus' disciples followed him and followed his example. "He ate. He taught. He laughed. He healed. He prayed. He told jokes. He told stories. He visited friends. He fed thousands. He partied. He went to weddings. He went to the local synagogues. He went on retreat with his disciples. He cried. He went to funerals. He gave advice. He answered questions. And in all of his comings and goings, his disciples watched him doing this and observed. They were immersed in a life with Jesus. It should come as no surprise, then, that we see them doing the *exact same things* in the book of Acts."[12] They walked together, talked together, ate together, and traveled together. We know that Jesus traveled by foot to Jerusalem at least three times, a one-way distance of about 100 miles (160 kilometers), which would have taken about a week. Following Jesus was more than a seminary education. He gave his disciples the pattern for life and ministry. Not only did they receive from him excellent content, but they also learned how to live, relate to one another, and treat others. The educational model of the Western world tends to focus on *information* (biblical and theological content). The assumption is that when people understand correct theology and know the right things, it will translate into correct behavior and ministry effectiveness. But in real life, we see that this is not always true. Seminary cannot fully qualify and prepare a person for ministry. Hershael York explains, "A seminary alone is not sufficient to qualify anyone for ministry, no matter how faithful the faculty or how hard it tries. A seminary is a rigorous academic program, but that is very different from being [in] a church in which the student can serve and demonstrate his gifts and calling while he is under its teaching, authority, and discipline."[13] Seminaries prepare candidates through teaching theological and scriptural depth. I have had wonderful training at three seminaries, and I am grateful for the men and women God used

10. Hull, *Jesus Christ, Disciplemaker*, 32–33.
11. Hull, *Jesus Christ, Disciplemaker*, 26 (emphasis added).
12. Breen, *Building a Discipling Culture*, 41.
13. York, "Why Seminary Can Never Qualify."

to shape my mind and my heart. But seminary cannot fully prepare a person. God's main instrument today is the church, primarily the local church. We will discuss this further in a later chapter.

Think about how Jesus trained the twelve disciples. For three and a half years, they watched Jesus heal the sick, heal the blind, heal the deaf, raise the dead, cast out demons, rebuke the Pharisees, teach the crowds, calm the storm, walk on water, teach in parables, feed the three thousand and the five thousand, and suffer and die on the cross, and rise again the third day. In Acts 4, the religious rulers brought Peter and James and questioned them for healing the beggar and proclaiming that Jesus was raised from the dead. In verse 13, we read that "they recognized that *they had been with* Jesus." Jesus' life and ministry became a *pattern* for them to follow. They naturally followed this pattern once he ascended to heaven. What they saw and heard, they emulated. God created us in this fashion. We emulate examples we consider *worthy* of following. Is *your* life *worthy* of following? Is my life worthy of following?

Listen to John's statement about their time with Jesus: "That which was from the beginning, which we *have* heard, which we *have* seen with our eyes, which we looked upon and *have* touched with our hands, concerning the word of life" (1 John 1:1, emphasis added). Three of the verbs ("we have heard," "we have seen," and "we have touched") are written in the perfect tense. The perfect tense indicates past tense action with continuing results in the present tense. In effect, John was saying that what they saw and heard in Jesus, they were still seeing and hearing in their minds. Jesus' life and example left an indelible impact on their minds and hearts. They could still see and hear him in their minds.

According to Langer and Jung, the language of imitation is synonymous with following. "Jesus consistently refers to his disciples as followers, while the writers of the Epistles tend to favor the language of imitation. The concepts remain very similar; though followers of Christ are now referred to as imitators of Christ, the essential descriptions of the Christian life remain firmly entrenched in the followership motif rather than the leadership motif."[14] They continue to explain that the New Testament writers avoided the contemporary usage of leadership words in favor of words that are descriptive of followers. "Overall, the New Testament conceives of discipleship as a chain of *followership* much more than

---

14. Langer and Jung, *Call to Follow*, 68 (emphasis added).

a chain of leadership."[15] This runs contrary to the contemporary books on leadership. Unless others are following you, you're just taking a hike. While there may be some truth to this, the idea of following others is secondary and of less value than leading. The point here is that we are following the model of others. Jesus' call was not to go and lead but to follow him. We are inviting others to follow us. In essence, we are leading, but the emphasis should be on following a pattern worthy of following. It is easier to preach a message once a week than it is to be a worthy example for others to follow. What we say in the pulpit should be lived out daily as an example to those we serve.

"ACCORDING TO THEIR OWN KIND" (GENESIS 1:11-12)

In Genesis 1, we see God's creation of the world—light, the expanse, vegetation, lights, birds, fish, and man. "And God said, 'Let the earth bring forth living creatures according to their kinds—livestock and creeping things and beasts of the earth according to their kinds.' And it was so. And God made the beasts of the earth according to their kinds and the livestock according to their kinds, and everything that creeps on the ground according to its kind. And God saw that it was good" (Gen 1:24–25).

Not only do animals produce after their kind, but leaders also produce after their kind. "We teach what we know—we reproduce what we are."[16] Do you want to become an effective pastor? Go with an effective pastor and learn from him. Do you want to become a great church planter? Spend time with a church planter, and you will become like the church planter. Do you want to become a cross-cultural missionary? Go and accompany a cross-cultural church planter. Do you want to become a small-group leader? Attend a small group with an experienced small-group leader. Do you want to become an effective evangelist? Go and spend time with an effective evangelist. Do you want to become a great teacher? Go and attend classes of an effective teacher.

This is where seminaries are so effective. Seminaries have good teachers. Their students become like their teachers. Many students will attend classes taught by certain teachers for their knowledge and expertise. Most seminaries produce good teachers. They know Greek and Hebrew. They know biblical doctrine. Seminaries do not always train great leaders

---

15. Langer and Jung, *Call to Follow*, 70.
16. Maxwell, *21 Irrefutable Laws of Leadership*, 138.

or church planters, but they do train great teachers and expositors of the Word of God. After attending my seminar on expository preaching, one pastor confessed to me that he preached like a seminary professor before, but members had noticed a difference in his preaching after following the principles on preaching in my seminar (which focus on calls to action). In the course on expository preaching, we train pastors how to design messages based upon the ancient text of the Bible and then build a bridge to the present world of people today with all their challenges and obstacles that they are facing.

Like attracts like. Passionate teachers attract people with teaching gifts. When I was in Bible college, I attended a Greek class taught by a well-liked Greek professor. He was very passionate about the Greek New Testament and knew the Greek language and grammar. Additionally, he had been taught by a renowned Greek scholar and commentator. His passion and insight attracted me. I took many of his classes. I began to sound like him when I taught. I spent hours studying the Greek New Testament. I followed this professor like the disciples followed Jesus. Unfortunately, when I finished seminary, I lost all contact with him. While he shaped my mind with his profound understanding of Greek, he could have shaped my soul and heart for ministry. Herein lies the weakness of formal training: little to no relationship. Are we sacrificing the heart and soul of the next generation of pastors, church planters, evangelists, and cross-cultural workers at the altar of speed, quantity, and credentials?

Paul Gupta of the Hindustan Bible Institute discovered this the hard way.

> What do you do when you discover that none of your graduates are evangelists or church planters, and that your training program produces completely different results than you intended? What do you do when you discover that you have recruited the wrong people for the mission you want to accomplish? Most institutions respond by making changes to curriculum and programs, hoping to recover their mission. *This rarely, if ever, works,* since the cause lies in the fundamental design or paradigm of learning in the institution.[17]

Gupta wanted to plant churches and saturate India with the liberating gospel of Jesus Christ. He discovered that their programs attracted the wrong students. These students were interested in degrees, not in planting

---

17. Gupta and Lingenfelter, *Breaking Tradition to Accomplish Vision*, 24 (emphasis added).

churches. They wanted credentials. So, they began looking for men and women who were new believers and were passionate about sharing their faith and starting new churches. They changed their training paradigm from formal to non-formal. They discovered the "power of training through practical, on-site experience. Adults learn far better *when they see and do ministry*."[18]

What was the result? "Each major adjustment they made over a fifteen-year period contributed in a significant way toward their goal of multiplying churches."[19] Gupta and his team defined what they wanted to see in the end and adapted their strategy and programs accordingly. Now, years later, they have started thousands of churches in India.

"SET THE BELIEVERS AN EXAMPLE."

In 1 Timothy 4:6–16, Paul instructs Timothy about being a good servant of Jesus Christ. Contrary to what many teach, Timothy was not a young pastor leading the churches of Ephesus. He was a church planter on Paul's team and was sent to Ephesus to teach sound doctrine and to establish godly leadership. Paul instructs Timothy in the appointing of elders and deacons. Timothy's role there is temporary. False teachers had invaded the church and were perverting the gospel.

In 1 Timothy 4:12, Paul instructs Timothy not to allow anyone to despise him due to his age. Instead, he is to set an "example" for believers. The word for "example" is the Greek word τύπος (*typos*), which can mean mark, copy, image, form, pattern, type, model, design, or example. Here the word means "an *archetype* serving as a model, *type, pattern, model*."[20] Timothy is to serve as a pattern for believers to follow. He is to be the pattern for how believers live and relate to God and one another. Timothy is to be a pattern "in speech, in conduct, in love, in faith, [and] in purity." He is to be the example of how a believer talks, conducts himself or herself, relates to God, and relates to others, especially to those of the opposite sex. Likewise, church leaders are to be the pattern of how a believer lives, talks, relates to God, and relates to others. The lesson here

---

18. Gupta and Lingenfelter, *Breaking Tradition to Accomplish Vision*, 38 (emphasis added).

19. Gupta and Lingenfelter, *Breaking Tradition to Accomplish Vision*, 41 (emphasis added).

20. BDAG, 1020.

is that believers, especially new believers, need a pattern to follow in how to live, how to relate to God, and how to relate to others.

NEVER GO ALONE

The significance of what Jesus did should be evident to us. Jesus rarely went alone. When traveling from one place to another, his disciples went with him. We also see this in the life of Moses. Joshua, Moses' aide, accompanied him up Mount Sinai. He accompanied him in the Tent of Meeting when Moses was praying and worshiping God. Elisha accompanied Elijah for about ten years and was also called his aide. The disciples accompanied Jesus wherever he went—to Jerusalem, to a wedding, in the synagogues, in the temple, to the woman at the well, etc. Timothy and Silas accompanied Paul on his missionary journeys. As a team, they worked together in proclaiming the gospel and starting new churches. Jesus traveled to Jerusalem at least three times with his disciples. From Capernaum to Jerusalem it was about 120 miles. They undoubtedly walked together along the way and talked and discussed many topics over the journey of several days.

The truth is we learn by being *with* other people. We subconsciously emulate people we like, and we become like them. Many Christian workers would rather spend time serving *by themselves* rather than allow others to get close to them. For personal impact to happen, transparency and time are necessary. We must invite others to follow us, and to do this, we must carve time out of schedules for this to happen. We are inviting people into a transparent relationship where we can speak into one another's lives.

Pastors, church planters, cross-cultural workers, and evangelists need to invite young Timothies to join them. Bringing someone along with you can be more difficult for you. Many times, it's easier to do something yourself alone than to bring someone else along with you. However, for others to learn how to serve and minister to others, they need an example to follow. Taking the time for others to accompany you will prove invaluable.

In 1987, my family and I moved to the small town of Guindulman, a rural town on the island and province of Bohol. I had decided to follow the example of Jesus after several months of cultural study, reflection on Jesus' example of training the Twelve, and prayer. Another missionary had gathered eleven believers on the outskirts of town and had returned to America. I began teaching them chronologically through the stories of the Bible, starting in Genesis. This was a method developed by the New Tribes Mission called the "Chronological Bible" storytelling method. By teaching the biblical stories, we could focus on the core theology of who God is, his character, who man is, the importance of a sacrificial substitute in place of the sinner, and the way of salvation. From creation to Jesus' ascension to heaven, seven months transpired. This allowed us time to develop relationships with the people we were teaching and build a theological foundation.

The Lord had opened the doors for evangelistic Bible studies in three different areas of our town—one along the coast in someone's home, one in the mountains in a Roman Catholic chapel, and one just a few houses down from where we lived in a billiard hall. After some time of prayer, I approached three men in our small church. Jose, Alberto, and Nestor agreed to join me in going to these evangelistic Bible studies. I instructed them that they would not need to preach or to teach; I would do that. But I needed their help distributing Bibles and the printed lessons and hanging our pictures of the stories on the wall for people to see. They would also help people find the passage in the Bible. They heard these stories as we met as a church every Sunday. They listened to the lessons a second time in the Bible study. I intentionally went to their homes and waited for them, sometimes for an hour. The Lord had given me a vision for this church, and I needed some good men to train to become the future pastors. Within three months, they began teaching with me. I would teach part of the lesson, and they would teach the other part. I coached them on the way home. I shared with them all the good things they were doing. I corrected them in areas that they needed correction. I provided them with suggestions for improvement. We did this for four months.

At the end of four months, a group of students from Liberty University visited our small town and gave a puppet show illustrating the gospel. In the middle of their presentation, I gave a gospel presentation and challenged those attending (about three thousand people) to join a home Bible study. We had chosen two key locations for the puppet show—one downtown near the market and one in the mountains. At about the same time, a young man who was part of the church joined our team, and three interns from our Bible school in the capital city of Tagbilaran, three hours away, also joined our team. We were now a team of eight.

The puppet show resulted in many open doors. Soon we were teaching over twenty evangelistic Bible studies all over the town—in the central area of the town and even in the faraway villages. After one Bible study attended by seventy people, a man walked up to me and invited us to visit his village several kilometers away. He asked, "Can you come to our village and teach us the Word of God?" The following Sunday, we went there and began with creation. We had two motorcycles, yet there were eight of us. Some of us had to walk or ride public transportation.

In 1989, I took five of these men with me to a pastors conference in Mindanao (the next island south). We rode a boat there together and back. Then, on two motorcycles (a Honda 125 and a Kawasaki 100) with our bags tied on the back carriers of the motorbikes, we started the ride home. I was rejoicing in my heart all the way back with what God was doing. These men were growing in their relationship with God, in their understanding of God's Word, in their character, and in their ability to communicate the gospel and God's Word. I had begun teaching them the seminary courses I had taken from Liberty University. I taught them hermeneutics, Old and New Testament introduction, expository preaching, and biblical doctrine. As I rejoiced in my heart at what I had seen, I prayed, "Lord, let me do this for the rest of my life." Little did I know what God had planned.

In 1990, just after two and a half years of service with me, we ordained Jose as the pastor of the church. He is still the pastor today. In 1995, we finished our ministry with this church and entrusted it to him and the leaders of the church. In the same year, I was returning a book to a colleague's office, and I noticed another book on his desk called the *Program Summary Manual*,[21] published by Bible Training Centre for Pastors, based in Atlanta, Georgia. Dennis Mock, the author and president, had written ten courses for pastors in Kenya, following the same order I had followed in the courses I taught the men in Guindulman. Yet, he had written five more. Randy Gardner (now the president) visited us that same year, and we decided to partner together. I reasoned, why should I continue writing the curriculum when someone else had already finished what I wanted to do?

The point of all of this is that *ministry is caught as much as it is taught*. We learn from others. We can only learn from others as we are *with* them. Jose, Alberto, Nestor, Nestor, Sammy, and others learned from me as they saw an example that they could follow. I would surmise that the most significant lessons you have learned in your life have come through a

---

21. Mock, *Program Summary Manual*.

close person who has taught you by example. If we never spend time with others, they will never learn the potential that they could otherwise learn from us. Many want to shortcut this process by offering training online, over video, or only during a short visit. While these forms have merit, they focus only on content. How can a person follow from your example if all they see is you teaching in a classroom setting and not in real-life settings? When we do life together (or life-on-life training), the greatest impact is made in a person's life.

While this may seem to be a much slower way of ministry, it is actually much greater than what we expect. After our time in Guindulman, we moved to Tagbilaran and started a second church. I also had the privilege of training the pastor of that church, and he is still the pastor of that church today. Later, I became the Asian coordinator for BTCP (Bible Training Centre for Pastors) and traveled around Asia starting training centers. Again, I implemented the "come and see" strategy. The Lord led me to another three men: Henry, Max, and Jun. In 2001, I invited these pastors to oversee the training in their regions. Henry would oversee Luzon, Max would oversee the Visayas, and Jun would oversee Mindanao. I visited the Philippines two to three times a year. We traveled together all over the Philippines. We traveled in boats together, ate together, slept in hotels and in homes together, rode in planes together, preached in churches together, visited pastors together, spoke at graduations together, and traveled in vans and taxis together. Max Caindoy passed away in 2019. During his service of nineteen years together with us, he trained over five hundred gospel workers. During his final hours, fishermen from islands north of Bohol visited him in the hospital in Cebu. He encouraged them not to be the traditional pastor who does all the work of the ministry. Instead, he encouraged them to equip others for the work. Max trained over 120 fishermen from twenty-six small islands north of Bohol for seven years. They would fish on the way to the main island of Bohol before class and sell the fish at the market for food and gasoline to return home later that week. Max spent two days a month with them and became their spiritual father. They learned from him not only the content of Scripture but also the pattern for living and for ministry.

This was the DNA of the ministry I wanted to implement: the *discipleship relationship*, where I modeled to them the values and the pattern that I wanted them to follow and implement with others. Jesus' method of "come and see" is still a powerful way of training disciples. By the beginning of 2004, we had grown to over a thousand church leaders in training throughout the Philippines. The ministry had spread through a web of relationships, not through any ingenious marketing technique of mine. Now, by God's grace, the Philippines is our largest field with twenty coordinators, over two hundred training classes, over 2,400 students, and over two thousand graduates. The discipleship relationship principle is still a powerful way of ministry, but it is slower, more personal, yet with a much greater multiplying impact. It takes time to model the Word of God. Proclaiming the gospel and preaching the Word is relatively easy. Living it out as an example is time-consuming. There are no shortcuts to a ministry of multiplication.

As BTCP refined their strategy to working only with partners in 2005, we became a partner and started Crossing Cultures International in 2006. By God's grace, we now oversee the training of over ten thousand pastors and church leaders in forty-one countries. We have added more courses. Over twenty-four thousand church leaders have completed all of our training courses. Recently, we organized our fourth global conference in Chiang Mai, Thailand. Over two hundred staff, trainers, students, and graduates from fifteen nations and twenty-five people groups attended the conference. In 2006, we were a team of five—my wife and me, and Henry, Max, and Jun. God is able to do more than we can think or imagine. I never dreamed that God would answer my prayer in the way that he has answered it.

I am still committed to the power of a godly example. People learn from other people. I still bring others with me. It is much easier to do ministry by yourself, but bringing someone with you is much more powerful. Through this, God multiplies his ministry through his Word through godly men and women, empowered by his Holy Spirit. Do you want to see your ministry multiply? Begin by prayerfully choosing a few good men or women and bringing them with you wherever you go. We do not need to be perfect; we just need to be a humble, godly servant, willing to wait for God to work through his Spirit in and through the lives of those who accompany us.

DISCUSSION QUESTIONS:

1. Who has made the greatest impact in your life?

2. What qualities of this person do you admire the most?

3. If you could choose one person to spend a week with, who would it be? Why?

4. What is the greatest lesson you have learned from someone else who has spent time with you?

5. Who could you invite to come and follow you as Jesus did his disciples?

6. Write out a plan for how you can implement this principle in your ministry.

PRINCIPLE #2

A Close, Personal Relationship

After this he went down to Capernaum, with his mother and his brothers and his disciples, and they stayed there for a few days. (John 2:12)

> The royal road to a man's heart is to talk to him
> about the things he treasures most.
>
> —Dale Carnegie[1]

The basis and foundation for effective ministry is *relationships*. Do you want to build a solid ministry? Build solid, close, personal relationships. Through close, personal relationships, *trust* is built. When people trust you, they open *their hearts* to you. There is transparency. While we cannot dispute the power of the gospel, the teaching of the Word of God, and the effective use of one's spiritual gift, without trust and relationships, ministry effectiveness is mitigated. Someone inebriated can proclaim the gospel and the hearers may believe. But how much more effective is the messenger when there is a close relationship and trust with his or her hearers? Close relationships pave the way for transparency and vulnerability. When there is transparency and vulnerability, the messenger can apply truth to the relationship where the greatest transformation can take place. This principle follows the first principle. When you invite people to come with you to follow your example, the door is opened for a *close relationship*.

---

1. https://www.allgreatquotes.com/quote-92277/, line 1.

COME AND SEE

Jesus is the model *par excellence* for close relationships. This is one of the miracles of Scripture: that God wants to dwell with his people. In the Old Testament, the presence of God was visible in the form of a cloud by day and a pillar of fire by night during the wilderness wanderings. Later, after Solomon built the temple, God dwelled in the Most Holy Place. When Jesus came, he dwelled with his people (John 1:14). Note what Jesus did at the beginning of his ministry. He spent *time with* his disciples. The disciple whom Jesus loved is the only Gospel writer who recorded this. Rocky Wyatt notes that the "words follow Me imply there is a relationship. If you follow someone consistently, you see them in every life situation. You have the opportunity to benefit from their teaching. When they face difficult circumstances, you learn from their response. You learn about their priorities and disciplines."[2]

> The next day again John was standing with two of his disciples, and he looked at Jesus as he walked by and said, "Behold, the Lamb of God!" The two disciples heard him say this, and they followed Jesus. Jesus turned and saw them following and said to them, "What are you seeking?" And they said to him, "Rabbi" (which means Teacher), "where are you staying?" He said to them, "Come and you will see." So they came and saw where he was staying, and *they stayed with him that day*, for it was about the tenth hour. (John 1:35–39, emphasis added)

Prior to this, John the Baptist baptized Jesus in order "to fulfill all righteousness" (Matt 3:15). Immediately after Jesus' baptism, the Holy Spirit, in the form of a dove, descended upon him. God the Father said that Jesus is his beloved Son with whom he was well pleased. Immediately, Jesus was led into the wilderness, where he fasted and prayed for forty days and nights and then was tempted by the devil. Afterward, Jesus returned to the area where John the Baptist was preaching.

Jesus began his ministry among men by spending *that day* with these former disciples of John the Baptist. John had identified Jesus as the Messiah, and naturally his former disciples were interested in who Jesus was. Michael J. Wilkins contends that at the beginning of the Jesus movement, his first disciples expressed personal initiative in following Jesus, but "full recognition of Jesus' identity was a developing process

---

2. Wyatt, *Pastoral Training in the Church*, 7.

for these disciples."³ Alexander B. Bruce states that the Baptist "spoke of this coming One in language fitted to *awaken* great expectations."⁴ John's disciples' interest was aroused through John's preaching and through his identification of Jesus as the Messiah.

Rather than launching a full-blown public ministry with a complete marketing plan with an all-out expense, Jesus began by spending time with his first followers. There was no great marketing plan, no search for great candidates for his staff. There was no business plan with budgets. Not that these are wrong, but Jesus, God in the flesh, spent time with these curious followers. This truth is mind-boggling: *the Creator of the universe desires to spend time with his creation.* He developed a close relationship with them.

To be a disciple of Jesus during his ministry, one had to leave all and follow him. The disciples were keenly interested in understanding who Jesus was and were committed to following him, regardless of what the implications were or what they believed about the Messiah. By spending time with them, Jesus got to know them and came to understand their gifts, abilities, and personalities. Even though Jesus was God in the flesh, he accepted the limitations of human existence while also being fully capable of knowing what is in a person (John 2:24–25).

"This, the first of his signs, Jesus did at Cana in Galilee, and manifested his glory. And his disciples believed in him. After this he went down to Capernaum, with his mother and his brothers and his disciples, and *they stayed there for a few days*" (John 2:11–12, emphasis added).

After his first miracle of making water into wine at a wedding, Jesus spent several days with his family and disciples. Word began to spread about him after his first miracle. Spending time together allowed his disciples to get to know the Messiah and be with Jesus, who was God in the flesh. Why did Jesus spend time with his disciples? Why not launch fully into a ministry driven by preaching and healing among the crowds? He knew what was in them and knew them. *To show a reproducible model to them, Jesus had to spend time with them.* The miracle of Jesus spending time with his disciples is the truth of God wanting *to be with his people.* We see this throughout Scripture.

God walked in the cool of the garden with Adam and Eve. Enoch walked with God and was taken. Abraham was God's friend. God came

---

3. Wilkins, *Following the Master*, 101–103 (emphasis added).
4. Bruce, *Training of the Twelve*, 3.

and visited Abraham before destroying Sodom and Gomorrah. All these examples are Christophanies, or appearances of Christ before his incarnation.

Christ, in his pre-incarnate form, wrestled with Jacob. God appeared to Moses in the burning bush. Moses built the Tent of Meeting and God came and tabernacled with his people Israel. When Daniel's three friends Shadrach, Meshach, and Abednego were thrown into the fiery furnace, Christ walked with them and protected them from the flames.

God has always desired to dwell with his people. "And the Word became flesh and *dwelt* among us" (John 1:14). God created us for us to know him and for him to know us. Before the creation of the world, God the Father, Son, and Holy Spirit existed in perfect harmony, with perfect love and perfect communication. God did not create us because he needed us, but because he wanted to share his relationship and blessings with us.

God the Father, Son, and Spirit and their perfect relationship and harmony with one another is *the* model for us to follow today in our ministries.

"After this Jesus and his disciples went into the Judean countryside, and *he remained there with them* and was baptizing" (John 3:22, emphasis added).

After Jesus' visit with Nicodemus, Jesus and his disciples remained for several days in the Judean countryside. They baptized people who repented of their sins, and he also spent time with the disciples. *Relationship and ministry existed side-by-side together.*

At the beginning of Jesus' ministry, Jesus spent time with his disciples. Why? He did so to develop a close relationship with them. They would get to know him as he fully made himself as God known to them (John 1:18). A major part of following Jesus is getting to know him as the Messiah. Another part of getting to know Jesus is him revealing to us what is in our hearts. We do not fully comprehend who we are or what is in our hearts. God uses opportunities and hardships to flesh out what is inside us. Like a mirror, the Holy Spirit uses the Word of God and hardships to reflect upon who we are and Who we need to become like.

Discipleship for most ministries is a *program*. It is a *series of lessons* over a few weeks that introduces a person to who Jesus is; what he accomplished through his death, burial, and resurrection; and other lessons pertaining to the Christian life. Discipleship programs include lessons on prayer, the church, evangelism, and salvation. All of this is good but not complete.

From the above passages, we can conclude that discipleship is *relational*. Wilkins notes that "Discipleship is not simply a program. Discipleship is becoming like Jesus as we walk with him in the real world. And the real world begins in my home, in my closest relationships, in the moment-to-moment circumstances of life."[5] Reading over the verses about Jesus' ministry with the Twelve reveals that discipleship is relational, and it is *life on life*. Discipleship *programs* fall far short of Jesus' way of making disciples.

In the centuries leading up to the New Testament and Jesus' usage of μαθητής (*mathētēs*) ("disciple"), the Greek world already had a paradigm in place with master teachers or great thinkers or leaders. Wilkins explains that the "relationship between a great thinker or leader and his followers involved a commitment that affected the follower's *entire* life. The follower was truly a 'disciple' of the leader and was known primarily for the character of the *relationship* shared with the master."[6] Later, he concludes by stating that the "commitment assumed the development of a *sustained relationship* between the follower and the master, and the relationship extended to imitation of the conduct of the master. This is the notion of the word understood by a Greek audience at the time of the writing of the New Testament."[7]

Jesus' decision to build a close relationship with his disciples was like lighting a candle. *The relationship became the catalyst for following him and embracing his mission in the world.* Bruce succinctly explains the effect. "They were *enthusiasts*: their hearts were fired, and, as an unbelieving world might say, their heads were turned by a dream about a divine kingdom to be set up in Israel, with Jesus of Nazareth for its king. That dream possessed them."[8] The relationship Jesus kindled with them was the catalyst for this.

From these passages, we can deduce the following principles. Effective ministry begins with developing *relationships*. There must be trust. The disciple maker cannot understand who he or she is discipling if there is no relationship. A disciple maker must commit time to unravel spiritual gifts, areas of weakness, areas of passion, ungodly habits and

---

5. Wilkins, *Following the Master*, 123.
6. Wilkins, *Following the Master*, 76 (emphasis added).
7. Wilkins, *Following the Master*, 78 (emphasis added).
8. Bruce, *Training of the Twelve*, 16–17.

desires, hidden sins, and the remnants of any abusive behavior or damage done to the disciple. Making disciples is *relational*, not just a program. As Jesus endeavored to determine a person's spiritual condition, as with the woman at the well, we disciple makers also must find out where a person is spiritually, what their hang-ups are, their habits, sins, and damage. Effective training and disciple making begins where the disciple is, not the program. However, for every disciple, common lessons need to be learned. Understanding a person's religious upbringing is also essential because false beliefs may need to be uncovered. This only comes through a close relationship.

Developing a close relationship allows us to work with the disciple, like peeling back layers of an onion to the core of a person's being. In discipling a person, we must be able to know that person in a way that will facilitate their becoming more like Jesus Christ.

While discipleship lessons will impact a person's cognitive understanding of knowing Christ, the disciple maker's relationship with the disciple will have the greatest impact. People learn from other people. The most life impactful lessons we have learned have been through a relationship with someone else who spent time with us and taught us. I look back over my life and know that the lessons I learned about my relationship with Christ came most powerfully through those people and mentors who took the time to get to know me and disciple me. Here is the missing element of seminary, which usually focuses solely on knowledge and understanding. What men and women need most is a relationship with their teacher, not just the lessons they teach.

Jesus was always available for his disciples. His mission was foremost in his mind, as his focus was on suffering and dying on a cross in Jerusalem. But next to this was his relationship with his disciples. The Sermon on the Mount was a teaching session for his disciples. "Seeing the crowds, he went up on the mountain, and when he sat down, his disciples came to him. And he opened his mouth and *taught them*" (Matt 5:1–2). At the beginning of his ministry, Jesus called fishermen to follow him. "Follow me, and I will make you fishers of men" (Matt 4:19). We should not be surprised by their reaction because Jesus had spent time with his disciples on and off prior to this. "Immediately they left their nets and followed him" (Matt 4:20).

JESUS' CIRCLES OF RELATIONSHIPS

In Jesus' ministry, he had circles of relationships. The *crowds* followed him, and he taught the crowds. He commissioned *seventy*, two by two, to proclaim the gospel, heal the sick, and cast out demons (Matt 10; Luke 10). The Gospels narrate most of Jesus' ministry with the *twelve* disciples. Of the Twelve, *three* (Peter, James, and John) were the closest. Jesus invited them into the most intimate times of his life. During the transfiguration, the three followed Jesus and witnessed this life-changing event.

Jesus' example of circles of relationships is a model for us to follow—from the wider circle of casual relationships to the more intimate relationships with our most trusted and entrusted disciples. The first step is to identify the crowds. Who are the crowds that follow us? For a pastor, it may be his congregation. The next step is to identify the seventy. Who are the core workers or volunteers? They are committed to the mission and vision of the church or the organization. The next step is to identify the twelve. Who are those followers who are most committed to the mission and vision and are engaged in significant ministry? Finally, who are the three—the most intimate relationships and the persons most committed to the mission and vision of the organization? For each level, we must have a greater relationship with them. For the crowds, we must be available and reach out to each one. From the crowds, we will find the seventy—the ones who volunteer to fulfill the mission. From the seventy, we will find the twelve. They are very committed to the mission and vision. They are ready for closer relationships and greater accountability. We call them, meet with them, and spend time with them to develop a close relationship with them. Finally, from the twelve, we will find our three—the most committed and invested in the mission and vision. They are also the ones that we must spend the most time with. As the number decreases, the relational time increases. As the number increases, the more the relational time decreases. As the number decreases, the closer the relationship becomes. As the number increases, the more distant the relationship becomes, but still the disciple multiplier must be able to model and invite them into a transparent relationship. A pastor or ministry leader must learn to discern who he or she should spend time with the most and who their closest relationships should be.

RELATIONSHIP BEGINS WITH INVITATION

This is a pattern we see in Jesus' way of making disciples. "Follow me." Instead of looking for volunteers, Jesus sought out his followers and invited them to join him. Personal invitation is effective because it focuses on investing in someone's life. A powerful way to multiply disciples is by invitation. In American culture, ministries look for volunteers. The initiative is with the follower to step forward. In honor-shame cultures, people avoid stepping forward because they do not want to bring shame to themselves or their group by implying that they are better than those around them. A more powerful way to multiply a ministry is by *invitation*. "Come and see." There is commitment other than making the time to be with the disciple maker.

MODELED BY PAUL

"You, however, have followed my teaching, my conduct, my aim in life, my faith, my patience, my love, my steadfastness, my persecutions and sufferings that happened to me at Antioch, at Iconium, and at Lystra—which persecutions I endured; yet from them all the Lord rescued me" (2 Tim 3:10–11). For at least sixteen years, Timothy followed Paul and was his assistant in Paul's church planting ministry. We are introduced to Timothy in Acts 16:1–5. Timothy was from Lystra. His mother was Jewish, while his father was Greek. He had believed in the Lord Jesus Christ during Paul's first visit to Lystra (Acts 14:8–23). In Lystra, Paul healed a disabled man who had never walked. As a result, the whole town thought that Barnabas and Paul were gods, and they came to worship them. Once Paul preached the gospel to them, they stoned him and left him for dead. They made many disciples in Lystra, among whom was Timothy.

Timothy was "well-spoken of by the brothers at Lystra and Iconium" (Acts 16:2). He had good character and was committed to Paul's mission of preaching the gospel to the gentiles. Paul had him circumcised out of respect for the Jews in the places they would be visiting. He wanted Timothy to be culturally acceptable to the Jews. Of Timothy, Paul testified that there was "no one like him" because he was "genuinely concerned" for believers (Phil 2:20). Timothy looked out for the interests of others. He had proven character because he had served with Paul in the gospel ministry as a son with a father (Phil 2:21–22). In the Roman and Jewish world, fathers taught their children (cf. 1 Thess 2:9–12). Timothy demonstrated respect and exemplified the character qualities that a father would want in his son. He could be entrusted with ministry and resources because Timothy was sent on missions and proved faithfulness (Phil 2:23–24; 1 Thess 3:6ff.).

A character like this is developed in a person through a close relationship. Mass marketing does not develop this level of character, as Paul said that he had no one like Timothy.

The second principle of multiplication is developing close relationships. Close relationships allow for more transparency and vulnerability. The disciple maker gets to know his/her disciples and understands their strengths, spiritual gifts, abilities, personality, and weaknesses. The starting point of making disciples of Jesus is getting to know the disciple. Once we understand the disciple, we can apply the truth and content of the gospel and the Word of God in that person's life. Close relationships allow for greater impact.

In 2002, a group of three men—Mickey, Craig, and Ralph—approached me about joining their accountability group. At first, I dismissed their invitation. Then I went to Bangkok, Thailand. As I was riding the elevator, the bellman offered to send a prostitute to my room because "she would make me feel really good." I then realized that I needed to have other men hold me accountable. The gospel is worth protecting. One night with a pretty girl in a hotel room is not worth the shame I would face once this is known. By God's grace, a commitment to moral purity, and through accountability relationships, God has protected me from moral failure. My travel schedule was not as intense as it later would be, but the more I traveled, the more I realized I needed authentic relationships with other men as protection. It would make me think twice because I knew I would have to face these men. In the beginning, we met for one to two hours. We discussed many things personal. Then the shift came. They were hungry for a greater understanding of Scripture and what it meant to be a disciple. We met every Wednesday night when I was in town. Soon we were meeting for three hours. I was answering their questions and explaining difficult passages and doctrines. Mickey and Craig became elders in the church we were attending. Ralph passed away during a scuba diving accident. Mickey has confided in me that our time together helped him grow as a disciple more than at any other time in his life. We do not meet together anymore, but I treasure those times because we grew close together. There are many men and women like Mickey and Craig who crave for an authentic and transparent relationship. Preaching is only a one-way street of communication. We need to unravel the layers in a person's heart and the only way that this happens is through close relationships.

DISCUSSION QUESTIONS

1. Think of the people you have had a close, personal relationship with. Did they initiate the relationship, or did you?

2. How did their relationship with you impact your life?

3. What steps can you take to develop close relationships with those whom you want to make disciples?

4. Whom can you develop a close, personal relationship with to help them grow as a disciple?

5. Prayerfully make a plan to choose at least one person with whom you can develop a close relationship and meet with them.

PRINCIPLE #3

Effective Biblical Training

> By the Holy Spirit who dwells within us,
> guard the *good deposit* entrusted to you. (2 Tim 1:14)
>
> Go therefore and make disciples of all nations, baptizing them in the name of the Father and of the Son and of the Holy Spirit, *teaching them* to observe *all that I have commanded* you. (Matt 28:19)
>
> And he gave the apostles . . . to equip the saints for the work of the ministry, for building up the body of Christ, until we all attain to the unity of *the faith* and the knowledge of the Son of God . . . so that we may no longer be children, tossed to and fro by the waves and carried about by every wind of doctrine by human cunning. (Eph 4:11–14)

EVANGELICALS' UNDERSTANDING OF SALVATION, basic theology, and basic Bible content is at an all-time low. This is ironic, especially considering the accessibility of good books and resources. We have more resources available for our digital devices than at any time in the history of the world. In my Logos library, I have over ten thousand books. I can access them on my mobile phone or tablet wherever I travel. I can download books and read them on planes, in a hotel room, at a pastor's home, or under a tree in the middle of nowhere.

With the abundance of accessible resources, we would think that Bible knowledge and understanding would be at an all-time high. Instead, the opposite is true. Further, the *sentiment* towards Bible knowledge and doctrine is at a low. The search for cultural relevance and contextualization has led many ministries to abandon or lessen the importance of doctrine and embrace relevancy versus Bible exposition and theological instruction. Without the firm foundation of theology and the gospel, we have no relevance for any culture.

When attending a planning meeting at a local church, one church leader remarked to me, "We don't want any doctrinal police around here," when I suggested making available good Bible training available to those who wanted more than what the church offered. The 1960s through the 1980s were filled with opportunities to attend Bible conferences. Then, like a pendulum swinging in the opposite direction, many churches and ministries abandoned these conferences for a more relevant and simpler message. The seeker-sensitive church was born. Messages were more practical and relevant. People became less interested in Bible content and theology. In many ways, this a welcome change because the Bible has a simple message and some scholars tend to make things complicated. This appealed to the masses, and people flocked to these churches, especially since they met a felt need. The music was something they were familiar with—it was appealing and stimulating. Even many of the songs were called "7-11 songs"—seven words repeated eleven times. Messages were shorter and more about family, finances, and other topics that people immediately needed to know. The majority of these churches avoided anything doctrinal or complicated. Religious words were omitted, and everything was organized to make seekers comfortable and welcome. This was a welcome change to Evangelicalism, but it went a bit too far. The Willow Creek Church Association examined their methodology and concluded that their teachings were deficient in terms of discipleship.

In 2008, former pastor Bill Hybels admitted their failure. "'We made a mistake,' he told the crowd gathered for the 2008 Global Leadership Summit (GLS). A detailed Willow study had found that the church had helped many people find new faith in Jesus, but had failed to teach them how to practice the spiritual disciplines needed to grow their faith."[1]

According to R. Albert Mohler Jr., biblical illiteracy is at an all-time high. "While America's evangelical Christians are rightly concerned about the secular worldview's rejection of biblical Christianity, we ought to give some urgent attention to a problem much closer to home—*biblical illiteracy in the church*. This scandalous problem is our own, and it's

---

1. Quoted in Smeitana, "Willow Creek Elders."

up to us to fix it."² He continues to describe the problem: "Fewer than half of all adults can name the four gospels. Many Christians cannot identify more than two or three of the disciples. According to data from the Barna Research Group, 60 percent of Americans can't name even five of the Ten Commandments." He continues to identify the root of the problem: "Christians who lack biblical knowledge are the products of churches that marginalize biblical knowledge. Bible teaching now often accounts for only a diminishing fraction of the local congregation's time and attention. The move to small group ministry has certainly increased opportunities for fellowship, but many of these groups never get beyond superficial Bible study." His conclusion is apropos: "We will not believe more than we know, and we will not live higher than our beliefs. *The many fronts of Christian compromise in this generation can be directly traced to biblical illiteracy in the pews and the absence of biblical preaching and teaching in our homes and churches.*"³

Wayne Grudem wrote his book on systematic theology for this very reason, i.e., so that every believer could understand Christian doctrine.

> I am convinced that there is an urgent need in the church today for much greater understanding of Christian doctrine, or systematic theology. Not only pastors and teachers need to understand theology in greater depth—the whole church does as well. One day by God's grace we may have churches full of Christians who can discuss, apply, and live the doctrinal teachings of the Bible as readily as they can discuss the details of their own jobs or hobbies—or the fortunes of their favorite sports team or television program. It is not that Christians lack the ability to understand doctrine; it is just that they must have access to it in an understandable form. Once that happens, I think that many Christians will find that understanding (and living) the doctrines of Scripture is one of their greatest joys.⁴

Many churches are looking for only the teachings in the Bible that are "relevant" to the needs of people. *The whole Bible is relevant to our lives* when the Bible is correctly handled (cf. 2 Tim 2:14–15). The failure to bridge the Scriptures from the ancient world of the Bible to the world of people today has been a failure. Preachers either focus exclusively on the text, with its background and word studies, or allegorize it, looking

---

2. Mohler Jr., "Scandal of Biblical Illiteracy" (emphasis added).
3. Mohler Jr., "Scandal of Biblical Illiteracy" (emphasis added).
4. Grudem, *Systematic Theology*, 18.

for a contemporary message, robbing it of its historical context. Listen to a "relevant" preacher, and you will likely hear verses taken out of context. The preacher designs his message and then looks for verses he thinks should go with the message. The result is that the Bible has become a smorgasbord for picking and choosing what the reader feels is good. In many cases, the reader has become the *determiner* of truth rather than the *discoverer* and *proclaimer* of truth. We have become like our postmodern culture, who believes that they are the ones to *determine* what truth is rather than discover what truth is.

I remember how shocked I was when returning from the Philippines in 1999 when we attended a small group. The small-group leader asked this question: "What does this verse mean to you?" A verse taken out of context can mean anything to the reader. The correct question to ask is: What does the passage mean and then how do I apply it to my life? New believers need to be taught how to understand a verse in its contextual setting. This takes some work and reflection.

JESUS TAUGHT HIS DISCIPLES THOROUGHLY.

The Sermon on the Mount is one of Jesus' main teachings to his disciples. The Gospel of Matthew is organized around five messages of Jesus. Matthew demonstrates that Jesus is the fulfillment of the Old Testament passages about the Messiah.

Matthew 5:1–2 opens with these words: "Seeing the crowds, he went up on the mountain, and when he sat down, his disciples came to him. And he opened his mouth and taught them, saying . . ." From Matthew 5, Jesus continued teaching his disciples through chapter 7. Like Moses gave the law as a part of the Mosaic covenant, Jesus taught his new law under the new covenant, inaugurated during Jesus' ministry (see Matt 26:26–30; Luke 22:14–23). Jesus had a rather extensive teaching ministry with his followers.

The word for "disciple" (μαθητής, *mathētēs*) means a learner or student. A disciple is "one who is rather constantly associated with someone who has a pedagogical reputation or a particular set of views, *disciple, adherent*."[5] A disciple, then, is a learner, from a teacher whom he or she has committed themselves to follow. As we pointed out in chapter 1, being a disciple is *relational*. But our focus in this section is on *what* the

---

5. BDAG, 609.

disciple is learning. The *content* of what a disciple learns is equally important as *the one from whom one learns* this content, because the one from whom you learn it could be imparting the wrong teaching(s) to a person. The word "disciple" occurs two hundred sixty-one times in the New Testament, *all* in the Gospels and in the book of Acts. Other words related to the noun for "disciple" (μαθητής, *mathētēs*) are μανθάνω (*manthanō*, "to learn") and ἀκολουθέω (*akoloutheō*, "to walk behind" or "to follow"). This word is used eighty-nine times, primarily in the Gospels and in the book of Acts. We have already seen that the words for "pattern" or "imitate" are essentially words for following someone.

Jesus is addressed as "Rabbi" thirteen times and is called "teacher" over forty times. Twenty-nine times Jesus is described as "teaching" (διδάσκω, *didaskō*) his disciples about God and the world around them. It's no wonder, then, that Jesus commands his disciples to make disciples of all nations *by teaching* them to obey everything he had commanded them. Wyatt explains Jesus' teaching: "Jesus was constantly teaching in the synagogues (Mt 4:23). He also taught at many outdoor events like the Sermon on the Mount (Mt 5–7), the feeding of the five thousand (Mt 14:13–21), and the feeding of the four thousand (Mt 15:29–39). He would often illustrate truth with real-life scenarios like the poor widow who gave all that she had to live on (Mk 12:41–44), the blind man (Jn 9), and the withered fig tree (Mk 11:12–25)."[6]

Jesus taught the truth and what he heard from God the Father. He taught in stories or parables. He taught truth in relation to the error of the Pharisees and Sadducees. He took every opportunity to teach the truth of God in every setting. Jesus was the Master Teacher.

Even though Paul indicates in Ephesians 4:11 that Christ gave some to be teachers, teaching has fallen on hard times. In many small groups' ministries, directors and trainers advise small group leaders *not to teach but to facilitate* and discuss.

From the 1980s to the year 2000, one could find a Bible-teaching church almost anywhere in the USA. You could read signs that said, "We are a Bible-believing and Bible-teaching church." There were Bible conferences, Bible seminars, Bible studies, and Bible teaching throughout the country. Then, in the 1990s, a new church type emerged that focused more on being relevant—how to parent children, manage your finances, have a happy marriage, etc. What churches offered was contemporary

---

6. Wyatt, *Pastoral Training in the Church*, 8.

relevancy but at the expense of Bible doctrine and teaching. Should we sacrifice doctrine for relevancy? Is this an either-or situation or both-and? Believers need to know sound doctrine, live holy lives, and bear much fruit through the Holy Spirit's work in and through them. Bearing fruit and living a holy life is based upon knowing basic theology. Being relevant is important, and meeting the immediate needs of people is important. Learning how to manage one's finances, raise children, operate a business, and other practical topics are all important lessons we need to learn. The gospel and sound doctrine have relevance for each of these. Without a well-informed robust life with sound doctrine, we are merely teaching good moral lessons that any religion could teach. I attended a contemporary church once while the pastor was teaching from Nehemiah. The moral of the story was good principles for leadership. Nothing was mentioned about Christ or the gospel. Unless we are gospel focused and Christ centered in our preaching and teaching, we are simply giving good moral lessons. The story of the Bible is much larger than one's finances, raising children, and leadership. If we only preach good moral lessons, we are missing the major storyline of the Bible: the glory of God in redeeming lost people for himself and for his glory. Likewise, indoctrinating believers in sound doctrine without showing them how this relates to real life is also missing the mark because sound teaching has relevancy for our daily lives. In many situations, doctrine is only taught as a cognitive exercise and not as an engagement of the heart. Each of the ten major doctrines has a life-changing component.

Theology proper teaches about the character of God. The application is to know him relationally. Bibliology teaches inspiration and inerrancy. Our response is to meditate on God's Word and obey it. Each doctrine has an emphasis and an application to our lives that should be life transformational.

Ryrie explains this succinctly. "The phrase 'sound doctrine' that Paul used means healthy doctrine (e.g., 2 Tim. 4:3; Titus 1:9). Healthy doctrine or healthy theology is always expected to result in holy living. When Paul prayed for churches, he prayed for an increase in knowledge, for he realized that this would produce holy living (e.g., Phil. 1:9–11; Col. 1:9–10). Healthy theology is expressed not only in creed but in fruitful living, and holy living must be based on healthy theology."[7]

---

7. Ryrie, *Basic Theology*, 10.

PRISCILLA AND AQUILA CORRECTED APOLLOS

Apollos was an eloquent defender of the gospel. We read that "He had been instructed in the way of the Lord" (Acts 18:25). He was zealous in preaching the gospel, but his teaching about baptism was deficient. He only knew about John's baptism but not about believer's baptism. He preached boldly in the synagogue in Ephesus. When Priscilla and Aquila heard him, they invited him to discuss this more and they "explained to him the way of God more accurately" (Acts 18:26). He received their correction and continued on to Achaia with the letters from the brothers in Ephesus. He then "powerfully refuted the Jews in public, showing by the Scriptures that the Christ was Jesus" (Acts 18:28). If we heard someone teaching wrong teaching, would we take the time to invite the person to discuss what they've taught and show them from the Scriptures their error and the "way of God more accurately?"

PAUL EMPHASIZED THE IMPORTANCE OF TEACHING SOUND DOCTRINE.

One of the phrases Paul uses in the Pastoral Epistles is "sound doctrine." The word translaned "sound" is the Greek word ὑγιαίνω (*hygianō*) and refers to good physical health and teaching, sound or free from error.[8] In 1–2 Timothy, Titus, 2 Peter, 2–3 John, and Jude, the writers address the problem of false teachers and false teaching. False teachers crept into churches and began to twist the gospel. Prevalent philosophy was used to understand the gospel, resulting in a perverted message. False teachers denied the humanity of Christ, mixing in current philosophical understandings of an evil, physical world.

The following are the instances where Paul uses *hygianō*.

1 Timothy 1:10: "the sexually immoral, men who practice homosexuality, enslavers, liars, perjurers, and whatever else is contrary to *sound doctrine*."

1 Timothy 6:3–4: "If anyone teaches a different doctrine and does not agree with the *sound words* of our Lord Jesus Christ and the teaching that accords with godliness, he is puffed up with conceit and understands nothing."

---

8. BDAG, 1023.

2 Timothy 1:13: "Follow the pattern of the *sound* words that you have heard from me, in the faith and love that are in Christ Jesus."

2 Timothy 4:3: "For the time is coming when people will not endure *sound teaching*, but having itching ears they will accumulate for themselves teachers to suit their own passions."

Titus 1:9: "He must hold firm to the trustworthy word as taught, so that he may be able to give instruction in *sound doctrine* and also to rebuke those who contradict it."

Titus 1:13: "Therefore rebuke them sharply, that they may be *sound in the faith*."

Titus 2:1: "But as for you, teach what accords with *sound doctrine*."

Titus 2:2: "Older men are to be sober minded, dignified, self-controlled, *sound in faith*, in love, and in steadfastness."

Titus 2:7–8: "Show yourself in all respects to be a model of good works, and in your teaching show integrity, dignity, and *sound speech* that cannot be condemned, so that an opponent may be put to shame, having nothing evil to say about us."

In addition, we also find the phrase "the faith," which is a reference to the *content* of true biblical teaching.

Paul explains that Christ gave godly leaders to the church so that there would be unity in *the faith*: "until we all attain to *the unity of the faith* and of the knowledge of the Son of God, to mature manhood, to the measure of the stature of the fullness of Christ" (Eph 4:13). Maturity is associated with understanding the faith.

Jude writes to exhort the believers to contend for *the faith*: "Beloved, although I was very eager to write to you about our common salvation, I found it necessary to write appealing to you to *contend for the faith* that was once for all delivered to the saints" (Jude 3).

While the word for "faith" can refer to the act of believing and the gift of faith, it is also used as the body of beliefs Christians are to hold on to. In 1 Timothy 4:6, Paul indicates that Timothy has been "trained in the words of *the faith* and of the good doctrine that you have followed." "The faith" refers to the set of beliefs that Jesus and his apostles taught. "τοῖς λόγοις is qualified by two genitives, τῆς πίστεως καὶ καλῆς διδασκαλίας. πίστις is used here with the same objective sense it has elsewhere in Paul (cf., e.g., Gal 1:23, 'preaching the faith'). Since the essential response demanded by Christianity is πίστις, Christianity itself and the sum of its message are appropriately called πίστις."[9]

Galatians 1:23: "They only were hearing it said, 'He who used to persecute us is now preaching *the faith* he once tried to destroy.'"

1 Timothy 1:19–20: "holding faith and a good conscience. By rejecting this, some have made shipwreck of *their faith*, among whom are Hymenaeus and Alexander, whom I have handed over to Satan that they may learn not to blaspheme."

1 Timothy 4:1: "Now the Spirit expressly says that in later times some will depart from *the faith* by devoting themselves to deceitful spirits and teachings of demons."

1 Timothy 4:6: "If you put these things before the brothers, you will be a good servant of Christ Jesus, being trained in *the words of the faith* and of the good doctrine that you have followed."

1 Timothy 6:10: "For the love of money is a root of all kinds of evils. It is through this craving that some have wandered away from *the faith* and pierced themselves with many pangs."

1 Timothy 6:21: "for by professing it some have swerved from *the faith*. Grace be with you."

2 Timothy 2:18: "who have swerved from the truth, saying that the resurrection has already happened. They are upsetting *the faith* of some."

2 Timothy 4:7: "I have fought the good fight, I have finished the race, I have kept *the faith*."

Knowing and understanding the content of the Christian faith is necessary for effective witness. When believers understand the truths of the faith, they are much more confident in sharing the gospel and exercising their spiritual gifts. We have witnessed this repeatedly in the lives of those we have trained around the world. An ordinary fisherman who has no confidence in sharing the gospel becomes a passionate evangelist of the gospel after he understands the content of the gospel. Greater understanding leads to great confidence and passion. When a believer's understanding and conviction of those truths combine, he or she becomes a powerful witness. While active witness of the gospel can lead to the believer's greater understanding of the gospel (cf. Philemon 6), a lack of sufficient understanding can lead to tentativeness, misunderstanding, and the belief and sharing of false doctrine. When believers are confronted with their lack of understanding, they are usually encouraged

---

9. Knight, *Pastoral Epistles*, 194.

to learn more about their faith, especially if they have a close friend or mentor who can guide them. In Philemon 6, Paul encourages Philemon to share his faith so that he would understand every good thing "that is in us." Sharing "the faith" results in a greater understanding of who we are in Christ and every good thing that God has entrusted to us. Obedience in sharing results in greater comprehension. Believers who do not share their faith will not be able to fathom what God has given to them and thus will not have the confidence they need to share with others. This is why modeling and understanding sound doctrine is so important.

In 1 Peter 3:15, Peter exhorts believers to "always be prepared to make a defense [ἀπολογία, *apologia*] to anyone who asks you for a reason for the hope that is in you." Believers should be able to defend their *hope*, i.e., the future reign of Christ in the coming age. Believers also need to be able to defend basic beliefs. Most believers cannot defend the deity of Christ from the Scriptures. Before Nabeel Qureshi believed in Christ, he could not find a believer who could show where in the New Testament Jesus claims to be God. In sharing with a classmate, Nabeel explained, "Jesus was not God. He was just a man." Nabeel went on to challenge the young lady he was talking to, named Betsy, to show where Jesus says he is God. She could not.[10] With the influx of Muslim immigrants and other religious groups, how can we ever reach them with the gospel if church members are not trained to articulate the basic doctrines of our faith?

WHY IS IT IMPORTANT?

Sound doctrine instructs us on what we believe about God, the Bible, Jesus Christ, the Holy Spirit, angels and demons, man, sin, salvation, the church, and future things. Theology guides us about with whom we can work and fellowship. Second John was written to instruct the church not to cooperate with false teachers. Who are the false teachers? Any teacher who denies sound doctrine.

Sound doctrine instructs us on whom we can partner with and give financial support to. Sound doctrine instructs us on what false teachings are. Knowing the truth will inform us of what the truth is not. Everyone is a theologian.

> Theology is for everyone. Indeed, everyone needs to be a theologian. In reality, everyone *is* a theologian—of one sort or another.

---

10. Qureshi, *Seeking Allah, Finding Jesus.*

And therein lies the problem. There is nothing wrong with being an amateur theologian or a professional theologian, but there is everything wrong about being an ignorant or a sloppy theologian. Therefore, every Christian should read theology. Theology simply means thinking about God and expressing those thoughts in some way. There will be a more precise definition in the first chapter, but in this basic sense everyone is a theologian. Even an atheist has a theology. He thinks about God, rejects His existence, and expresses that sometimes in creed and always in lifestyle. The follower of a non-Christian religion has substituted his counterfeit deity for the true God and shows off that theology in various ways.[11]

Everyone is a theologian to some degree. The question is this: Are they a good theologian with an accurate understanding based upon Scripture, and are they able to articulate and defend these beliefs?

Everyone *can become* a good theologian because the Bible is a normal book written for ordinary people. The New Testament was written in Koine Greek, the common man's language, not in classical Greek, the language of philosophers and professionals. The Bible was written in the vernacular of the people. This implies that God meant for his Word to be understood by the masses. In Mark 12:37, we read, "And the great throng heard him gladly." The common people heard and understood Jesus' words. This brings us to the teaching called the "perspicuity of Scripture," or the "clarity of Scripture." God designed that Scripture be understood. Ordinary, common men wrote the Bible in a common language for all to understand. Theology can be communicated in a clear way for people to understand. This has not always been the case. Grudem states, "The clarity of Scripture tells me that its doctrines can be taught in a way that ordinary people are able to understand."[12] Theology is a tool that the disciple maker can use in making disciples who can articulate and defend the faith. The Bible is simple to understand in many passages, yet in some places it can be difficult. While we may not understand the Bible perfectly, we can understand it sufficiently. During this age, we will not understand theology and God exhaustively, but we will understand him sufficiently. In Deuteronomy 29:29, Moses states it perfectly: "The secret things belong to the Lord our God, but the things that are revealed belong to us and to our children forever, that we may do all.

---

11. Ryrie, *Basic Theology*, 9.
12. Grudem, *Systematic Theology*, 131.

The words of this law." While God has not revealed everything, we can understand what he has revealed with constant use (cf. Heb 5:14). This is where churches and ministries need to align with Scripture. An aversion to theology will only lead to error or a revolving door of people coming and going. When a church attendee exhausts all that is available to them, they, with a consumer-like mentality, will look for something else that will help them in the next stage of growth—or they will remain stagnant.

Brian Wagner acknowledges this same reality. "He [Paul] admitted that knowledge and prophecy concerning such revelation is only partial until 'that which is perfect' arrives (1 Cor 13:9). Yet partial revelation does not necessitate ambiguity in what is partially revealed, but it does confirm that Paul believed that the Scripture does not deal with every issue comprehensively."[13]

Pettegrew explains that "the doctrine of the perspicuity of Scripture does not mean that the teaching of Scripture is everywhere equally simple. There is a difference between clarity and simplicity. Scripture is clear, not mystical or hidden. But it often takes work to understand what the biblical authors meant in a certain passage. Commenting on Paul's writings, the apostle Peter admits, 'There are some things in them that are hard to understand, which the ignorant and unstable twist to their own destruction, as they do the other Scriptures' (2 Pet 3:16)."[14] Taking the time to explain these more difficult teachings will bring great benefit to believers who can then, in turn, defend and explain these beliefs in, sometimes, many critical situations.

WHAT IS SOUND DOCTRINE?

What are the teachings that make up sound doctrine? What essential teachings are we to impart to those we are discipling and training? In order for us to see a ministry of multiplication, we must impart a theological understanding of God's revelation. Millard Erickson explains the importance of theology. "Theology in a Christian context is a discipline of study that seeks to understand the God revealed in the Bible and to provide a Christian understanding of reality. It seeks to understand God's creation, particularly human beings and their condition, and God's redemptive work in relation to humankind. Biblical, historical, and

---

13. Wagner, "Perspicuity of Scripture," 75.
14. Pettegrew, "Perspicuity of Scripture," 213.

philosophical theology provide insights and understandings that help lead toward a coherent whole. Theology has practical value in providing guidance for the Christian life and ministry."[15]

Every two years, Ligonier Ministries and LifeWay Research surveys Americans' understanding of theology. In 2022, the results were shocking. About one half believes that God changes and that he is not immutable, that humans are born innocent, and that church membership is not important.[16] We live in an era where sound theology is an absolute necessity to inculcate.

Here is a list of doctrines that believers must understand and be able to articulate. This is not a comprehensive list, but it is a starting point.

1. Bibliology

    a. The Holy Spirit guided men as they prophesied and wrote down God's Word (2 Pet 1:20–21).

    b. The Bible is God's inspired Word in its original form and is useful for ministry (2 Tim 3:16–17).

    c. God has preserved his Word (Isa 40:8; Matt 5:18).

    d. The Bible is God's final authority for what we believe and practice (Acts 17:11).

2. Theology Proper

    a. God is Spirit, eternal, omnipresent, omnipotent, infinite, all-loving, gracious, merciful, and punishes sin (Gen 1:26; 3:22; Isa 48:16; Matt 28:18–19; Mark 12:29; John 1:14; Acts 5:3–4; 2 Cor 13:14; Titus 3:4–7; Heb 1:1–3; Rev 1:4–6).

    b. God has revealed himself in three persons—Father, Son, and Holy Spirit—three co-equal persons, but differing in roles (Deut 4:35; 6:4; Isa 44:5–8; Matt 28:18–20; 1 Pet 1:2–4).

3. Christology

    a. Jesus is fully God and fully man (John 1:1, 14, 18; 10:30; Rom 9:5; Phil 2:6; Col 1:15; 2:9; Titus 2:13; Heb 1:3; Matt 28:19; 2 Cor 13:14; John 1:14).

    b. Jesus was born of the virgin Mary (Matt 1:16–25).

---

15. Erickson, *Christian Theology*, Kindle loc. 224–28.
16. https://thestateoftheology.com.

c. Jesus lived a sinless life (Heb 4:15; 2 Cor 5:21).

   d. Jesus' death on the cross was sufficient once and for all to pay for our sins (2 Cor 5:21; Heb 7:25; 9:14, 22, 23–28; 10:11–14).

   e. Jesus will return to defeat Satan and establish his kingdom (Rev 19–20).

4. Anthropology

   a. God created man in his image (Gen 1:26–27) and gave him personality (mind, will, emotions).

   b. God created man, male and female. Our sexuality is a part of our identity (Gen 1:27).

   c. God created marriage, where a man and a woman will bond together in marriage to have children and oversee the world that God created (Gen 1:27; 2:18–25). The word translated "suitable" means "corresponding," meaning of the same substance (bones, flesh, blood) but differing in sexuality.

5. Hamartiology

   a. When Adam sinned, he, as the representative head of the entire race, became a sinner, and so every person is born a sinner, separated from God (Rom 3:10–23; 6:23).

   b. Man cannot save himself through good works or through religious works (Titus 3:5; Eph 2:8–9).

6. Soteriology

   a. Man is saved by grace through faith in Jesus Christ's once-and-for-all sacrifice on the cross and resurrection (Eph 2:8–9; Rom 3:21–26; 2 Tim 1:9; John 3:16; 1 John 5:11–12).

   b. When a person believes in Christ, his sin is removed, and the righteousness of Christ is donated to him as a gift (Rom 3:24; 5:1; 8:1).

   c. We have assurance of salvation through faith, by God's power, evidenced by but not conditioned upon good works (John 10:29–30; Col 3:1–3; 1 Pet 1:5).

7. Eschatology (the doctrine of future things or last things)

    a. Christ's return is imminent (1 Thess 4:13–18).

    b. Believers will experience the resurrection to eternal life (1 Cor 15:42–58).

    c. Unbelievers will face the Great White Throne judgment and be cast into the lake of fire (Rev 20:11–15).

    d. God will reign with his people in the new Jerusalem, the new heavens, and the new earth forever and ever (Rev 21–22).

Like guardrails on the road, understanding basic Bible doctrine and content can protect us from driving over the cliff. Doctrinal understanding gives us direction and a foundation upon which to build God's ministry.

Advocates of the church planting movement contended that seminary training is disadvantageous to the planting of churches at the beginning stages. Adding formal seminary training will supposedly kill a church planting movement. God the Holy Spirit will teach new leaders and lead them into the truth by themselves. While it is true that the Holy Spirit will lead us into all truth, he leads us into truth through his Word (2 Tim 3:16–17) and through other teachers (Eph 4:11–16). Why does Paul exhort Timothy (1 Tim 1:5) to stop the teaching of false teaching and to start teaching sound doctrine in the churches of Asia Minor if the Holy Spirit would lead these men by themselves? The Holy Spirit uses Holy Spirit–filled and Holy Spirit–led men and women in teaching others in the Word of God. This movement also contends that non-formal training is preferred. "A decentralized theological education which is punctuated by practical experience is preferred . . . Higher education may benefit church leaders at some point, but it can hinder a Church Planting Movement in its early stages."[17] Garrison recognizes the importance of leadership training. "Leadership training is vital to Church Planting Movements. With new churches being produced so rapidly, there is a never-ending demand for the training of new leaders. For that reason alone, it is not surprising that Church Planting Movements have featured various types of *practical, continual on-the-job training*."[18]

---

17. Garrison, *Church Planting Movements*, 44.
18. Garrison, *Church Planting Movements*, 234 (emphasis added).

While seminary specializes in delivering great content and producing great teachers and preachers, most of the time, there is no discipleship relationship between the teacher and the students. I know this is a generalization, but this has been my experience and the experience of many of the pastors and global workers I have known. Professors are consumed with preparing for classes and grading papers and tests. There is little time for developing relationships with students or mentoring them.

This is where the concepts of this book can greatly contribute to formal institutions and various movements. Some movements are advocating such speed in multiplication without the necessary training. Mentoring can include instruction in sound doctrine and biblical content. Many from these movements arena already have the mentoring relationship. Why not add more biblical content and training in sound doctrine? In our ministry, we have provided training for pastors of churches that were started by those of the church planting movement. We observed that many of these pastors could not articulate sound doctrine and were deficient in ministry skills. But after three years of training with us in local church-based training classes, the training in sound doctrine provided a solid theological foundation and stabilization to their churches and ministries.

A SUGGESTED BIBLICAL CURRICULUM

First, believers need to know basic hermeneutics. They need to know how to observe the text, interpret the text, and apply the text to their lives. We need to understand the truths and principles that God the Holy Spirit has placed in his Word. We discover truths. We do not determine truth. We read the Bible like a normal text, seeking to find the meaning of the text through meanings of words determined by the context. We do not look for hidden meanings, nor do we allegorize the text. Other areas of hermeneutics that need to be understood are the importance of the historical and cultural background (the author, occasion, themes, structure), the literary context (understanding different genres of Scripture), and determining word meanings according to the context and the semantic domain of the word being studied.

Believers need to understand the overall message of the Bible, and the contents, structure, theme, and message of each book of the Bible.

Old and New Testament survey courses can help them understand how each book or letter contributes to the overall message of the Bible.

Believers need to understand doctrine as discussed above. What does the Bible teach about God, the Bible, Christ, the Holy Spirit, angels and demons, man, sin, salvation, the church, and future events? We need to understand these topics because they become foundational in our lives for spiritual growth.

Believers need to know how to grow spiritually, who they are in Christ, and the difference between salvation as a one-time event and sanctification as an ongoing process with the goal of becoming more like Christ. We also need to understand and practice spiritual disciplines—prayer, fasting, service, Scripture memorization and meditation, and silence. We also need to know our spiritual gift and how we can use that gift in serving others.

Believers need to understand Jesus' ongoing mission in the world and how we can be a part of that by praying, giving, and going. We need to understand missions in the local church and the concept of people groups—reached people groups, unreached people groups that have been engaged by a ministry or church or churches, and unreached people groups that have not been engaged.

Believers need to understand the content of the gospel, what are the false gospels, and study the different evangelistic methods today that one can use in sharing the gospel. While not every believer has the gift of evangelism, every believer can share the gospel. Believers need to know how to disciple new believers and what tools are available to do so.

As a believer matures and grows in his or relationship with Christ, God will call some to be church planters, pastors, global workers, evangelists, women ministry leaders, men's ministry leaders, student ministry workers, etc. When a person devotes himself to an office or position, there should be commensurate training available for each of these ministry positions. There are abundant resources available to help a person become effective in these areas. For a pastor, servant leadership is essential as well as effective pastoral ministry and effective preaching of biblical messages. All of these positions necessitate the need for effective communication tools. I have written a course on advanced expository preaching based on a method known as "crossing the homiletical bridge." This method teaches one how to develop messages that are based upon the Scripture, but are relevant to the needs of the audience (I do believe in being relevant after all!). When a person learns this method, they can then begin to learn topical preaching, which focuses on what the Scriptures teach on a variety of topics. The danger here is that many relevant preachers determine their message and then look for the verses that back up their topic. The only problem is, upon examination of the verses that they have used, one sees that that particular verse has nothing to do with that topic. We have to make sure that we are servants for the Word of God and that the Bible is not a servant for our vision and purposes.

We must also work with our trainees not only to equip with the tools for effective Bible study, preaching, knowing, and understanding the contents of the OT and NT and the spiritual disciples; we must also help them in determining a plan for ongoing personal growth. By examining their greatest areas of interest and need, we can help them formulate a plan with books to read and seminars to attend. Guiding them in the right direction after they have mastered study skills and intentional thinking will help facilitate their ongoing growth.

NEW TESTAMENT WRITERS WARNED AGAINST FALSE TEACHERS.

Jesus warned against false Christs. In Matthew 24:5, Christ states, "For many will come in my name, saying, 'I am the Christ,' and they will lead many astray." Paul warned the Ephesian elders, "after my departure fierce wolves will come in among you, not sparing the flock; and from among your own selves will arise men speaking twisted things, to draw away the disciples after them" (Acts 20:29–30). Paul commanded Timothy and Titus to guard the good deposit and to stop false teachers from teaching (1 Tim 1:3–4; Titus 1:9–16). He warned of Hymenaeus and Philetus, who had swerved from the truth teaching a realized eschatology saying that the resurrection had already taken place (2 Tim 2:16–19). Peter also warned of false teachers (2 Pet 2:1–3), as did John (1 John 2:18–27; 3:4–10; 4:1–6) and Jude (3–16). When believers are grounded in sound doctrine, they will be able to recognize false teaching.

If we want to see a ministry of multiplication, we must entrust faithful men with the essential truths of the faith. A ministry that avoids doctrinal instruction will run into disunity, which will mitigate against the increase and multiplication of a disciple making ministry.

From AD 100 to 300, one of the reasons the early church grew as it did was because of its emphasis on teaching. Before a new believer was baptized, he had to undergo two to three years of instruction by a catechist. Listen to Alan Kreider's assessment.

> So how were Christians made? By a process of formation that, as time progressed, was increasingly self-conscious. It was rooted in the habitus of the communities—their reflexive behavior. It was embodied knowledge rooted in predispositions that guided the Christians' common life and expressed themselves in practices. These predispositions shaped worship practices that became essential, formative parts of the communities' habitus. These predispositions also expressed themselves in concentrated form in the initiation processes culminating in baptism that formed the candidates for communal membership. Christians maintained that if they were attractive, it was not because they were born that way. It was because they had been reborn—changed, converted—to be attractive. Outsiders could see the results of the formation *but not the formation itself, which happened privately, secretly, out of the public eye.* In this chapter and the next, I will contend that the Christians' habitus was formed patiently, unhurriedly, *through careful catechesis* as well as through the communities' reflexive behavior, and that it was renewed in the regular worship of the Christian assemblies.[19]

TRAINING IN VIJAYAWADA, INDIA

In 2012, we were invited by two brothers, Vinay and Isaac, to come to their city of Vijayawada, India, to train the pastors and leaders of churches associated with their father's ministry. Their father, Abraham, was a gifted evangelist who had led evangelistic campaigns where over eight thousand people believed in Jesus Christ and were baptized. Thirty-three men and six women enrolled in our class. Vinay and Isaac were students of mine in a class in Hyderabad started by Shepherding the Nations, based in the Los Angeles area. We discussed starting this class together, and after praying, I invited them to co-teach with me. For five years, my wife and I traveled there two to three times a year. I faced many health issues, which I believe were spiritually related. Since I was six years old, I have had severe asthma. Some nights I awoke with an asthma attack. Two times while visiting there, I had pneumonia. The Lord strengthened me during this time and enabled me to continue training these men. We met

---

19. Kreider, *Patient Ferment of the Early Church*, 134 (emphasis added).

from 8:30 a.m. until 6 or 7 p.m., without air conditioning, even during the hot season, when the temperatures soared to 118 degrees Fahrenheit (48 degrees Celsius). There were many challenges, but we implemented the "come and see" strategy. We visited the students in their homes, ate with them, and visited their churches. We attended a wedding and a funeral. We visited preaching points (groups not yet a church). We prayed for women to conceive and have children. God answered our prayers. God displayed his power and grace to these people.

From the beginning class on hermeneutics, it was apparent to me that there were a lot of doctrinal misunderstandings. In every week we taught, many questions involved difficult passages and doctrine. One doctrine they had a difficult time understanding was *grace*. Many pastors wanted to teach a gospel that involved works to keep the people coming back to the church services. My co-teachers said to me many times that all the pastors in that area have a difficult time understanding and teaching grace, i.e., that salvation is based upon God's grace in giving us forgiveness and salvation, not by our works or good deeds but simply by his favor. This is such an elementary teaching. If pastors are not teaching the gospel of grace, what are their people believing, and how are they living and relating to one another? Over five years, we taught, illustrated, read, and explained Bible passages, including difficult passages. They eventually understood and began teaching this important truth. Six of the men in this class became trainers. They have now trained over one thousand other pastors and workers. Theological understanding and a solid theological foundation are necessary for a ministry of multiplication.

In 2001, I started these same classes at Crosstown Community Church, now known as The Crossing Church. I served there for six years as the part-time missions pastor. My first class began with twelve students and was unannounced to the church congregation. A pastor informed me that if my ministry were to be successful, it would be through my initiative and leadership. After book 1 on Bible study methods and rules of interpretation, I continued with Old Testament survey. The attendance grew from twelve to forty. Word began to spread to others through my students. Eventually, I started a second class and invited one of my students, Bob, to co-teach with me. At the end of book 1, I entrusted the class and the training to Bob. Bob went on to finish not only this group, through all ten books of the Bible Training Centre for Pastors' curriculum, but he also taught three other groups of leaders through this curriculum. One of his students became a teacher. I started a second class.

Out of this class came a missionary, elders, a missions pastor (Norris Brown), a pastoral care pastor, and another student named Scott Phipps, who started a missions organization that focuses on family ministry, evangelism in a Muslim country, and partnerships with other national pastors and global workers. Eventually, that one class blossomed to touch the lives of over two hundred people. The focus on modeling, developing close relationships, and training in doctrine has given ordinary believers the biblical understanding, ministry skills, and character for long-term effective ministry.

DISCUSSION QUESTIONS

1. Do you agree with the teachings listed above? What would you change?

2. Do you agree with Barna's findings that America is at an all-time low in Bible and doctrinal understanding? Why or why not?

3. If you were to design a curriculum for the content portion of making a disciple, how would you design it? What courses do you think are necessary for multiplying disciples?

4. How can local churches teach their members essential doctrines of the faith? Or is this the function of only seminaries?

5. How could those in the church planting movement arena train emerging leaders in theology so as to provide guardrails to their movement?

PRINCIPLE #4

Giving Guided Opportunities

> And he called to him his twelve disciples and gave them authority over unclean spirits, to cast them out, and to heal every disease and every affliction ... These twelve Jesus sent out, instructing them, "Go nowhere among the Gentiles and enter no town of the Samaritans, but go rather to the lost sheep of the house of Israel. (Matt 10:1, 5)

> The seventy-two returned with joy, saying, "Lord, even the demons are subject to us in your name!" And he said to them, "I saw Satan fall like lightning from heaven ... Nevertheless, do not rejoice in this, that the spirits are subject to you, but rejoice that your names are written in the heaven." (Luke 10:17–20)

> Everyone wants to be a hero.
> Yet only a few understand the
> Power in being a hero maker.[1]

> *Many potentially effective servants of the Lord lack one major thing—opportunity!*

IN THIS CHAPTER, WE will focus on giving our trainees (i.e., disciples) opportunities for service with accountability. For most believers, ministry is offered as an optional opportunity for those who take the initiative to seek out those opportunities. The initiative to get involved is left to the volunteer. But it was not that way with Jesus. We will look at

---

1. Ferguson and Bird, *Hero Maker*, 15.

examples in Scripture and endeavor to extract principles that we can apply to our situation.

Shortly after I surrendered my life to Christ, I served as the assistant to the youth director in the church where I trusted Christ. I was very new, young, and in need of a lot of coaching. I remember well my first message—Amos 4:12, "Prepare to meet God." This was my five-minute message to the other young people that day. Not everyone received it well, as I remember. The opportunity gave me greater desire, yet revealed many of my shortcomings. About two years later, after I had finished my first semester at Liberty, my former Sunday school teacher offered me the opportunity to teach the middle school boys' class. There were about fifteen boys there that Sunday. I had taken a course called Inductive Bible Study with Dr. Paul Fink, and it had changed my life. Previously, I had not received any training in studying the Bible. I was left to my own, and it revealed my shortcomings. After the class with Dr. Fink, I had a tool to use and some understanding of how to study the Bible. The lesson that coming Sunday was from 2 Peter 3:8–13. That was forty-five years ago, but I still remember it vividly. As I prepared for the class, a hunger and thirst grew within me, resulting in a burning passion to study God's Word. As I taught that Sunday, I do not remember the response from the boys' class, but I do remember the result it created in me. I was hooked. A flame ignited within me to teach people the Word of God. A gift that God had given me was suddenly fanned into flame (cf. 2 Tim 1:6). That flame continued to burn within me as I received more training, as I had more opportunities to use this gift, and as I received feedback and critique from those listening. I do not remember the Sunday school teacher taking me aside and coaching me afterward. He may have given me a verbal commendation of "Good job, David." Meeting with people individually after their opportunity to coach them on what they did well and where they need to improve can help further develop the person.

There are many benefits to giving opportunities to people, especially to our trainees. A blog called *Basics by Becca* lists ten benefits of giving people opportunities: 1) they motivate personal growth; 2) they help you achieve your goals; 3) they enable networking; 4) they allow discovery of your passions; 5) they help you in moving forward; 6) they help you reach your dreams; 7) they help you become a leader; 8) they encourage risk-taking; 9) they enable you to be your best self; and 10) they help you create success stories.[2] While some of these benefits overlap with one another, the benefits are obvious for personal growth and development.

MOSES, JOSHUA, AND JETHRO—"WHAT YOU ARE DOING IS NOT GOOD!" (EXOD 18:17)

Has this ever happened to you? Moses was leading two to three million people—an extremely large group. His father-in-law arrives and observes what is happening, and his first statement is, "What you are doing is not good!" Let's look at the context.

In Exodus 17:8–16, Joshua defeats the Amalekites. While Joshua was fighting the battle, Moses stood on top of the hill with the staff of God in his hands. As Moses became tired, he lowered the staff, resulting in Joshua beginning to lose the battle. When Aaron and Hur helped him hold up the staff, Joshua overwhelmed the Amalekites. The staff revealed Moses' weakness—he needed other men to stand with him. However, when we read Exodus 18, we see that he had not learned this lesson.

In Exodus 18:13, Moses sat down to judge the people and to help them resolve their problems while the elders stood around him. If we do all the work, everyone will watch and congratulate us for our hard work. It is often easier to do the work ourselves, but our output is limited. There is only so much work we can accomplish. Many pastors hire their staff from outside the church and seek volunteers to help with the work. But rarely does this result in multiplication. This process is not reproducible, nor does it equip the people to do the work. It sends a clear message to the church—*they are not qualified*. This practice perpetuates the unbiblical divide between clergy and laity. We need to find a seminary graduate because ordinary church members are just lay people. I am not against seminary graduates, because I am one myself. Nor am I against hiring seminary graduates. But we must be careful in how we go about it so that we do not send the wrong message.

When Jethro arrived at the place the Israelites had camped, he observed what Moses was doing and remarked that what he was doing was not good. "You and the people with you will certainly wear yourselves

---

2. C., Rebecca, "10 Advantages" (https://basicsbybecca.com/blog/taking-opportunities). See also "Take Opportunities" (https://www.morningcoach.com/blog/take-opportunities-while-they-are-there) and "Importance of Opportunity" (https://www.linkedin.com/pulse/importance-opportunity-quantum-research-grip-b7cjf/) for similar benefits.

out, for the thing is too heavy for you. You are not able to do it alone." Jethro's statements are insightful.

First, they would wear themselves out. They would overwork themselves and burn out. The Barna Group collected data from pastors between 2021 and 2022 and discovered that about 42 percent of pastors considered quitting full-time ministry due to the immense stress brought on by the job itself.[3] Could this be a result of the traditional mindset of the pastor doing all or most of the work of the ministry or due to the unrealistic expectations of the congregation of the pastor? When the pastor takes on all the work of the ministry, and all the people stand around and watch, what Jethro warned is what really happens. "You will certainly wear yourselves out." When the pastor views himself as a doer rather than an equipper, this is what happens. Most pastors and Christian workers devote most of their time to sermon preparation, staff management, and ministry growth. When *our* goal is only to increase conversions, baptisms, and offerings, we fail to fulfill our clearest job assignment. In Ephesians 4:11–16, the pastor's role is to "equip the saints" to do the work of the ministry. When we focus on *doing* the work to maintain and grow the ministry, we fail to reach our goals. As the ministry grows while we fail to *equip* the saints, our capacity diminishes, and we set ourselves up for burnout and failure. Something must give—our family, our health, or our effectiveness—or all three. The back door of the church becomes as big as the front door. While we may be seeing growth by addition and not by multiplication, subtraction through dissatisfaction happens because the pastor certainly cannot meet all the expectations for all the members.

Sadly, this is the model most global workers have taken with them to other countries. I have visited churches and looked at the global workers they are supporting. Praise God that they are diligently doing the work of the ministry, leading people to Christ, discipling them, and organizing them into a local church. (Many of them are doing this in reached areas rather than unreached areas. That's another topic.) If you survey their work, you will discover that most are focused on *doing*, not *equipping*. I know this is a generalization, but I have helped churches by creating an evaluation tool to discover what their supported cross-cultural workers are doing, what the priorities of the church are, and where they should allocate most of their resources. The majority are doing the work where

---

3. Barna, "Pastors Share Top Reasons" (https://www.barna.com/research/pastors-quitting-ministry/).

nationals could be doing the same work, and probably better since they know the language and the culture better than the global workers do.

Another trend today is satellite churches. In a satellite church, the lead pastor's face and body are shown on the screen. The pastor feels that he is the most effective speaker of the church. While this may be the case, it ends up all depending upon him. A broadcast message has limitations. While it may be *good*, it may not be the *best*. The greatest impact we will make is through face-to-face, in-person contact. Jesus' way of making disciples involved in-person conversation. While online classes are good, they are not the best. Personal contact will always have the greatest impact. Even John realized the limitations of correspondence. "I had much to write to you, but I would rather not write with pen and ink. I hope to see you soon, and we will talk face to face" (3 John 13–14). The words translated "face to face" are literally "mouth to mouth" (Gr., *stoma pros stoma*). John knew then the limitations of papyrus and ink. They just do not communicate everything we are trying to say. This is why person-to-person contact and conversation are so important and effective.

Additionally, broadcast services eliminate others from the opportunity to speak and develop their skill of communication. It all depends upon the "gifted" speaker. The truth is we are all replaceable. God can raise up another gifted speaker. How much better is it if he uses us to do that? If we continue to lead in capacities like this, the less opportunity we can give to others to develop and grow. Rarely does a person step into a position effectively from the start without having prior experience. People need to grow *into* the position with effectiveness. Or the gifted person begins to lead in a capacity they may have the gifting for, but are too young and do not have the maturity necessary for the role. They need coaching in a close relationship. The lead pastor can allow someone to shadow him, and the lead pastor can coach and mentor him until his potential is revealed, encouraged, and strengthened.

We rob people of the opportunity to grow and develop their skills and abilities if we keep on leading in these capacities. How much more effective would it be if a pastor like this would personally groom another person to take his place and then be there when the transition takes place? After the transition, the pastor needs to fully empower, entrust, and celebrate this new leader's role, or he has the potential to encourage the church to have divisions and become a stumbling block to the community. In the next chapter, I discuss entrusting the work to our trainees.

Equipping others is an act of service where we function as *servants* by giving others guided opportunities with coaching. We serve others by equipping them and by giving them opportunities. Furthermore, we coach them and help them develop into the capacity that God has given them. Much of our idea of what a leader should be comes from the executive world of business—the CEO. However, Jesus cautioned his disciples from following this model and revealed his value of a servant (Matt 20:20).

James, John, and their mother came to Jesus and asked that they be seated at Jesus' right and left in his coming kingdom. Jesus answered that only God the Father has the authority to give those positions. They were not to follow the culture of the gentiles, who "lord it over them, and their great ones exercise authority over them" (Matt 20:25). Instead, if they wanted to be great in God's kingdom, they needed to serve. Those who serve others will become great in Jesus' kingdom (Matt 20:26–28; cf. Mark 10:45). We need to take this position. Jesus never used his authority for personal gain or exploitation. He served his disciples. We can follow his example of service and only use our authority and position when necessary.

Second, Jethro said, "You are not able to do it *alone*." The first thing that God saw that was not good after creation was that man was *alone*. So, God created family. He provided a companion for Adam suitable for him. Here, Jethro recognizes Moses' capacity limitation. We were not designed to serve in ministry *alone*. Even Jesus, the Son of God, did not serve in ministry alone. He had his seventy-two disciples, his twelve disciples, and his three closest disciples. Yet, many pastors are *alone* and feel *alone* in ministry. Even God himself exists as Father, Son, and Holy Spirit—the three-in-one God, the triune God. How could we ever think we can serve all *alone* and accomplish all the ministry by ourselves?

In my travels, I have met many pastors who are doing this exact thing—*serving alone*—and are burnt out. God did not design us to exist and to serve in this way. Many pastors feel that they have been trained for this work and no one can do it as capable as they can. Possibly, this is true—*right now*! It is not easy to train people to do what we are doing.

Years ago, I was talking with a missionary in the Philippines about him working on his vehicle. I suggested he find a mechanic to repair his truck, so that his time would be freed to focus on evangelism and discipleship. He said that if he asked a mechanic to do it, the mechanic would not do it as well as he does it and may instead create more problems. He would eventually have to repair his vehicle, and it may take more time and be more costly. Yes, this may be true in ministry also—*at least at first*. But it does not have to stay this way. It may take more time in the beginning, but as the disciple grows in the Lord and in their new ministry assignment, we are freed to focus on other areas.

Equipping others is hard work. I remember visiting a pastor in the Philippines. He led a church of over two hundred members. He did all the work—preaching, teaching, evangelizing, counseling—you get the picture! The church attended, watched, and celebrated his work and love for the Lord. But he was burnt out. He was ready to quit. I explained that we could help him, but it would mean more work. He wasn't too excited about that. But I clarified that after one year, his work would pay off. He could entrust ministry to the men he was training. He accepted the challenge. We visited him sixteen months later. His smile was contagious. He said, "I've never been happier in all my life. I'm accomplishing more than I have ever accomplished, and I myself am doing less work than I ever have done. The men I have been training are doing the work very effectively."

I once talked with a missionary in Fiji who responded the same way this pastor did. He was ready to quit and return home. The work load had negatively affected his health. I encouraged him to equip leaders. He did. When I visited him again, he shared with me the great joy he had. Everything was not perfect, but the entire church was working together as a body. He was personally doing less work but accomplishing more, as the leaders he was training were stepping up and leading the various ministries of the church.

Many pastors may love doing all the work for four reasons: 1) the glory and attention they receive from doing everything, especially if they do it well; 2) the insecurity and fear they feel if they train someone else to do the work; 3) they simply love the work of teaching and preaching the Word of God, and they love the people of God; and 4) they really do not know how to have a ministry of multiplication or do not think that this is possible. Some simply do not want to equip others to take their place. But we all have a shelf life, and one day someone *will* replace us. It is better to have a hand in the training of the replacement than to allow it just to happen, because rarely does it turn out well this way. Many ministries are left for years without a replacement, or if they do find someone, it does not always work out the best.

JESUS GAVE HIS DISCIPLES GUIDED OPPORTUNITIES.

Equipping others includes giving them *guided opportunities*. Our modeling and close relationship must be accompanied by *accountability*. During Jesus' ministry, he mobilized his disciples. There were at least two occasions when Jesus sent out his disciples. After calling the Twelve, he sent them out (Matt 10:42; Mark 6:7–32; Luke 9:1–10). In the second commissioning, Jesus sent out seventy-two disciples (Luke 10:1–20). In Matthew 9:35–39, Jesus tells his disciples that the harvest is plentiful, but the laborers are few. A few verses later in chapter 10, he instructs them what to do. He gives them authority over demons. The opportunity came with *detailed instruction and authority*. A. B. Bruce explains, "This mission of the disciples as evangelists or miniature apostles was partly, without doubt, an educational experiment for their own benefit; but its direct design was to meet the spiritual necessities of the people, whose neglected condition lay heavy on Christ's heart."[4] In other words, Jesus sent them out on mission for two purposes: 1) to develop them as future apostles, and 2) to minister to the needs of the Jewish people, who were languishing under the heavy burdens of their time. Over the last fifty years, there have been many teams of believers who have traveled to other lands to minister to the needs of people (mission trips). It is well known that *those who go are the most affected* by the exposure to a different culture and the intense nature of the mission trip. Various kinds of mission trips appeal to different people according to their abilities and maturity. Bruce goes on to explain that there were four things Jesus focused on for their mission.

First, the scope of their mission was Israel. "Go nowhere among the Gentiles and enter no town of the Samaritans, but go rather to the lost sheep of the house of Israel" (Matt 10:5–6). In Luke 9:6, we read that they went through all the villages and towns, "preaching and healing everywhere." This caught the attention of Herod the Tetrarch in Tiberias (Luke 9:7–9). Jesus defined the scope of their mission: they were to go to lost Jewish people in the towns and villages throughout Israel. The disciples were unprepared for a greater mission that included Samaritans and gentiles. We see their prejudice even in Acts 10, where Peter initially refused to visit Cornelius even though he was a God-fearer, i.e., a gentile convert to Judaism. Bruce notes that "the principal reason of the prohibition lay

---

4. Bruce, *Training of the Twelve*, 99.

in the present spiritual condition of the disciples themselves."[5] This implies that Jesus tailored the mission to their level of spiritual maturity, and at the same time, to the lost people of Israel. "Their hearts were too narrow, their prejudices too strong; there was too much of the Jew, too little of the Christian, in their character."[6] The implication is that we must know our trainees and tailor their assignments according to their abilities and spiritual maturity. We want to use the opportunity to stretch them so that they see a greater vision of what God desires and, at the same time, have this become a tool of inspection in their own lives that can lead to greater personal growth.

Second, according to Bruce, their work was extensive, and their message was limited. We could also say that their work was focused—on the spiritual powers of darkness. They were given authority to "Heal the sick, raise the dead, cleanse lepers, cast out demons" and "proclaim as you go, saying, 'The kingdom of heaven is at hand'" (Matt 10:7–8). They called the people to repentance (Mark 6:12). There were no restrictions on their healing ministry. Every sick or demon-possessed person would be touched. All of this was to be done in Jesus' name, under his authority and direction. Their message was simply, "The kingdom of heaven is at hand." They did not yet comprehend the full meaning of this. They did not understand the necessity of the cross and Jesus' sufferings. They did not understand about the resurrection. Their work and message were assigned according to their level of understanding with accompanying authority. We tend to do the opposite—overkill on the content and give little of the authority. In giving assignments to our trainees, we must ascertain what level of authority, teaching message, and ministry we should entrust to these growing servants. In many ministries, little authority is given. Little authority may be required. We must determine that through prayer and the leading of the Holy Spirit. Over the centuries, there has been much abuse, especially in the areas of finances, and many are tentative in this area. Authority is to be given according to the scope of the ministry with accountability.

In Numbers 27:15–20, God instructs Moses to give authority to Joshua. God tells Moses that Joshua would be his successor because he had disobeyed the Lord in striking the rock instead of speaking to it (27:12–14). Then, the Lord instructs Moses to lay hands on Joshua

---

5. Bruce, *Training of the Twelve*, 101.
6. Bruce, *Training of the Twelve*, 101.

before the congregation, commission him in their sight, and invest him with some of his authority (27:18–20). Ashley explains that "sense basic to all these rituals may be the transfer of something (a blessing, guilt, leadership) from someone to someone (or something) else."[7] Here, leadership is being transferred to Joshua in the sight of the nation. Joshua's authority over Israel was derived from Moses. While this may be used as a pattern for final conferring of authority and leadership, the concept of giving authority to someone is taken from one person to another. This was also practiced in the early church. When the early apostles appointed leaders to care for the Grecian Jews, they laid hands on them, imparting authority and accountability to them, in the sight of the gathered assembly.

Third, later, when they returned, they reported to him what happened. The opportunity also required accountability. Jesus invited his disciples to come aside by themselves to rest and to reflect upon all that had happened (Mark 6:30–31; Luke 9:10). With their involvement in Jesus' mission, it had gained possible undue attraction not only from the crowds of people but also from the authorities. It was time to debrief and reflect upon what had happened. In our training missions with our trainees, we must also give time for interaction, reflection, and debriefing. What did the disciples learn from the mission? What could they do better next time? What did God do in them? What did he do through them? This is necessary for personal development and growth. Otherwise, we go on to the next event without rejoicing in all the good things God had done and reflecting upon the areas where we need personal growth and development. In many instances, people are left to their own to process these things. What I am suggesting is that the trainer-mentor take an active role in the processing of what has happened, or we may lose the opportunity for the disciple-trainee to grow and to develop into what God wants to do in that person's life.

Fourth, after the second mission, the seventy-two returned. "The seventy-two returned with joy, saying, 'Lord, even the demons are subject to us in your name!'" (Luke 10:17). Jesus rejoiced with them in what happened. "I saw Satan fall like lightning from heaven" (Luke 10:18). He indicated to them that he had entrusted to them his authority over all demonic beings. He also tempered their excitement. "Nevertheless, do not rejoice in this, that the spirits are subject to you, but rejoice that your

---

7. Ashley, *zBook of Numbers*, 552.

names are written in heaven" (Luke 10:20). We naturally rejoice in great victories like the disciples witnessed.

In 2009, I took a group of pastors with me to Myanmar. I divided everyone into teams of two and sent them to various churches. The scene I witnessed that afternoon when everyone returned was similar to what we see in Luke 10. Everyone was rejoicing in what God had done. One pastor prayed for someone who was sick, and God healed him. Another one preached the gospel, and a Buddhist monk trusted Christ as Lord and Savior. One after another gave testimony to what God had done. The temptation is to vanity and pride after such happenings. When we see God work in incredible ways like this, we can begin to think that we are something special. More important than this, said Jesus to his disciples, is that we are children of our heavenly Father, and our names are written in the book of life! Our relationship with God the Father through Jesus is the most important truth. Otherwise, we begin to value our ministry performance over our relationship with our heavenly Father. Or we define our significance by our performance, and when our performance is not good, we question our calling.

Bruce explains this very succinctly. "The admonition to the seventy is indeed a word in season to all who are very zealous in the work of evangelism, especially such as are crude in knowledge and grace. It hints at the possibility of their own spiritual health being injured by their very zeal in seeking the salvation of others. This may happen in many ways. Success may make the evangelists vain, and they may begin to sacrifice unto their own net. They may fall under the dominion of the devil through their very joy that he is subject unto them."[8] Judas Iscariot was a member of this group. He cast out demons just like the other disciples did. No one suspected him to be the one to betray Jesus in the garden of Gethsemane. This is the risk we take in mobilizing would-be servants of the Lord. We must have a cautious eye so that our trainees are not filled with pride and fall into the trap of the devil (1 Tim 3:6). This teaches us the importance of caution and carefully instructing our trainees and following up with them after opportunities like this.

The most frightening aspect of giving opportunities to the people we are equipping may be the *authority* we have to entrust to them. We cannot control all the ministry anymore. Maybe this is frightening for you. Equipping others and giving them opportunities means that you also

---

8. Ashley, *Book of Numbers*, 108.

must entrust them with authority. This means that you lose some control. This should be encouraging because we do not control what is not ours anyway. The church or the ministry does not belong to us. It belongs to Jesus Christ. He said, "I will build *my* church," not *your* church. We are only servants and stewards of his work, and we will give an account of how we serve. This is the point of 1 Corinthians 3:5–17, where Paul addresses the issue of division and then pivots to the workers in 3:9. From 3:9–15, he explains that God will judge the quality of our work. Our rewards will be determined by our labor (3:8). Regardless of the size of our work, God will reward faithful hard work! Paul's exhortation is to the quality of our labor (3:10). "Let each one take care how he builds upon it." Then in verse 12 he compares our work to various materials—excellent quality materials and inferior quality materials. God will judge the quality of our work on that "day." Work that survives judgment will be rewarded, while work that does not survive judgment will not be rewarded (3:14). This should encourage us to be sober-minded and humble. As Jesus instructed his disciples, we see that everything is turned upside down. The first shall be last. The servant is the greatest in his kingdom. How great it will be before the Lord if we have followed his example and equipped disciple makers as he did. Or vice versa, how sad it will be if we have done everything by ourselves and not equipped others. Like the servant with the one talent, out of fear, we hid ours in the ground (kept it to ourselves doing all the work) and did not develop others.

As we begin to model Christlikeness for others, develop a close relationship with them, instruct them in sound doctrine, and give them guided opportunities, one thing that is obvious is that our role changes. Initially, a person may be enamored with our leadership and giftedness and follow everything we say. Then the relationship changes to that of a close friend, and the person we are mentoring may appreciate us taking the time to get to know them. But as they grow in the Lord, in their understanding of Scripture, and in their ability to serve and handle God's Word, that enamor begins to dissipate, and the reality that we are fragile human beings becomes apparent. In 1 John 1:7, we read that "if we walk in the light, as he is in the light, we have fellowship with one another, and the blood of Jesus his Son cleanses us from all sin." In other words, the light (God's truth) displays our weaknesses and areas in our lives that need growth and improvement. But notice in this verse the word "we." Most Westerners view this (and most of the Bible) from an individualistic perspective (just listen to Christian songs—"my battle," "my giants," "my faith," etc.). This is not the case in the majority of the world of the Bible and in much of the world today. The Bible was written from a collective shame-honor culture, where people did everything to avoid shame and did everything to gain honor. (Read Philippians from this perspective and you may see it in a new light. Note how Paul addresses the church and talks about honor.) This type of social jockeying results in a more collective society, where one's worth and dignity are not determined by my opinion but by the group that we are part of. Thus, everyone endeavors to meet the expectations of the values of the group rather than pursue their own dream or uniqueness. Thus, in 1 John 1:7, "If *we* walk in the light as he is in the light, *we* have fellowship with *one another*, and the blood of Jesus his Son cleanses *us* from all sin" (emphasis added). We are walking in the light together, and as we walk in the light together, we see each other's weaknesses and sin. We need the blood of Jesus to cleanse us from all sin. Then, as we begin to give guided opportunities with accountability, the relationship changes again. This is where we must be strict and gracious—strict with areas of ministry assignment that have been mutually agreed upon, and gracious when our mentor makes a mistake. Jesus gave detailed instructions to his disciples. Mentors can sometimes fail in that they assume the trainee knows what to do or knows what is expected. We must provide clear instructions and guidelines; otherwise it is difficult to hold someone accountable for what they are not aware of. One new role emerges during this process: the role of management, where the trainer manages the trainee and his work. Management involves encouragement, equipping, oversight, and accountability. Another way of describing this is to move from being the quarterback or player to being the coach. The potential for aged men and women who have been in full-time ministry for years is that they will have hungry candidates to mentor and coach. As a new pastor begins to realize his limitations, his need for someone to coach him grows—if he is teachable and desires to be effective.

The most detailed list of instructions by Jesus to his disciples is given in Matthew 10. Jesus sent them two by two, which empowered them to work side by side, which developed their giftedness and ability to work together. First, they were to go with minimal equipment and depend upon the goodwill of those who welcomed them into their homes. In other words, they would need to depend upon God to provide for them through the goodwill of those they ministered to. God would provide the necessities of life to them. They would take care of the disciples. Jesus allowed the disciples to be blessed by the generosity of their hosts

(10:8–15). They would bless those who received them. Those who rejected them would face judgment from God (10:15). Second, he warned them of facing difficulties and persecution (10:25). They would face demonic attack, persecution, hardships, and rejection. They would need to exercise caution yet live with love, kindness, and simplicity ("be wise as serpents and innocent as doves"; 10:16). This was no vacation. They were sent on mission by Jesus to deliver his message and to do his work. When facing difficult situations, the Holy Spirit would instruct them what to say. There were evil men that they were to be cautious of, yet they were to be kindhearted, ready to love and serve others. Third, they were not to go in fear, but to walk in faith (10:26–33). They were to only fear God. God would take care of them. He knows the number of hairs on their heads. He cares for them. Fourth, their cooperation in this mission was evidence that they were willing to take up their cross and follow Jesus (10:34–39). Persecution would even be evident in a family. Not all would welcome their message. He asked them to love him more than anyone else in the world. Those willing to lose their lives would find their lives (10:39). Fifth, rewards were guaranteed (10:40–42). Those who received them would also be receiving Jesus, who sent them. Even if a person gives a cup of cold water in his name, he will receive a reward (10:42).

I wonder how many Christians would go on a mission trip today if these were the instructions given. Just take the minimal supplies. Depend on your hosts. Eat whatever they feed you. Whoever receives you is a sign that they have received or will receive me. Those who accept you and provide for you will be richly rewarded. There will be difficulties and persecution. Those who reject you will be severely punished. Don't go in fear. Trust the Lord. He will see you through this. These were the instructions Jesus gave his disciples for their first mission trip!

Bill Hull explains the necessity of this step from Jesus' sending of the disciples. "A person who is just learning the ropes of laboring not only *needs* supervision but in most cases *desires* it. Because of our fallen human nature, when we are given an assignment we need to give an account of our experience. A vital part of leadership is assisting trainees in learning and improving skills. As a leader, I would be sinning against the ones I train and those my trainees touch if neglect to supervise."[9]

---

9. Hull, *Jesus Christ Disciplemaker*, 174.

Michael J. Wilkins suggests this was the time that Jesus began to "sift" his followers.[10] The number of followers were growing and not all their expectations were in line with Jesus' mission. Many followers wanted to take him by force and make him king, assuming that he would lead a revolt against the Romans. Establishing lines of accountability where guided opportunities are given can reveal areas of needed growth. Some, like John Mark, may realize that they are not up to the task, quit, and return home (Acts 13:13). Thankfully, John Mark did return and reconcile with Paul during Paul's later years and Paul recognized John Mark's usefulness in the ministry (2 Tim 4:11). Barnabas may have been premature in his invitation of John Mark, not accurately accessing his readiness.

ELIJAH GAVE ELISHA GUIDED OPPORTUNITIES.

In 1 Kings 19:19-21, we read that Elijah returned from Mt. Sinai from his new commission from the Lord. Elijah threw his cloak upon Elisha. "Throwing a prophet's cloak around a person symbolized the passing of the power and authority of the office to that individual. That Elisha realized the meaning of this act is obvious from his reaction. Immediately he started to abandon his former occupation and follow Elijah. Elijah gave him permission to say farewell to his family."[11] "So after he made the break and killed his oxen, his means of livelihood—a final act of total commitment—and went with Elijah (1 Kings 19:21), what did he find himself doing? Serving Elijah. It is true that those who would lead must first learn to serve. And it is equally true that to train men a person must be willing to spend time with those men in hours of conversation and association in the normal affairs of life."[12] Elisha spent the next ten years with Elijah as Elijah developed schools or groups of the prophets (see 2 Kgs 2:3) who taught the Word of God to Israel. Elijah and Elisha had taught them the Word of God, and they in turn taught Israel the Word of God. Elisha continued this tradition and continued to train new prophets. They multiplied to the extent that they had to expand the building where they met with him (2 Kgs 6:1-7). Many of these prophets lived during the times of the minor prophets. It is possible that Elijah and Elisha had trained them in these groups of disciples of the prophets.

10. Wilkins, *Following the Master*, 114.
11. Constable, "1 Kings," 529 (emphasis original).
12. Eims, *Lost Art of Disciple Making*, 31.

BARNABAS GAVE SAUL GUIDED OPPORTUNITIES.

This is one of the greatest examples in Scripture. In Acts 9:31, all the disciples feared Saul until Barnabas vouched for him. As a result of Barnabas' vouching for Saul, Saul was able to boldly preach the gospel throughout Jerusalem. As a result, the church "multiplied" (Acts 9:31). Barnabas encouraged Saul to preach the gospel, and he did so, boldly. "So the church throughout all Judea and Galilee and Samaria had peace and was built up. And walking in the fear of the Lord and in the comfort of the Holy Spirit, it multiplied [*plēthynō*]" (Acts 9:31). *The church multiplies when we equip others by giving them guided opportunities.*

Later, in Acts 11:19–31, the church of Jerusalem sent Barnabas to the church in Antioch. In Acts 11:20, we read that some of the evangelists preached the gospel to Greeks, i.e., gentiles. A significant number of people turned to the Lord and believed in Jesus. Barnabas realized that he needed help in leading this church since it was a multiethnic church. He also knew that God had called Saul as an apostle to the gentiles, so he decided to give Saul the opportunity to serve with him. In Acts 11:25, we read that Barnabas left to find Saul and diligently searched (from ἀναζητέω, *anazēteō*). "But it is specially used of searching for human beings, with an implication of difficulty, as in the NT passages."[13] This is also found in Luke 2:44–45, where Mary and Joseph looked for Jesus and found him after great difficulty. This shows the *intentionality*, deliberate determination, and genuineness of Barnabas in offering this opportunity to Saul. When Barnabas went to Tarsus, he would have traveled about three hundred kilometers (about two hundred miles) across land and sea, which would have taken him five or six days to accomplish. Bruce surmises, "He therefore went to Tarsus in person to seek him out—a task of some difficulty, perhaps, since Saul appears to have been disinherited for his joining the followers of Jesus and could no longer be found at his ancestral home."[14] Polhill comments that "Barnabas was a 'bridge-builder,' one who was able to see the positive aspects in both sides of an issue and to mediate between perspectives."[15] He also notes the difficulty that Barnabas faced in finding Paul. "The verb Luke employed (*anazēteō*) means *to seek out* and implies he had some difficulty in finding him. Quite likely Paul was off somewhere busily engaged in missionary activity. When

---

13. Moulton and Milligan, *Vocabulary of the Greek Testament*, 32.
14. Bruce, *Book of the Acts*, 227.
15. Polhill, *Acts*, 272.

GIVING GUIDED OPPORTUNITIES

Barnabas finally located Paul, he brought him back to Antioch where the two were heavily occupied in preaching and teaching to 'great numbers' (v. 26)."[16] He brought Saul to Antioch, and they taught great numbers of believers in Antioch. So much was their influence that the disciples were called "Christians," a distinct group of Jesus followers different from Jews. Toussaint states, "The significance of the name, emphasized by the word order in the Greek text, is that people recognized Christians as a distinct group. The church was more and more being separated from Judaism."[17] As a result of their ministry in Antioch for one year, the leadership team multiplied (see Acts 13:1). In Acts 13:1, we read that there were prophets and teachers at Antioch from diverse ethnic backgrounds, which included five gifted leaders—two Jews, an African, a European, and a Palestinian. Not only did Barnabas and Saul grant opportunities to others to serve based on their giftedness, but ethnic distinctions also did not matter. They did not project themselves as superior to these new leaders but were listed together as equals. Since Barnabas is listed first, he was the leader of this team, as they focused on worshipping the Lord and praying together. This was a tremendous development in the early church. There was no racial prejudice as they were co-equals serving together on the leadership team.

Later, during their first missionary journey, the order of their names was changed from "Barnabas and Saul" to "Paul and Barnabas" (Acts 13:13). Poyhill comments that "Barnabas' greatness is displayed by his willingness to let Paul be the leader. So Paul and his companions sailed to Perga in Pamphylia."[18] Barnabas was humble and servant enough to allow Paul to develop into a great missionary leader and allowed him to lead their missionary team. In Acts 11:22–24, we read that Barnabas was sent by the Jerusalem church. His name had been changed from Joseph to Barnabas because he was an encourager. When he arrived in Antioch, Barnabas also exhorted (from *parakaleō*, also meaning "to encourage") them to "remain faithful to the Lord with steadfast purpose." Barnabas focused on the good things that God was doing in the new church of Antioch ("he saw the grace of God"). Barnabas recognized Paul's giftedness, and when he saw that Paul was ready, he allowed him to lead the team. Barnabas also saw John Mark's potential and wanted to give him an opportunity, but he may not have been ready for this commitment. Barnabas's desire for John Mark

16. Polhill, *Acts*, 273.
17. Toussaint, "Acts," 383.
18. Polhill, *Acts*, 388.

to rejoin the team after the Jerusalem Council led to his and Paul's conflict and subsequent separation into different teams (Acts 15:37–41).

How can we apply this to our ministries today? Do you consider yourself a gifted pastor? Do you allow younger men to get close to you, or do you keep people at a distance? Enlist a young man to shadow you and follow you around. Then begin giving him opportunities with feedback and coaching. You can become a servant to this up-and-coming leader. Your intentional choice to mentor this young man and model effective ministry and Christlikeness to him will communicate tremendous servanthood and respect to him. Let him see how you relate to your family, staff, and leadership team.

How often does this happen today when the senior leader gives way to an aspiring visionary leader like Paul and allows him to lead the team and take his place? Barnabas was a "good man, full of faith and the Holy Spirit." Barnabas was also a humble man, allowing Paul to serve with him, to see his potential, and to allow him to lead their missionary team. This is a rare occurrence in Christian ministries. In forty years of ministry, I have never witnessed this happen. I have seen older men serve with younger men, but only at the younger man's invitation. Is it that we are thinking so much of ourselves that we do not see the potential of others? Or is it that we are protecting our position, prestige, and possibly paycheck? We have arrived at the highest position of the ministry, and we do not want to give it up to someone else possibly because we are selfish and self-centered. Could we be standing in the way of God?

Barnabas's choosing of Saul was intentional and deliberate. He went to Tarsus to diligently look for Saul. Barnabas focused on the good things that God was doing in people's lives ("when he saw the grace of God"). Barnabas, with the eyes of faith, saw the potential in people and helped bring those good qualities and giftedness out of them. He did this with Saul, whose name was later changed to Paul, and also with John Mark. He gave John Mark a second chance to continue to develop him. Paul later stated that John Mark was useful for the work. Barnabas was quick to notice the potential in others and give them a second chance.

In giving people guided opportunities, we must also be *deliberate* and *intentional*. Opportunities sometimes come by God's sovereignty in our lives. But through prayer and the leading of the Holy Spirit, we can become instruments in the hand of the Lord in developing a Saul or John Mark. Second, we must rejoice in the good things God is doing in the person's life. We should focus on the positive aspects of that person. We can look at the cup as half full (positive characteristics) or half empty (negative characteristics). Third, we can serve with grace by giving people a second chance after they have failed if they are teachable and correctable. Fourth, we should look into the person with faith for what God can do through them.

Dave Ferguson calls this the ICNU ("I see in you") conversation. It requires that we are Spirit-led and take a keen interest in people's lives enough to see the potential in them. Ferguson shares the potential of this practice. "I can't stress enough what a difference it can make when someone you respect takes the time to see something in you and to call that out in you. Most people did not grow up in a family in which they experienced this, nor do they work in an environment where this happens. Our ICNU culture helps those who are affirmed with the confidence to step forward and ask for permission, wanting to hear, 'Yes, you can do it.'"[19]

Do you consider yourself a successful children's worker or women's ministry leader? Find someone to shadow you and to mentor. Allow them to accompany you, ask questions, and give them guided opportunities where there is feedback and coaching. Coaching provides encouragement of where they have done well and where they need improvement.

This approach follows well with Paul's instructions to Titus in Titus 2: the older men are to teach the younger men, and the older women are to teach the younger women. In a culture that values youth, this could provide a correction to our culture's misplaced values, show an example to the world of respect, and pass the baton to the next generation. Whether you like it or not, the next generation will lead because we all have a shelf life. We cannot serve forever in our current positions and ministries.

PAUL GAVE TIMOTHY AND TITUS GUIDED OPPORTUNITIES.

In Acts 16:1–3, Paul enlisted Timothy as his assistant during his second missionary journey. Timothy was "well-spoken of by the brothers" (Acts 16:2), and Paul probably led Timothy to Christ since he called Timothy his "true child" (1 Tim 1:2; 2 Tim 2:1). Paul sent Timothy to different cities to follow up on contacts and projects. When Paul was in Athens, he sent Timothy to visit the Philippian church and the Thessalonian church (Phil 2:19–24; 1 Thess 3:1–5). He sent Timothy to find out about their

---

19. Ferguson and Bird, *Hero Maker*, 104.

faith and to find out how they were doing. Paul described Timothy as one who was genuinely concerned for other believers and that he had served with him as a son with a father. He had proven worth (Phil 2:22). This resulted from Paul giving Timothy opportunities to serve with him. Timothy served faithfully and demonstrated proven worth. It was not by accident that Timothy served faithfully and demonstrated worth. Paul's involvement in Timothy's life and Paul's providing him with opportunities led to his development. Rarely do we think this way. Pastors hire a staff they expect to be already equipped. Paul also knew Timothy to be timid, and he needed to stir up the gift of God in him (2 Tim 1:6). He knew that he had stomach issues and advised him to drink wine for his stomach illnesses (1 Tim 5:23). Paul knew Timothy's limits and weaknesses. This only comes through close discipleship relationships.

In Titus 1:5, we read that Paul left Titus in Crete to finish the job of establishing the churches and developing solid leadership. Paul gave Titus opportunities to serve with him. In 2 Corinthians 8:6, Titus was sent to collect the offerings from churches to give to the poor believers in Judea. Paul left Timothy in Ephesus to teach sound doctrine, appoint godly leadership, and establish the church (1 Tim 1:5). They were entrusted with collecting offerings for the project in Judea, teaching sound doctrine, organizing ministries, and making sure that churches were operating with order and purpose. Both were left to finish developing these churches. Their roles in these churches were temporary, in place only until pastors and elders could be trained and appointed to teach with sound doctrine, competence, and character. In these cases, Timothy and Titus had reached the higher level of responsibility and trust required for the task. We learn from this that varying levels of responsibility are to be entrusted as trainees or disciples grow into these responsibilities with the accompanying capacities of competency and trust. In the entrusting of opportunities, we must make sure that we are giving sufficient and clear instruction, varying levels of responsibility according to the person's capability and maturity, and then require the accountability that accompanies each level of opportunity. When giving someone the opportunity to share a testimony, less instruction will be needed as opposed to asking someone to lead a small group or to preach a message. As we develop varying levels of opportunities, each should be tailored to the trainee with the accompanying instruction, accountability, and coaching afterward.

Who in your ministry needs a guided opportunity? You can meet with the person before the opportunity and review what they need to do.

Give them guidance. After they have taken the opportunity, meet with them again and coach them through the good things they did and where they need to grow and improve.

During our first church plant in the Philippines, I started three evangelistic Bible studies in our town. I was teaching the stories of the Bible, bringing out the theology of who God is, what God demands for our sins to be forgiven, who man is, and what our proper response should be to God's gracious provision of Jesus Christ. At the same time, I was teaching these lessons to our small church, started by a colleague who returned to the USA for a home ministry assignment. I began praying and asking God whom I could bring along with me. The Lord led me to invite Jose, Alberto, and Nestor to accompany me in these Bible studies. In the beginning, they helped people find the Scripture passage. We also used pictures of the stories created by tribal people from other parts of the country. They set those up. Three months after we started the Bible studies, I asked these three men to help me teach the lessons. I gave them opportunities to serve with me. I taught part of the lesson, and they taught the other part of the lesson. On the way home, I coached them, telling them all the good things they said and did and giving them suggestions on how to improve and grow. Four months later, the Bible studies finished those lessons. God opened new opportunities for us. We grew to over twenty evangelistic Bible studies within a year. There was no way I could lead those Bible studies by myself. With three new trainees, I sent them to lead these Bible studies. Three other young men from the Bible college in the capital city also joined us, and another young man from the church joined us. There were eight of us leading Bible studies all over the town. We went two by two. Sometimes we walked. We also took public transportation. God began using these men greatly. Three of them are still pastors today.

As we give guided opportunities, we are entrusting ministry and authority to them. One of the more difficult things to do is to give authority. In 2006, I started Crossing Cultures International (CCI). In the beginning, I oversaw everything. As the ministry grew, I had to learn not only to entrust the ministry responsibility but to give authority to the people I had entrusted ministry to. I have experienced the blessing of the Lord to see us hire new servant leaders. At our last global conference, I found myself grieving due to the loss I would experience by entrusting ministry, authority, and people to others—people I have spent a lot of time with, teaching, training, modeling, and correcting. I have grown very close to these men, and now I am entrusting them to others. In reality, they belong to Jesus, and I am his instrument in training and in shaping them to serve him in his work.

Some men and women never reach their God-given potential because no one allows them the opportunity to serve. No one sees the work of God in their lives. No one sees their potential. If you do all the preaching and teaching, everyone will be conditioned to be a spectator. Transform spectators into servants by giving them opportunities, even if the opportunity is for a few minutes.

DISCUSSION QUESTIONS

1. Can you think of someone who gave you opportunities to serve? How did it help you develop?

2. Were the opportunities guided or were you left on your own to figure things out? If guided, how did that help you? If not guided, what were the results?

3. Who can you give guided opportunities to in your ministry? Make a plan that is deliberate and intentional, with detailed instructions according to the task, and plan to meet with the person afterward to coach that person to grow and improve.

4. Create a plan for your ministry with varying levels of responsibilities, training content, opportunities, coaching, and accountability.

PRINCIPLE #5

Entrusted Ministry

And when they had appointed elders for them in every church, with prayer and fasting they committed them *to the Lord in whom they had believed.*
(Acts 14:23)

EARLIER, I SHARED ABOUT three men I began training and coaching. One of them is Jose. When I met Jose, he had been a follower of Christ for less than two years. He was a fairly new convert. I invited him to accompany me to a Bible study at the seaside. I would do the teaching. He would help people find the passages of the stories in the Bible that we were studying. He went with me every Sunday. Sometimes, I waited for him for up to an hour before going to the Bible study. I did not mind waiting for him because this gave me time to visit with his family and get to know them better. I had been teaching the same lessons with the church. Three months into this Bible study, he began teaching with me. On the way home, I coached him on how to grow and improve. As he continued to demonstrate faithfulness, I entrusted more responsibility to him. Later, he led several Bible studies, and I began training him in preaching every Sunday. I gave him the message, and he preached the message I wrote. We evaluated his message on Monday. After several months of doing this, he began developing his own messages. We met afterward to assess his message. He was growing steadily, and I felt he was ready to lead the church. I met with the other global workers, and everyone agreed. We ordained him as the pastor in April 1990. Jose is still serving as the pastor today as I write this. In May 1990, we returned to the USA for one year of "home assignment." When we returned in 1991, the church was still growing. There were new Bible studies. There were new people who had trusted in Christ and new baptisms. I could see that the hand of the Lord was upon Jose. In some ways, I rejoiced about this, but in others I was not emotionally ready.

Before we left for the USA, I oversaw the church. When I returned, I was no longer in charge. At first, I had a hard time not being in charge anymore, but eventually I saw the wisdom in him leading the church and our transitioning away and letting him lead. That was the goal—to have a qualified and competent national leading the church. In cross-cultural church planting, this is referred to as the "phase-out stage," the "exit strategy," "departure," or "passing the baton." We remained there another four years to help the church develop an evangelistic outreach. He and I had conflicts along the way, but we worked those things out, and we are still close friends today.

In his book *Passing the Baton*, Tom A. Steffen states that the issue with church-planting efforts in cross-cultural settings is the *lack* of a definitive plan and definition for phase-out. "Without such a definition of phase-out, the church planters had no way to identify their necessary role changes, much less work through them. Furthermore, the agency did not include a phase-out philosophy in its recruiting, selection and training of church planters. Consequently, most of its church planters stayed on as evangelists and teachers, rather than becoming partners; they emphasized phase-in rather than phase-out."[1] We can apply this not only to cross-cultural global workers and national pastors, but also to pastors of established churches and ministry leaders of non-profit organizations. Having a definitive phase-out plan guides the leader in intentionally raising up the next pastor or ministry leader. If we are not deliberate and intentional, we are leaving the phase-out to chance, speculation, and possible failure and frustration.

Entrusting ministry assignments to someone can be challenging, especially if you are in the same ministry. But we must realize that we are not going to live forever. We will all die. We have a shelf life. Someone will take our place, or the church or ministry will die with us. If someone is ready to take our place now, why not entrust that ministry assignment to them now? We have modeled effective ministry and Christlikeness

---

1. Steffen, *Passing the Baton*, 13.

for them. We have developed a close relationship with them. We have trained them in sound doctrine. We have given them guided opportunities. They have demonstrated faithfulness. They have proved themselves. It is time to entrust the ministry to them. There will always be ministry opportunities. There will be people who need to hear the gospel until we go to heaven. There will be believers who need discipling and pastoring. The opportunity to develop a successor will not available. Gifted leaders will seek out other opportunities if we continue to hold on to our positions.

Once, while talking with a local Tampa pastor, he told me that many pastors do not realize when their time is up. They keep leading the church even when they should turn it over to someone else and let them lead without interfering with their leadership. I was meeting with another pastor years ago, and we were discussing the weakness of satellite campus churches where the senior pastor does all the preaching and does not entrust this to others even when there are capable men to lead the campus churches and lead the preaching and proclamation of the gospel. I asked him what would happen to a church with multiple satellite campuses if the senior pastor died. While we were discussing this, a senior pastor of a large church with multiple campuses did pass away that very hour. Several years passed before the church recovered, but they were forced to allow campus pastors to carry the responsibility of preaching and teaching, which actually turned out to be a good thing. Once they found a new senior pastor, he did not take over that responsibility from the campus pastors. The campus pastors continued to carry the responsibility of preaching and teaching. Either we can intentionally plan for this by equipping pastors with effective preaching, or we can let what may happen and allow them to pick up the pieces afterwards. The more responsible and productive route would be to create an intentional plan. If we fail to do this, we can be certain that our ministry will not multiply. Many churches measure their success by conversions, offerings, baptisms, and volunteers. It is time to start measuring success not by how much we do, but by how much we give away and how many we entrust and empower with ministry, and by how many we send.

Pastors can become addicted to the ministry. They can fall in love with leading the church, preaching every Sunday, and overseeing all the ministries and programs. We can become addicted to the authority, influence, and popularity. We can become enamored with the attention and glory and not realize that the church does not belong to us, but the church belongs to Jesus Christ. Jesus promised in Matthew 16:18 that he would build his church, not ours.

On the other side of that is disillusionment. Members can develop unrealistic expectations and unhealthy images of what a pastor should be and do. Pastors can become stressed out with all the unrealistic expectations people place on them. Members can have a hero image of the pastor and project expectations onto their spouse that he or she should be like their pastor or their pastor's wife. Churches can become personality driven, much like what we find in 1 Corinthians 3. Expectations can become so high that only Jesus could ever meet the expectations members have for their pastor. The reality is that no pastor has all the spiritual gifts and abilities needed to do all the ministry. The Holy Spirit has given each believer spiritual gifts requisite for the ministry assignment that God desires to entrust to each of us. In areas where we are deficient, we need someone to serve alongside us.

So how do we entrust ministry to a potential candidate? First, we must follow the first four principles. Live as a godly model for those you want to entrust ministry. Bring people with you. Do you want them to be an effective teacher? You need to be the example of an effective teacher. Do you want them to become a Christlike servant? You need to be the example of a Christlike servant. Do you want them to be an effective soul-winner? You be the example of an effective soul-winner. Next, develop a close relationship with them. Developing a close relationship will reveal the person's strengths, weaknesses, and spiritual gifts. Next, equip them with sound doctrine. Discover what they understand about the main biblical teachings. Your goal is that they learn how to articulate these biblical teachings. Writing enables a person to develop ideas on paper (or digital paper). The writer has time (unless it's a test) to read, reread, edit, and finalize. More important, though, is that they learn how to explain and orally defend these teachings. When sharing the gospel with a person or counseling a client, there is no time to rehearse, edit, write, or rewrite. Finally, give them guided opportunities. Giving them opportunities will further reveal to you where their deficiencies lie.

When I began church planting in the Philippines, all my deficiencies became apparent (my wife already knew them all!). Ministry tends to do that. When we begin to serve, our strengths are apparent, and so are our weaknesses. Like Moses holding the staff, he had to eventually lower it because he was limited. Ministry reveals our weaknesses and our need for others to serve with us. When Aaron and Hur helped Moses lift up the staff, Joshua and his army defeated the Amalekites. Unless we learn how to invite others to hold up the staff with us, we will not win the battle. Winning the battle by ourselves is virtually impossible. Just look at what happened to Elijah. One day after winning the battle over the prophets of Baal, he was ready to die under a tree in the wilderness.

THE IMPORTANCE OF QUALITY EVALUATION

In Romans 15:14–33, we see Paul's ability to carefully evaluate the church in Rome. Paul did not start this church, nor had he visited this church. But due to persecution, many workers there had traveled to other parts of the Roman Empire, where Paul was stationed. We see this in Acts 18:2–3, where we read, "And he found a Jew named Aquila, a native of Pontus, recently come from Italy with his wife Priscilla, because Claudius had commanded all the Jews to leave Rome. And he went to see them, and because he was of the same trade, he stayed with them and worked, for they were tentmakers by trade." Undoubtedly, they talked together, and Paul learned enough of this church to make this assessment.

Paul was confident (from πείθω, *peithō*, to be "convinced" or "persuaded") that the Roman church was characterized by goodness, that they understood the gospel and sound doctrine ("filled with knowledge"), and that they were competent to instruct one another. He assessed their character, knowledge and understanding, and competency. Paul's purpose in writing to the church in Rome was to unpack the gospel and defend his ministry to the gentiles. He was direct in some of the areas where they needed a reminder (15:15). He shared how God confirmed his gospel proclamation to the gentiles through signs and wonders. He had accomplished the mission from Jerusalem to Illyricum (modern Albania). In Paul's ministry in Ephesus, he focused on equipping servant leaders. They, in turn, carried the gospel to the outlying towns and villages of Asia Minor. Paul chose strategic urban areas and entrusted to his disciples the responsibility to reach inland and to towns and villages. Paul also knew when he had finished the work God had called him to (Acts 14:26). Thus, it behooves us to know clearly what our work is and when the work is finished. If these are not clearly defined, there will be ambiguity about the different roles of leaders and when the work is finished. If we do not have a definitive plan for what we will do, everything will be left to happenstance. We will never know when we are done and when to exit and turn over the ministry to our trainees.

Because the work was so extensive and there was persecution and hardship, Paul was hindered in coming to Rome. He requested that they pray for him that his ministry in Judea would be successful. He also wanted them to allow him to come and base his operations in Rome in order to reach Spain (15:28). He desired that they refresh him when he comes (15:32) and that they support him with all that he needed for travel (from προπέμπω, *propempō*) on his journey to Spain (15:24). Paul was finished the work in the eastern part of the empire, and now he wanted to start over in the western part.

In 1 Corinthians 3:1–4, Paul assesses their spiritual maturity as lacking because they were divided. He assesses that they were carnal or worldly. Paul also evaluated the churches of Galatia. False teachers had invaded them with a false gospel. Like wild animals, they were biting and devouring one another (both present-tense verbs indicating ongoing action) (Gal 5:15). Paul sent Titus and Timothy to establish the churches in Crete and Ephesus.

The point here is that we must learn how to evaluate and assess believers and churches. What is their understanding of Scripture and theology? What is their understanding and usage of their spiritual gifts? How effectively are they serving? How is their relationship with Christ and with other believers? What is their level of spiritual maturity? Are they able to handle conflict in a biblical way with grace and gentleness, or do they flee to the nearest church, bringing their problems with them? Evaluation and assessment will help us determine what ministries they should serve in, what opportunities we should entrust to them, and when we should exit. From reading Paul's letters, it is evident that Paul knew his role, knew what spiritual maturity looks like, and knew how to evaluate and assess a local church. This is something that we need to learn how to do with a scriptural basis.

THE NEW TESTAMENT CONCEPT OF PROVING

The most common word in the New Testament for *proving* is δοκιμάζω (*dokimazō*) (verb). Other forms of this word include δοκιμασία (*dokimasia*, "testing"), δοκιμή (*dokimē*, "proven character"), δοκίμιον (*dokimion*, "testing, genuine"), δόκιμος (*dokimos*, "approved, tested"), ἀποδοκιμάζω (*apodokimazō*, "to reject"), and ἀδόκιμος (*adokimos*, "unqualified"). δοκιμάζω (*dokimazō*) has two meanings: "to make a critical examination of something to determine genuineness" and "to draw a conclusion about the worth of the basis of testing, prove, approve, here the focus is on the result of a procedure or examination."[2] Of the twenty-two times δοκιμάζω is used in the New Testament, it is used nineteen times in Paul's letters and three times in Luke.

Δοκιμή (*dokimē*) is used for testing, an ordeal, or proven character. It is used for "a testing process" or "the experience of going through a test with special ref.[erence] to the result."[3] In 2 Corinthians 8:2, Paul indicates that they had experienced a "severe test of affliction." Paul wrote to test them and see whether they are "obedient in everything" (2 Cor 2:9). God tests us to reveal to ourselves where we need improvement and growth. He is the ultimate test giver.

Δόκιμος (*dokimos*) refers to "being genuine on the basis of testing."[4] We see this in 2 Timothy 2:15, where Paul exhorts Timothy to do his best to present himself to God as one "approved," one who has been tested and has passed the test and demonstrated maturity.

Δοκιμασία (*dokimasia*) refers to the act of testing, where Israel tested God in the wilderness (Heb 3:9). This has a negative connotation. The Israelites, due to their hardened hearts, refused to obey God and thus put him to the test. In other words, they challenged God with their disobedience.

ἀποδοκιμάζω (*apodokimazō*) is used eight times for Israel's rejection of Jesus and one time in Hebrews for God's rejection of Esau (12:17).

ἀδόκιμος (*adokimos*) is used eight times in the NT, translated by the ESV as "fail," "disqualified," "debased," "unfit," and "worthless." This word primarily focuses on the results of the testing without mentioning the one testing, except in 2 Corinthians 13:5, 6, and 7, where the Corinthian church was to examine themselves or that they had tested Paul.

Δοκίμιον is used twice in the NT (Jas 1:3; 1 Pet 1:7), where God tests the genuineness of our faith. It is used of the "process or means to determine the genuineness of someth.[ing]" or the "genuineness as a result of a test."[5]

---

2. BDAG, 256.
3. BDAG, 256.
4. BDAG, 256.
5. BDAG, 256.

GOD TESTS US BELIEVERS.

Guffield and Van Cleave explain that the "Greek words: *dokime, dokimazo, dokimos, dokimion* (used thirty-nine [39] times in the New Testament), are words from the work of the assayer with his crucible. In the life of the Church, believers are in God's crucible, being tested and approved. (See 1 Thes. 2:4; Rom. 16:10; 1 Cor. 12:19; 2 Cor. 10:18; Jas. 1:12)."[6]

In 1 Thessalonians 2:4, there are two instances of the word δοκιμάζω. In the first instance, Paul and his team had been tested and found trustworthy with the gospel. Wanamaker explains that "The perfect verb δεδοκιμάσμεθα expresses the fact that Paul has been examined and found acceptable by God to be entrusted with the gospel."[7] Paul does not indicate what test this was, but since he had just arrived from Philippi, he may be referring to their imprisonment in Philippi, or a prior experience in his first missionary journey, or some unknown event. After being humiliated in Philippi, God gave them the boldness to continue to Thessalonica, where they proclaimed the gospel "in the midst of much conflict" (2:2). Paul shares that they visited the Thessalonians not out of impure motives (2:3, 5–6). Paul approached them as spiritual parents (2:7–12) and was ready to sacrifice for the spiritual growth of the Thessalonian believers.

In the second instance, Paul used the participle τῷ δοκιμάζοντι (*tō dokimazonti*), which is a relative clause modifying God. God is the one who is in the ongoing process of testing our hearts. In James 1:3, we see the purpose of the desired outcome of the testing. There the focus is not on God doing the testing but on the actual testing itself. "The testing of your faith produces *steadfastness*." We can be certain that the one who does the testing is God, but here the purpose is the focus—steadfastness. The Greek word ὑπομονή (*hypomonē*) was a virtue in classical Greek. Hauck explains that "as ὑπομονή later came to hold a prominent place in the list of Greek virtues, so there predominates in ὑπομένειν the concept of the courageous endurance which manfully defies evil."[8] This is God's goal in testing believers through "various trials." James illustrates this from the lives of Abraham (2:21), the prophets (5:10), and Job (5:11). Indeed, the man who perseveres through the trials is blessed because after "he has stood the test he will receive the crown of life, which God has

---

6. Duffield, and Van Cleave, *Foundations of Pentecostal Theology*, 457.
7. Wanamaker, *Epistles to the Thessalonians*, 95.
8. Hauck, "Μένω," 581–82.

promised to those who love him" (Jas 1:12). In 1 Peter 1:7, Peter uses the illustration of a fire in a crucible testing gold as an analogy of God's testing of our faith. The tests themselves are "various trials." The purpose of the testing is to prove that the believer's faith is genuine. God allows tests to demonstrate the genuineness of our faith, i.e., that we are not fake. In 1 Corinthians 3:13, the "day" will reveal the quality of the workers' work because it will be tested by fire. The workers' work is compared to various building materials; some is of good quality, and some is consumed by fire.

BELIEVERS SHOULD TEST THEMSELVES.

In 2 Corinthians 13:5, Paul encourages the church to "examine" (πειράζω, *peirazō*) and to "test" (δοκιμάζω, *dokimazō*) themselves to see if they are true believers. Believers are to "test" their own works (Gal 6:4), to show if the work is worthy of boasting. The church is to test prophecies (1 Thess 5:21) and the "spirits" (1 John 4:1). They are to evaluate traveling teachers to see if what they are teaching is doctrinally sound. In the context of 1 John, their teaching needs to line up with Jesus' incarnation and humanity. Paul challenged the Corinthian church to participate in the giving project for the poor saints in Judea in order "to prove by the earnestness of others that your love also is genuine" (2 Cor 8:8).

CHURCH LEADERS SHOULD TEST THEIR TRAINEES.

In 2 Corinthians 8:22, Paul explains that he is sending "our brother whom *we have often tested* and found earnest in many matters" (emphasis added). Paul tested his disciples to prove their genuineness and character. Concerning deacons, he instructs Timothy to "test" them first and "if they prove themselves blameless," they can serve the local church (1 Tim 3:10).

Thus, we have seen that God tests us to refine us and make us better servants, and we are to test those serving with us to help them grow in Christ. How does God test us? As we read in 1 Thessalonians 2, God tests our hearts. He tests our motives and our desires. We have also seen that God uses hardships and difficulties to test us. God tests us just as the master goldsmith turns up the heat under the caldron with gold to cause the impurities to come to the top. As these impurities come to the surface, we begin to see how God sees us and what is in us. God uses hardships and difficulties to reveal to us what our motives and desires are so that we examine ourselves to see where we need to grow and improve. According to Black,

> Gold ore is smelted in order to remove the impurities and expose the precious metal. Trials serve to refine the Christian and test his or her faithfulness. This analogy is common in the Old Testament: e.g., Psalm 66:10 ("For you, O God, tested us; you refined us like silver") and Zechariah 13:9 ("I [God] will refine them like silver and test them like gold"). Peter's use of the smelting analogy adds an emphasis on the importance of faithfulness. Gold, however valuable it may be, is a perishable commodity, doomed to perish with the earth. By contrast, genuine faith endures for eternity and results in praise, glory, and honor.[9]

Grudem clearly explains this in his commentary on 1 Peter:

> Gold perishes even though it is refined or *tested* (*dokimazō*, from the same word group as *dokimion*, above) by fire—in fact, gold is one of the most durable of all substances. Yet Peter says that it 'perishes', because he knows that this entire creation is on its way toward final destruction (see 2 Pet. 3:7, 10–12). Genuine faith is more valuable to God than gold because he is a God who delights in being trusted.[10]

MONEY AND TESTING

Money is a key factor in revealing a person's faithfulness and qualification for ministry. The Bible mentions money and possessions about 2,500 times. In the Gospels, Jesus used money in parables to teach how money reveals what is in a person's heart. In the Parable of Ten Minas in Luke 19:11–27, Jesus uses this story to teach how he will reward his faithful stewards at his second coming. Each of the servants were entrusted with a mina. According to Bock, a mina is "equivalent to one hundred drachmas or about one hundred days of an average working wage."[11] One man invested his mina and made ten minas more. The nobleman praised him for his faithfulness and rewarded him with ten cities. Another servant invested his mina and made five minas. The nobleman praised him and rewarded him with five cities. Another servant was afraid and did not

---

9. Black and Black, *1 & 2 Peter*, n.p. (Logos edition).
10. Grudem, *1 Peter*, 69.
11. Bock, *Luke*, 485.

invest the mina entrusted to him. The nobleman chastised him for being a wicked servant because he did not invest what was entrusted to him. The nobleman took the mina given to him and gave it to the one who made ten minas. When a person does not use what has been entrusted to him, God takes it away from him and gives it to another. In a similar story in Luke 16:1–13 about the dishonest manager, Jesus teaches the principle of faithfulness. A person who is faithful with little will be faithful with much. Likewise, a person who is dishonest with little will be dishonest with much (16:10). How a person uses money reflects their relationship with God. A person who is not faithful with money will not be entrusted with "true riches" (16:11). What are true riches? True riches are ministry opportunities and responsibilities. If a person cannot handle money, how can they be entrusted with ministry responsibilities? How a person uses money in ministry is a revelation of their values. Are the funds being used with integrity and transparency, or are they being used to fulfill the personal desires and lusts of the spender? In his book on *Mastering Church Finances*, Craig Larson shares that "he realized that in God's eyes managing money was not a distraction from real ministry but *a proving ground for real ministry*. By handling financial responsibilities well, I showed myself capable of handling spiritual responsibilities well."[12] He continues to explain that "Money means comfort, power, security, status, opportunity, freedom, pleasure, choice. That is why Christ makes radical claims on our checkbooks. No other issue so clearly, objectively addresses the clash between this world's values and Christian values."[13] Not only is integrity with money important, but also how a person uses money in ministry is vitally important. In what programs will a person invest? What events will they organize? Aligning the use of money with the church's mission, vision, and values is of utmost importance. This is why training, opportunity, and coaching of a trainee are so essential.

Ministry Watch exists to evaluate ministries and inform and educating believers on excellent organizations. Their website states, "Ministry Watch is an independent donor advocate facilitating the information needs of donors. It provides information on organizations alleging to be charitable and its key leadership in order to identify materially misleading behavior, or wasteful spending practices. We also identify and highlight organizations that are above board and running efficiently."[14]

12. Larson, *Mastering Church Finances*, 8 (emphasis added).
13. Pohl, "Spiritual Side of Mammon," 42.
14. https://ministrywatch.com/about-ministry-watch/.

They have a grading system that informs donors about the practices of an organization. Ministry Watch advocates for transparency, accountability, and the credibility of Christian organizations. They list ministers and ministries that have failed to maintain integrity, and they highlight those who have maintained it. Organizations that are members of the Evangelical Council for Financial Accountability (ECFA) have to pass rigorous tests for accountability to be approved by them. According to their website, "The founding ministries of ECFA understood this simple truth. How organizations treat financial transparency, board governance, and stewarding charitable gifts can create trust with their donors or break it irreparably. In today's world, demonstrating trustworthiness is more important than ever in effectively reaching the world for Christ."[15]

During my training of Jose, Alberto, and Nestor, I gave them responsibilities involving money to test their faithfulness. I asked them to go to the city three hours away on public transportation with a list of things to buy. I knew the prices of those things they were to buy. I gave them more than enough to cover their transportation, food, and the things they were going to buy. Would they return with the proper accounting? They did. Jose returned with the things I had asked him to buy along with the amount of the money I had given him, with all the expenses recorded on paper. He passed the test. I also gave them other responsibilities involving teaching God's Word, visitation of members, and government requirements. They had to go to the government building (municipal building) to obtain permission for some of the outreaches we had planned. This involved talking with the right people in charge of that responsibility and coming back to me with the proper paperwork. For their teaching and preaching responsibilities, I checked to see if they were prepared, and if they had accurately taught the lesson that day.

PAUL'S ILLUSTRATION OF THE ATHLETE AND PROVING

In 2 Timothy 2:5, the athlete is one of the seven illustrations that Paul uses for Christian leadership. While it takes self-discipline to be a successful athlete, the focus in 2:5 is on competing according to the rules. No athlete would be crowned unless he had followed the rules of the competition. There were gymnasiums and competition sites in every

---

15. https://www.ecfa.org/About.aspx.

Roman city. Disqualification occurred when an athlete did not compete according to the rules. Paul stated this in 1 Corinthians 9:27. He disciplines himself so he will not be disqualified. A Christian worker is similar to an athlete. What areas of a Christian worker's life need to be guarded so that we do not become disqualified? We have already discussed the area of finances. Many Christian workers and leaders have fallen due to financial reasons, whether intentional embezzlement or lack of training in handling finances. Every Christian worker needs to learn and implement consistent ways of financial stewardship. Another area is in the area of sexual purity. King David experienced immense hardship due to his adulterous affair with Bathsheba. In Matthew's genealogy, he remembers that Bathsheba was not David's wife but Uriah's wife (Matt 1:6). No one forgets this sin. We must take precautions against this by committing to a pure relationship with our spouse and avoiding any areas of temptation. This also means that in all of our devices, we avoid pornographic material, which can incite a person (especially men, who are driven by sight) to temptation. A third area that needs to be carefully watched is personal spiritual growth. In 2 Timothy 2, Paul begins by exhorting Timothy to find his strength in his relationship with Christ (2:1) before exhorting him to entrust the faithful message to faithful men and women. Many Christian leaders have fallen because they did not maintain their intimacy with Christ. Another area to avoid is pride and arrogance. Paul addresses this in 1 Timothy 3:6 in his list of qualifications for the overseer of a church. We must train our trainees in these areas so that they will be able to have many fruitful years of service. Many a Christian leader has fallen due to these issues: pride, abuse of power, financial impropriety, immorality, and failure to remain close to the Lord.

Proving faithfulness is more than an exam or a quiz. Testing in ministry involves the examination of a person's motivation, reliability with finances, faithfulness in handling the Word of God, and how a person treats other people. Ministry involves three areas of responsibility: programs, people, and finances. Programs refer to the lessons or methodology in communicating the gospel and God's Word. There are programs for children, young people, single adults, newly married couples, married couples with children, empty-nesters, and the elderly. People include the members of a church or the people who come to events. Finances are what is necessary to run the program or ministry event with the people who come to the event. How a person handles all of these is key to understanding a person's genuineness and fitness for ministry. How does a person handle the finances for a particular activity or event? Is there proper accounting with receipts? Does a person humbly steward well in these areas, or are they careless with money, harsh in their working with people, or unprepared in their messages and teaching responsibilities?

In 1986, we moved to the Philippines, and one of the first things I learned was proper accounting for personal and ministry funds. Glenn Kurka, the director of our ministry then (now he is our vice president of corporate operations), met with me and showed me how to record income and expenses using a ledger book. He trained me in recording the date, the vendor or person receiving the funds, and the amount. He also encouraged me to obtain a receipt for everything, and if the vendor did not provide one, I could write it down on paper. I added up the funds for all the categories each month and this revealed what it took to run the ministry. I also did this for our personal funds and balanced the books. Was the money in my hand the same as what was on the ledger? If it was not the same, I would search my pockets, think back through the month in my expenses, etc. I found doing this weekly was highly effective. It is easier to keep records weekly than try to remember for a whole month. Later, I bought a computer and learned how to do this with a program called Lotus 123, which was eventually bought out by Microsoft and is now Excel. I learned how to create spreadsheets that automatically calculated the balance by adding the income and subtracting the expenses. When Glenn saw my new computer, he asked, "What are you going to do with that?" I said to him and to my other coworkers, "Let me show you how it works." I showed him and others how to create spreadsheets and record ministry (and personal) expenses. They all smiled and within three months they all had a computer and were using my template! Today, we require all our national directors and coordinators to submit a monthly financial report. A few years ago, we created a spreadsheet for the whole year with a summary page. Our purpose was to help them see how much it costs to run the ministry and how to make a budget based on income and expenses. Since we started CCI in 2006, the ministry has continued to grow with income and with personnel. We now have over 150 team members. We are equipping church leaders in over forty-one countries, and God continues to expand our ministry.

Some of the men who have worked with us have proven unfit for our ministry. We had one coordinator who did not like to submit financial reports. Before we hired Glenn, I reviewed everyone's financial reports. I noticed a pattern with this one coordinator's reports. He had the same expenses on the same day of every month with the same amount for the same thing. I emailed him and asked him about it. His response was not adequate to me. I met with him personally and discussed this with him. I reminded him that it is God's money that he has entrusted to us, and we need to be faithful and accountable for what he has entrusted to us. Eventually, this coordinator decided to leave our ministry for another ministry and said that we were using a "worldly" way of accounting.

I also had doubts about another of our former directors. Even though he promised to raise funds within the country to fund all our visits, he requested more and more funds every year. One day, I received a message from an anonymous person wanting to discuss something urgent with me. I gave him my email address, and he wrote to me about this person. He said that his wife worked for our director and that this had been the worst situation she had ever worked under. The director continually humiliated the workers. He also asked them to record their expenses with inflated numbers. Class reports were also inflated. No one, however, would come forward to confront him with me, so I prayed about what to do. The Lord impressed upon me that he needed to retire to spend time with his family. I visited him, told him how God was leading me, and replaced him with one of the coordinators. He did not receive this very well and began undermining the new director. We continued to pray and ask the Lord to help us through this situation.

Towards the end of Paul's life, he urged Timothy not to be "hasty in the laying on of hands, nor take part in the sins of others" (1 Tim 5:22). We need to be careful not to promote people too quickly into a position that they are not ready for because the "sins of some people are conspicuous, going before them to judgment, but the sins of others appear later" (1 Tim 5:24). Some people are good at hiding their sins and weaknesses, while others' sins and weaknesses are obvious to all.

How do we test people and promote them in the right way? The first four principles in this book are necessary. We model for them what we expect from them. We develop a close relationship with them to help them discover their giftedness and where they will serve effectively. We give them guided opportunities. Giving them guided opportunities, in a way, is a form of testing. How do they do with these opportunities? How do they treat people? Are they gentle or harsh? Do they do well in explaining their expectations? How do they handle God's Word? Do they abuse God's Word? Or are they faithful to the authorial intent of the text? How do they handle finances? Do they do well with submitting receipts and proper accounting? Do they follow instructions well? How do they respond when you correct them? Are they faithful to God's Word, with resources, and with the opportunities that are given to them? Are they available when given opportunities? Are they teachable when you need to correct them? Faithful, available, teachable—these are three principles I have followed for forty years. Is the person trustworthy? Do they make the time when given an opportunity? Do they follow instructions? Do they receive correction well or are they defensive? At the core, these are the most important questions. As a person demonstrates faithfulness in these three areas (people, finances, God's Word), we can entrust more responsibility and more resources to them.

The problem I see in many ministries is the promotion of people too quickly along with a lot of funding. There is a proving process that God takes a person through, and he uses us in that process. Because we are not patient and want a large ministry now, sometimes we do not allow God his time in testing a person, and we promote people into high positions too quickly. We can easily sacrifice patience for expedience because we believe that large numbers or a large ministry signifies God's blessing and approval. Like the man who built his house on the sand in Jesus' parable, the storms of hardship and difficulties can reduce a ministry to nothing. I am confident that you can think of ministries that were once huge but are now much smaller due to failure in one of these areas (how they treated people, how they used God's Word, and how they used finances). Many ministries today are a shell of what they once were. They were impatient. They were not accountable.

One of our core training seminars is called "God's Financial Principles," produced by Crown Financial Ministries for pastors outside North America.[16] In the seminar, we train pastors about God's promise to provide, our responsibility to work, making and keeping a simple budget, listing our income and expenses, biblical stewardship versus the prosperity gospel and the poverty gospel, getting out of debt, learning to save, becoming a generous giver, and integrity and honesty with God's resources. By God's grace, we have trained about ten thousand pastors and church leaders through this seminar. In most cases, pastors have not taught about biblical giving. Many are reticent to teach on the subject with their church for fear of how people would respond. When they discover that the Bible addresses money and possessions over 2,500 and

---

16. Originally published as *The Bible and Money*.

they discover what the Bible says about stewardship, they teach this to their church. We give them messages and Bible studies for one month on this topic. Many of them have seen a fourfold increase in their church's giving. As a result, they have more resources to hire staff and reach their community for Christ. Most Bible colleges and seminaries do not train prospective pastors on this topic. One young church leader was sent by his church to a Bible school in Hanoi, Vietnam. He grew up in a rural area, so the city provided him with many opportunities and temptations. He obtained a smartphone, and someone showed him how to gamble online. The result was that he became so indebted that he quit Bible school and moved back home with a lot of shame. Later, he attended our seminar on biblical stewardship. He began paying off his debts, one by one, until he had paid them all, and now he is free. One of the greatest areas of stress for married couples is how their money is used. We have seen marriages restored through this training. Training pastors and church leaders should include this vital topic since how money is used has a lot of impact on our personal life, family, and church ministries.

DISCUSSION QUESTIONS

1. Do you think the proving process is necessary? Why or why not?

2. What process have you followed in the past in proving people you add to your team?

3. What are the benefits of a proving process?

4. Are there any disadvantages?

5. What areas do you think a person needs testing in?

6. If you designed a testing program for people in your ministry, what would it look like? Write out a plan.

PRINCIPLE #6

The Centrality of the Local Church

And I tell you, you are Peter, and on this rock, I will build my church, *and the gates of hell shall not prevail against it.* (Matt 16:18)

Now to him who is able to do far more abundantly than all that we ask or think, according to the power at work within us, to him be glory in the church and in Christ Jesus throughout all generations, forever and ever. Amen. (Eph 3:20–21)

IN 1961, MEMBERS FROM a local Baptist church in southern Virginia stopped by our house and invited my mother to a revival service. She was always curious about the contents of the Bible since she had never owned one. She attended that night, and after she heard the gospel, she trusted Jesus Christ as Lord and Savior. She was pregnant with me at the time. One could say that I started attending church even before I was born. My father was not really happy with her attending there, but she continued to attend every service. When I was six years old, I heard and understood the gospel and was convicted by the Holy Spirit that I was a sinner and needed God's forgiveness. When the invitation was given by the pastor that Sunday night, I walked forward, and a deacon named Charlie Bryant took me to a room in the back of the building and shared with me the Roman's Road to salvation (Rom 3:10, 23; 5:8; 6:23; 10:9, 10). I believed in the Lord Jesus Christ that night and was baptized a few months later. I grew up in that church and then moved to Lynchburg, Virginia in 1979. I enrolled in college at Liberty University. While I was there, I attended

Thomas Road Baptist Church. When I married Mindy, she and I attended Thomas Road as well. She had grown up in Limerick Chapel in Limerick, Pennsylvania. When we were ready to move to the Philippines, the Limerick Chapel pastors and elders laid hands on us and sent us out. I still remember the sending service on June 1, 1986. The next day, we moved to the Philippines. After language school, we moved to the island of Bohol and lived in a small town called Guindulman. There was a small group of believers that we began to teach and meet with, and we called that church Guindulman Christian Bible Church. It was located in Guindulman; we were following Christ, and we followed the Bible. Later, we moved to Tagbilaran, where we started a second church with professionals who had been taught the way of salvation by my missionary colleagues. We named that church Tagbilaran Bible Fellowship because we were located in Tagbilaran; all that we did and believed was based upon the Bible, and we loved to fellowship with one another. I had the privilege of training the pastors of both of these churches. When we returned to the USA, I became the missions pastor at Crosstown Community Church, which later became The Crossing Church. They allowed me to start a training ministry there in addition to the team I developed based upon Acts 1:8 (Jerusalem, Judea, Samaria, and the Ends of the Earth teams). The Lord allowed us to develop team leaders and we eventually trained over two hundred members of the church. Some became pastors, global workers, elders, or small-group leaders, and others served in various ministries. I have been an engaged member of a local church since I was born.

Mention the word "church" and it will be understood in many ways. Most people think of a place or building when the word "church" is mentioned. Some people think of the worship service as "church." They say, "I am going to church." Others think of the church as an organized religion or all Christians, Christianity, or Christendom. But what really is the church? The good news is that the Bible gives us a clear understanding of the word "church."

THE MEANING OF "CHURCH"

The word "church" comes from the Greek word ἐκκλησία (*ekklēsia*). ἐκκλησία is translated as "church," "assembly," or "congregation" in English New Testaments. In the Old Testament, the word translated "assembly" is from the Hebrew word *qāhal*, which means "assembly," "convocation," or "congregation."[1] In Deuteronomy 31:30, Moses sang his song "in the ears of all the *assembly* of Israel." *Qāhal* is found 122 times in the Old Testament. In the New Testament, ἐκκλησία (*ekklēsia*) is found 114 times. ἐκκλησία (*ekklēsia*) is used in reference to a legislative assembly (Acts 20:39), an informal gathering of people (Acts 20:32, 40), and a gathering of people with shared beliefs.[2] It is used for the "assembly" of Israelites. Hebrews 2:12 quotes Psalm 21:23 to the assembly of Israelites and Stephen refers to the "congregation" of the Israelites in his message to the Jewish leaders before they stoned him to death (Acts 7:28). While there are areas of commonality with the New Testament idea of church, the assembly of Israelites in the Old Testament is different from believers gathered together as the "church" of the Lord Jesus Christ.

The word "church" is used by Paul and other New Testament writers to refer to a local body of believers who meet together to worship the Lord, who are strengthened by the teaching of the Word of God, who fellowship with other believers, who make disciples of all people groups, and who observe the two ordinances of the Lord's Supper and baptism. Believers are under the authority of the Word of God, led by pastors and elders who shepherd, oversee, and lead this body of believers.

In Jeremiah 31:31–34, God promised a new covenant with the houses of Israel and Judah. He would put his law into their hearts, they would be his people, and everyone would know the Lord. Not all Israelites who gathered as an assembly in the Old Testament knew the Lord. They were a particular nation. They Holy Spirit did not indwell in them. In Ezekiel 36:27, God promised to put his Spirit in every covenant participant and cause them to walk in his ways. During the Last Supper, Jesus stated that the cup he would drink was the cup of this new covenant as it represented his blood that would later be shed and his body that would be broken (Matt 26:26–29).

Peter visited Cornelius, and he and his extended family and workers all heard the gospel, believed in the Lord Jesus Christ, and were all baptized by the Holy Spirit (Acts 10:34–48). In his defense of the circumcision party (Acts 11:1–18), Peter narrated what happened when these gentiles believed and the Holy Spirit fell on all of them "just as on us at the beginning" (11:15)—a reference to Pentecost, where the Holy Spirit fell on the believers waiting in the upper room (Acts 2). The

---

1. Brown, Driver, and Briggs, *Enhanced Brown-Driver-Briggs*, 874.
2. BDAG, 303.

coming of the Spirit fulfills the Old Testament promise of a new covenant and Jesus' statement where he said, "I will build my church" (Matt 16:18). While there are elements of continuity in the use of the word ἐκκλησία (*ekklēsia*) in the Old and New Testaments, there are also points of discontinuity between the two. The assembly with Moses was under a different covenant that was terminated with Jesus' death and has now been made obsolete (Heb 8:13; Rom 7:1–6). Jesus is pouring new wine into new wineskins, and his church is composed not only of redeemed believing Jews but also of Greeks and gentiles who have believed. This was shocking to the Jewish believers, but after seeing and hearing the sign gift of speaking in tongues by both Jews (Acts 2) and gentiles (Acts 10), they realized that this was a movement of God and did not want to become a hindrance to what God was doing. They glorified God and concluded that "to the Gentiles also God has granted repentance that leads to life" (Acts 11:18).

JESUS AND THE CHURCH

In Matthew 16:13–20, Jesus is discussing with his disciples about who he was. He asks them who people say he is (16:13). Then he asks them who they say he is. Peter confesses that Jesus is the Messiah, "the Son of the Living God." Peter affirms that Jesus is the Messiah, and he affirms his deity. Jesus commends Peter for his confession and explains that God the Father had revealed this to Peter (16:17). Then, Jesus states that Simon is "Peter" (Πέτρος, *petros*, masculine noun) and upon this "rock" (πέτρα, *petra*, feminine noun), Jesus would build his church (ἐκκλησία, *ekklēsia*). There are several interpretations of Jesus' statement "on this rock." Some understand this to be Peter as the "rock" on which Jesus would build his church (classical Roman Catholic interpretation). Others understand the "rock" as Peter's *confession* that Jesus is the Christ, the Son of the Living God. Others understand the "rock" to be *Jesus Christ himself* as the rock upon which he would build his church (cf. 1 Cor 3:11; Eph 2:19–22; 1 Pet 2:4–8). The last two have the greatest support. The point here is that Jesus is clear in stating that he would build (future) his church, and that who he is and what he would do (his atoning death on the cross) would be the foundation for the church.

THE CHURCH AS A LOCAL CHURCH OR LOCAL BODY OF BELIEVERS

By reading through Paul's letters, the general New Testament letters, and the book of Revelation, we can see that the apostles wrote to local churches or believers in a particular area. The focus in the book of Acts, in the letters, and even in Revelation is on the church or the local church or servants of the church. Here are statements usually at the beginning of the letter, addressing the church or the body of believers.

Romans 1:7" "*To all those in Rome who are loved by God and called to be saints*: Grace to you and peace from God our Father and the Lord Jesus Christ."

1 Corinthians 1:2: "*To the church* of God *that is in Corinth*, to those sanctified in Christ Jesus, called to be saints together with all those who in every place call upon the name of our Lord Jesus Christ, both their Lord and ours . . ."

2 Corinthians 1:1: "Paul, an apostle of Christ Jesus by the will of God, and Timothy our brother, *To the church* of God *that is at Corinth*, with all the saints who are in the whole of Achaia . . ."

Galatians 1:1: "and all the brothers who are with me, *To the churches of Galatia* . . ."

Ephesians 1:1: "Paul, an apostle of Christ Jesus by the will of God, *To the saints* who are in Ephesus, and are faithful in Christ Jesus . . ."

Philippians 1:1: "Paul and Timothy, servants of Christ Jesus, *To all the saints in Christ Jesus who are at Philippi*, with the overseers and deacons . . ."

Colossians 1:2: "To the *saints and faithful brothers* in Christ at Colossae: Grace to you and peace from God our Father."

1 Thessalonians 1:1: "Paul, Silvanus, and Timothy, *To the church of the Thessalonians* in God the Father and the Lord Jesus Christ: Grace to you and peace."

2 Thessalonians 1:1: "Paul, Silvanus, and Timothy, *To the church of the Thessalonians* in God our Father and the Lord Jesus Christ . . ."

Paul wrote First and Second Timothy to his apprentice Timothy in establishing the church at Ephesus. Similarly, he wrote Titus to his apprentice Titus in establishing the churches of Crete. The letter of Hebrews was a "word of exhortation" (i.e., message or sermon) to a church (Heb 13:22). James wrote to believers of the twelve tribes (Jas 1:1). Peter wrote "To those who are elect exiles of the Dispersion in Pontus, Galatia,

Cappadocia, Asia, and Bithynia." Similarly, the letter of Second Peter was sent "to those who have obtained a faith of equal standing with ours by the righteousness of our God and Savior Jesus Christ . . ." First, Second, and Third John were written to believers as well. First John does not indicate an addressee. Second John was sent to the "elect lady," which was most likely a local church. Third John was sent to Gaius, a church leader. In Revelation 2 and 3, Jesus sends messages to the churches in Asia Minor (Ephesus, Smyrna, Pergamum, Thyatira, Sardis, Philadelphia, and Laodicea). The ruins of these Roman cities still exist today in southwest Turkey.

The word ἐκκλησία (*ekklēsia*) is found 114 times in the New Testament, of which 108 references are to a local church or the church as a whole. ἐκκλησία is found nineteen times in the book of Acts, most of which refer to local churches. From Paul's statement in Romans 16:5, where he says to "Greet also the church in their house," it is evident that *the church is not a building but a group of believers who meet together regularly for worship, edification, and proclamation of the gospel under the authority of biblically qualified leaders who are under the authority of the Word of God.*

The church is also the new dwelling place of God the Holy Spirit. Believers are "living stones" (1 Pet 2:5). Every believer is a priest in service to God who offers spiritual sacrifices (1 Pet 2:4). The people of God are not composed of one particular nation, but are composed of every believer from every tribe, tongue, and nation. Every believer is indwelled by the Holy Spirit, and they belong to Jesus Christ (1 Cor 6:19–2). The church gathered is also indwelled by the Holy Spirit when they assembly together (1 Cor 3:16). The mystery that Paul proclaimed is that gentile believers are fellow heirs with Jewish believers and are members of the same body (Eph 3:6). The mystery is that Christ is in gentile believers, and he is the hope of glory (Col 2:7).

THE CHURCH IN A REGION

The "church" is also all believers in a region. In Acts 9:31, we read that the "church throughout all Judea and Galilee and Samaria" was being built up and multiplied. Luke does not specify individual local churches in this region, but the "church" throughout this region.

THE CHURCH AS THE BODY OF CHRIST

Paul also uses "church" to refer to all true believers. In instructing the church at Corinth about foods offered to idols, he cautioned them about not being offensive or becoming a stumbling block to anyone. "So whether you eat or drink, or whatever you do, do all to the glory of God" (1 Cor 10:31). Why? Christians are to live to glorify God and not cause an offense to "Jews or to Greeks or to the church of God" (1 Cor 10:32). The "church of God" is not a reference to any local church, but the church worldwide, the bride of Christ, all true believers who are born again and are followers of the Lord Jesus Christ.

PAUL'S MISSIONARY ENDEAVORS

Paul and his team members were engaged in the forming of local churches. In Acts 14:21–23, Luke summarized their first missionary journey: they proclaimed the gospel, made disciples, and appointed elders to lead these churches composed of followers of Christ. A significant component of their ministry was the training of leaders of these newly founded churches. The local church was central to Paul's ministry, and training pastors or elders to lead these churches was a significant part of his ministry. Making disciples always led to organizing these disciples into local Bible-believing churches.

PAUL AND HIS MINISTRY AT EPHESUS

For me, one of the most inspiring chapters in Acts is Acts 19, where Paul equipped leaders who went all throughout the province of Asia to preach the gospel, make disciples, and start churches. Initially, Paul entered the synagogue and for three months he "spoke boldly, reasoning and persuading them about the kingdom of God" (19:8). However, some of the participants there stubbornly rejected his teaching and spoke evil of the way of Jesus. As a result, he left the synagogue and moved his teaching ministry to the hall of Tyrannus. He reasoned daily with those who came through. The word "reasoning" occurs in 19:8–9 both as a participle describing his primary approach and as an activity with those who listened. "Reasoning" is from διαλέγομαι (*dialegomai*) and means "instructional discourse that frequently includes exchange of opinions."[3] Of its thirteen occurrences in the New Testament, it occurs ten times in the book of Acts, all with reference to Paul's teaching ministry. According to Schrenk, "In Socrates, Plato and Aristotle there is developed the art of persuasion and demonstration either in the form of question and answer (Socrates), the establishment of the idea by pure thought (Plato), or the investigation of the ultimate foundations of demonstration and knowledge (Aristotle). Because διαλέγεσθαι is the only way in which Greek philosophy can reach the λόγος or idea, it is of central importance."[4] Paul's approach was teaching with argumentation and persuasion, an apologetic form of teaching. This resulted in the whole province of Asia hearing the gospel (19:10). From Colossians 1:4, we know that Paul did not start the church in Colossae. He made disciples in the hall of Tyrannus, persuasively teaching the Word of God. The result was that he equipped disciple makers and evangelists who returned to their home areas and made disciples in those outlying areas as well. This is how all the churches of Revelation 2–3 were formed from Ephesus around the province's major towns and villages. Paul made disciples and entrusted to them the responsibility to preach the gospel and make disciples in outlying areas. He personally did not go to these towns. We can learn a great lesson from Paul's strategy. We should not do for our disciples what they themselves should go and do. Paul went to major urban areas, persuasively taught the Word of God, made disciples, and planted churches. Those disciples then, in turn, were expected to go and do the same in remote areas of the province. In essence, Paul worked with his disciples, whom he expected to continue to do the work. Thus, in Romans 15:18–20, we read that Paul had finished the work of making disciples ("I have fulfilled the ministry of the gospel of Christ") all throughout Greece, Asia Minor, Galatia, and the surrounding regions (from Antioch to Athens). Now, he was looking westward to Spain and desired to base his operations in Rome.

If we were to evaluate our work of making disciples over the last 220 years back to William Carey, we could make one colossal observation: we have not equipped the nationals well to take the gospel of Christ to the interior areas. Many Westerners have done this work of going to the interior, possibly implying to the national church that it is not their responsibility or that they are not competent. Like Paul, mission efforts

---

3. BDAG, 232.
4. Schrenk, "Διαλέγομαι, Διαλογίζομαι, Διαλογισμός," 93.

should concentrate on urban areas and place the responsibility of taking the gospel of Christ to the more remote areas on the nationals.

PAUL AND THE LOCAL CHURCH

Paul's training of servant leaders was local church based. Reading through Acts and Paul's letters reveals his passion to equip church leaders with sound doctrine and Christlikeness.

Wyatt concludes that "There is no indication that the church is responsible to disciple general members of the congregation, but another institution or organization is essential to train those who pursue pastoral ministry."[5] Later, he stated that "the biblical model clearly establishes the church as the primary place where we are to train men for ministry. The church is responsible for identifying faithful men and, ultimately, to affirm their giftedness and qualifications."[6]

When the new church in Antioch was formed of Jews and Greeks (Acts 11:19–21), the church at Jerusalem sent Barnabas to shepherd them (11:22–24). Barnabas recognized that he needed a helper, so he brought Saul to Antioch, and they taught great numbers of believers for one whole year (11:25–26). When they took the offering for the poor believers in Judea to Jerusalem, they entrusted those funds to the elders of the church (11:27–30). The church and its pastoral leaders were involved in these affairs. After the Holy Spirit called Barnabas and Saul to leave and preach the gospel to the gentiles, the church laid hands on them and sent them out (13:1–4). Thus, God's primary instrument in reaching the world today is the local church.

Every pastor can appreciate the value of pastoral training. No one doubts the value of theological and ministry training for the pastoral candidate. The typical process is that a young man (or woman) indicates his belief that God is calling him into full-time (vocational) ministry. He then approaches the leadership of his church. Then, with their encouragement and support, he finds a seminary to attend and moves to the location of that seminary. The seminary provides rigorous academic and theological training. He learns the Bible, theology, and ministry skills. Rarely is there ever any personal discipleship or mentoring. He may be involved with a local church in that area. He will be there for three to

---

5. Wyatt, *Pastoral Training in the Church*, 24.
6. Wyatt, *Pastoral Training in the Church*, 41.

four years. He often gets married, has children, and never returns to the church that nurtured and taught him the gospel. Wyatt laments that "the traditional process in our culture for training a man for ministry is often divorced from the life of the very church where he acknowledged his call to ministry."[7] This is compounded with internationals who attend American seminaries. The majority never return to their home countries. Anthony F. Casey laments the "brain drain" that happens when internationals pursue education abroad.

> In its essence, brain drain occurs when the best and brightest citizens of a country leave that country to pursue education or work abroad but never return . . . Even bottom-tier schools in America are often preferred to a university in Malaysia. Students leave with promises to return and make their country a better place. And they mean well. But it sometimes happens that they find life is better in the new country and, if offered a job, students find the money and standard of living are hard to pass up. So, they stay and send money back home but not their skills and service to their country.[8]

While we recognize the great benefits of seminary training, we should realize that this is not the only way. In reality, current pastors and churches have given up their role in equipping the next generation of leaders to institutions. In 2 Timothy 2:1–2, Paul is clear that current pastoral leaders are to equip and entrust sound doctrine to the next generation of leaders. This has not been an intentional step on the part of churches and pastors. Subconsciously, we have assumed that seminaries take this role that we could have in forming the next generation of leaders. Likewise, formal institutions would be delighted if local churches and pastors embraced this role. Formal institutions do not see themselves as the only ones to equip pastors and most recognize the central role of the local church. Additionally, seminary training is not always sufficient to equip a pastor. While a pastoral candidate studies the Bible and theology, seminaries do not always focus on the more practical areas of pastoral care, finances, and leadership. Formal training is many times divorced from real life. Most professors are not pastors. Many have not pastored a church but have focused on academics and the study of the Bible. Wyatt laments, "It is remarkable how many men successfully complete seminary with very little practical experience in pastoral responsibilities . . .

---

7. Wyatt, *Pastoral Training in the Church*, ix.
8. Casey, "Majority-World Theological Education."

They have never had to confront false teaching. Many have never done any supervised counseling. Very few have sat in on elder meetings. Most have never had to deal with bylaws and constitutions. They have likely never participated in a church budget process."[9] Most seminaries also do not include any form of a discipleship relationship with their students. I have attended three seminaries. Not one professor took the time to get to know me or mentor me, even though I desired this. The assumption is that everyone is doing fine on their own. Most students are pursuing good grades and fulfilling all their assignments. Seminary professors could grow in these areas by implementing the first four principles of this book and engaging in local church ministry. They could bring their students with them, just as Jesus did with his students.

NON-FORMAL LOCAL CHURCH-BASED TRAINING

An alternative to formal seminary training is a recent movement among churches called "local church-based non-formal training." Rowland, Jones, and Miller explain, "The church is the vehicle God has chosen to use to raise up leaders for his work in the world. Over the past centuries, we have allowed the church to move to the sidelines, and we are now lamenting the results."[10] Many organizations have created pastoral training programs to meet the need for churches in training and equipping their leaders. With a plethora of available resources, offering local church-based non-formal training is affordable and possible today. There are many benefits of providing ministry training in the local church.

First, non-formal training is relatively inexpensive compared to accredited seminaries. There are many pastoral training programs accessible and affordable today. The cost of going to well-known seminaries is about $120,000 for a four-year degree. For a family man, this is a nearly impossible situation, especially for minority pastors or pastors from developing nations. The student will have to go into debt, which he will pay off for the next ten years or more.

The second strength of local church based non-formal training is immediate ministry integration. While the trainee is learning, he is also applying what he is learning in his ministry context. The trainee does not learn massive amounts of information over a short period of time that he

---

9. Wyatt, *Pastoral Training in the Church*, xvi.
10. Forman, Jones, and Miller, *Leadership Baton*, 40.

will use later (and most likely forget). He can learn as he serves. When we use what we are learning, we are able to retain what we have learned.

Third, non-formal local church-based training does not require expensive relocation to a faraway city or country. The trainee can remain in his local church and vicinity and continue working in his job.

Fourth, non-formal local church-based training is more personal and relational. The pastor-trainer usually already knows the trainee. The trainee usually has roots and family in the area. The trainer can mentor the student and watch over him as he develops the ministry skills, is able to articulate sound doctrine, and becomes more like Jesus Christ.

Fifth, the scheduling can be flexible to the availability of the teacher and the students. Many of our classes in the USA and around the world meet one night a week or one whole day. Schedules and syllabi are distributed at the beginning of the class.

Sixth, the pastor who embraces this approach and equips his leaders fulfills his assignment from the Lord. In Ephesians 4:11–16, we read that Christ gave pastors to the church "to equip the saints for the work of the ministry." The pastor's role is not to *do* all the work of the ministry but to *equip* others and *oversee* the work of the ministry. Forman, Jones, and Miller state, "If we evaluate pastors primarily on how well they are doing ministry as individuals, we are emphasizing the wrong criterion. More importantly are questions like these: How well are our pastors equipping others to do ministry? How many people have they empowered to do ministry? Are they doing ministry through a team? How successful are the people around them?"[11]

Seventh, there is a greater potential for the church when members and leaders are equipped to do the work of the ministry. When God's people are equipped and they learn how to do the work, the whole church ministry benefits. Seminary is an option for those who can afford it and who are available. What about those who cannot afford it and are not available? What option do they have? Could there be men and women like Paul or Barnabas in our churches with great potential and giftedness who, when equipped, could serve the Lord using their gifts and abilities? This scenario is a definite reality. But we have failed to tap into the potential due to the tradition of equipping people in only one way. Our failure to equip others comes from a lack of vision of the potential of the people God has entrusted to us and from a lack of obedience to Ephesians 4:12.

---

11. Forman, Jones, and Miller, *Leadership Baton*, 35–36.

People are not equipped through a thirty-minute message on Sunday morning. Yet, many pastors focus their entire work on the Sunday morning service. Equipping necessitates us deciding to embrace this approach and a deliberate and intentional plan for equipping people. It has to come from an intentional decision and plan to do this. Otherwise, we will continue to indirectly communicate that seminary graduates are the only ones to serve, not the members. When we always hire outside the church, we are communicating to the church that they are not good enough or competent enough to serve. When we bring someone from the outside, they may have superior training, but they will lack the insider knowledge of the church's vision, core values, and DNA. Forman, Jones, and Miller explain this well: "By hiring an outsider, you may well be communicating that, when you really want to do something great, you are going to go out and find the best rather than develop the best internally. There is a huge difference between leadership acquisition and leadership development."[12]

Eighth and finally, the church benefits as we equip workers with biblical understanding and knowledge, ministry skills, and personal character for serving the Lord with their spiritual gifts and abilities. The whole church grows and benefits. As leaders are equipped and serve in various ministries, the entire church is strengthened and reaches a new level. In Ephesians 4:11–16, we read that as the members are equipped, the church grows with unity and Christlikeness. People will not be swept away by every new wind of false teaching. Members will learn how to speak the truth in love as they become more like Jesus Christ. When each part grows and does its part, the church grows into the full stature of Christ and builds itself up in love. The more the church looks like Christ and the more the church knows sound doctrine, the better it is in position to reach its community and the world for Christ.

Additionally, many seminaries and Bible colleges accept the training finished by trainees where there is good content and comprehensive training. This is called "advanced standing." With the guidance of a seasoned pastor and other pastoral leaders (elders), a person who finishes training with a local church can apply for advanced standing. The content of the courses will be examined by the school, and they will decide on how much credit to give them. In this way, a pastoral candidate can be equipped and discipled at his local church, prove his character and giftedness, and then enroll in a formal institution. In this way, local churches

---

12. Rowland, Jones, and Miller, *Leadership Baton*, 37–38.

and seminaries can partner together to equip emerging church leaders, future pastors, global workers, and church planters. The church is God's instrument in the world to accomplish his purposes. Seminaries, mission organizations, and non-profit organizations are partners that help accomplish the church's mission in the world.

In this chapter, we have seen the centrality of the church. We have seen that the local church is the most ideal environment to equip emerging church leaders. As each member learns their spiritual gift and finds a place to serve, and as each learns sound doctrine and how to defend their faith, the more the church becomes more like Jesus Christ and the more positioned the church will be to reach their community. We have seen the benefits of non-formal local church-based training.

For the last thirty-seven years, in different cultures with different educational and economic levels, I have been engaged with believers all over the world in non-formal local church-based training. This has been a great privilege as I have witnessed firsthand how God has used this to equip ordinary followers of Christ to make incredible impact in their local church and communities. I have witnessed how God can take the most unlikely person, equip them, and shape them to make an eternal impact in their community for the glory of God. Earlier, I introduced the first three coordinators to serve with us: Henry, Max, and Jun. Henry was a local pastor who had no formal Bible training but had a tremendous passion for serving God. After believing in Jesus Christ, he and his wife traveled to a nearby village and began teaching people the Word of God. They went house to house teaching the stories of the Bible. A friend of mine, Larry Salisbury, invited Henry to a class at the church he had planted. Reluctantly, Henry joined the class with about ten others, including Jay, who would become the pastor of the church Larry and Donna (his wife) started. Henry learned how to interpret and apply the Bible. He realized that he could have taught false teachings and would have led people astray. He finished the training at Larry's church plant and accompanied me all over the Philippines. Henry now leads our ministry all over the Philippines. God has taken this man with a big heart from his village in a small city and is using him throughout the country. He has become an example for other people who serve on our team. Max trained over five hundred pastors and church leaders. Many of these students are from the twenty-six islands north of Bohol. They are fishermen who have endured famine, hardships, persecution, lack of funds, and typhoons. They would fish on the way to class and spend two days with Max. He became their spiritual father. Now, all twenty-six islands have a Bible-believing church led by a qualified pastor. I have visited several of their churches. I learned their language well enough to communicate with them. None of these men would have ever had the opportunity to attend formal training, but through a discipleship relationship with Max and training consisting of over 520 hours, they are now competently serving the Lord Jesus Christ. Jun followed the same pattern in Mindanao. In Iligan City, he started a class with professionals at Metropolitan Heritage Baptist Church. Many of the members are educators and businessmen. Walter is a high school principal. He entered training and by the end of the first year, he and his wife were called by God to start a church in a nearby town. They began visiting there, sharing the gospel with the townspeople. By the time they finished the training, there was a church meeting every week. Later, he began the training there with young people and middle-age adults. One of his disciples started a church in a distant village. Whether living in remote areas with little education, or in urban areas in countries like the Philippines, or here in the USA with professionals, these people are now serving God competently in local church ministry. Some of my students here in the USA are now serving as pastors, elders, global workers, small-group leaders, and ministry leaders. The work is expansive. We have a huge assignment in making disciples of all people groups. The local church is God's instrument in the world. Many potential servants of the Lord are waiting for us to come and train them to turn the world upside down just like the early disciples.

DISCUSSION QUESTIONS

1. Did you attend Bible college or seminary? Did a professor befriend you and develop a discipleship relationship with you? What were the results in your life?

2. What benefits do you see in formal training?

3. If you were to design a pastoral training program for your local church, what courses would be included? How would you design it?

4. What benefits do you see in local church-based non-formal training besides those listed in this chapter?

5. Do you agree with the centrality of the local church in God's plan today? Why or why not?

PRINCIPLE #7

Engaging in God's Mission in the World

> Go therefore and make disciples of all nations, baptizing them in the name of the Father and of the Son and of the Holy Spirit, teaching them to observe all that I have commanded you. And behold, I am with you always, to the end of the age. (Matt 28:19–20)

> But you will receive power when the Holy Spirit has come upon you, and you will be my witnesses in Jerusalem and in all Judea and Samaria, and to the end of the earth. (Acts 1:8)

IN 1981, I HAD the privilege of serving in inner-city Philadelphia for twelve weeks. Liberty University promoted three teams to New York City, Washington, DC, and Philadelphia, the "city of brotherly love" (or "brotherly shove" as some say it). I grew up in rural Virginia, twenty minutes from North Carolina, and the largest cities I had ever seen were Roanoke, Virginia, and Greensboro, North Carolina. I have fond memories of going to the amusement park in Roanoke, the "star city of the South." After arriving in Philadelphia, Roanoke seemed like a small town. This was my first experience in a big city, and I was eager to learn. We handed out gospel tracts on the street, went door to door, talking with people and sharing the gospel with them (most of them never answered the door), and preached at the corners of Frankfurt and Pratt Streets, where the train and the bus depot are located. Thousands of people walked by as we used the microphone to proclaim the gospel to people. It was also my first encounter with a gang. We also served at an inner-city church, led by

Jack Raeside. Jim O'Neill led our team of fifty students. Our team of five within the larger group was assigned to the church led by Pastor Jack. I learned much that summer about the world, people, and myself.

The following fall, Glenn Kurka, a missionary serving in the Philippines, spoke during our chapel service. He promoted a short-term mission trip for the summer of 1982—it was called "Saturation '82." He was looking for Liberty students to spend the summer evangelizing the people on the island of Bohol. My girlfriend, who is now my wife, wanted to go because her aunt and uncle had served as cross-cultural workers in the Philippines for many years, and she had heard many stories and had learned Tagalog songs. God had been working in my heart about serving in cross-cultural ministry. When I was sixteen years old, I attended youth camp and heard a missionary from Africa share during the chapel time, and the Lord burdened my heart to do what he was doing. At first, I resisted, but the more I thought and prayed about it, the more convinced I was that God was calling me into cross-cultural ministry. I decided to go on this trip to the Philippines with the purpose of testing to see if this indeed was what God wanted me to do. We prepared during the school year and left in May 1982. Thirteen students from Liberty went on this trip, and thirteen Filipino students from Cebu joined us on the island of Bohol. We were divided into four teams and each team visited four towns. We lived with Filipino families, ate Filipino food, and visited door-to-door inviting people to come to the film showing that night. We learned simple words and phrases in the Cebuano language so that we could communicate with people. After six weeks of intensive evangelistic outreach, we returned home to our families. I was changed forever. Living in another culture for six weeks revealed to me a lot about myself that needed changing. This experience revealed to me that God's world is much greater than what I thought. I learned that there were believers in another country who had much less than I did economically, but they had great joy and passion in knowing Jesus and making him known. Living in the Philippines for six weeks was a life-changing experience and created the catalyst for spiritual growth within me.

The majority of people who go on a mission trip come back with a changed life. Going on a mission trip exposes believers to a different culture, different people, sometimes a different language, different religious beliefs, and a different economy. An effectively planned mission trip will enable the leader to disciple the participants on the team. People who go on a mission trip see themselves in a new light. They see that the world is much bigger than what they thought. They see that God is much bigger than what they thought. They are out of their cultural bubble into an environment that is many times radically different from what they know. This is a perfect opportunity for discipleship and personal spiritual growth. While short-term global workers may not have the training and maturity of a seasoned missionary, their love for one another, unity, and passion for the Lord will communicate volumes to the host ministry and country. Likewise, their immaturity, bickering, fighting, selfishness, and materialism when the team has not been properly trained and discipled will also impact the host church in a negative way. There have been casualties due to a lack of screening, training, and preparation prior to the trip, or the leader of the team failed to equip them to prepare for the trip. One excellent training tool for mission trips is Culture Link. Culture Link's mission is to disciple those who make disciples of all nations. They do this by enhancing "cross-cultural workers effectiveness by educating, equipping, and empowering."[1] Culture Link has equipped 2,500 leaders who have led teams to 129 nations. Colleges and seminaries now offer credit to participants. The curriculum introduces a seven-step process for planning an effective mission trip with a church's ministry partner. Topics include pre-field paperwork, cultural research, becoming cross-cultural, ministry preparation, team building, travel, packing, reflecting on servant leadership, going on the trip with daily devotions, re-entry, sharing your story, and debriefing after returning home. All of this contributes to the discipling of the team participants. Mission trips are a great way to equip and disciple emerging leaders.

GOD'S MISSION IN THE WORLD

God's mission in the world is to glorify himself by redeeming a people for his own purposes, so that through them his glory would be revealed to the nations. "God's glory—his own naturally overspilling life, seen in his Son—is mission's *rationale* and its motor. In whatever sense mission is about our going out into the world to make God known, it is only ever our being caught up in the already gushing tide of blessing that flows from the heart of the Father in the Son."[2] God is perfect in every way, and he is infinitely holy (Isa 6:3). He deserves our worship. According to the

---

1. https://culturelinkinc.org/about/. See also Ragan, *Help!*
2. Hames and Reeves, *What Fuels the Mission of the Church*, 22.

Westminster Shorter Catechism, "Man's chief end is to glorify God, and to enjoy him forever."[3] This is based upon Psalm 86:9; Isaiah 60:21; Romans 11:36; 1 Corinthians 6:20; 10:31; Revelation 4:11; Psalm 16:5–11; 144:15; Isaiah 12:2; Luke 2:10; Philippians 4:4; and Revelation 21:3–4. John Piper explains, "Worship, therefore, is the fuel and goal in missions . . . The goal of missions is the gladness of the peoples in the greatness of God . . . Passion for God in worship precedes the offer of God in preaching."[4]

The mission of God is all-encompassing, including his using his people to accomplish his purposes. In Ephesians 1:9–10, Paul explained that God's plan in Christ is to unite all things in him. Everything will become subject to Christ, who will hand over the kingdom to God (1 Cor 15:24–28). Christ will destroy all evil and death. Wright explains that "the Bible clearly reveals the God who drives the whole story of the universe forward with a sense of divine purpose and ultimate destiny, who also calls into existence a people who share in that divine mission, a people with an identity and role within the plan of God."[5] Mission relates to God's overarching purpose in the world through Christ and now through the church. God's plan is "that through the church the manifold wisdom of God might now be made known to the rulers and the authorities in the heavenly places. This was according to the eternal purpose that he has realized in Christ Jesus our Lord" (Eph 3:10–11). George W. Peters describes the difference between mission and missions this way: "Mission, in my usage, refers to the total biblical assignment of the church of Jesus Christ . . . [Missions is] the sending forth of authorized persons beyond the borders of the New Testament church and her immediate gospel influence to proclaim the gospel of Jesus Christ in gospel-destitute areas, to win converts from other faiths or non-faiths to Jesus Christ, and to establish functioning, multiplying local congregations who will bear the fruit of Christianity in that community and to that country."[6] The mission of the church is broad, while "missions" are the activities involved in accomplishing the mission.

Missions include all the activities the church engages in to accomplish God's mission. Missions include Jesus' instructions in the Great Commission passages, which we will examine later. Under the old covenant, Israel was to be God's holy people and obey his commandments.

3. "Shorter Catechism," question 1.
4. Piper, *Let the Nations Be Glad*, 11.
5. Wright, *Great Story*, xi.
6. Peters, *Biblical Theology of Missions*, 11.

By doing so, they would be his kingdom of priests to the nations. God invited the nations *to come and see* how he had blessed Israel, and this is what he would do to any nation that would follow his commands. In the new covenant, the church is God's instrument in the world through making disciples of all nations.

Wright argues for a missional hermeneutic in understanding the Bible. "A missional hermeneutic, then, affirms this great, divinely directed story as the interpretive context in which we must read all the Bible's constituent parts. The meaning of the Bible's story is to be found in the plan and purpose of the Bible's God. Or to put it the other way around, understanding 'the mind of God' requires understanding the Bible as the record of God's driving objective through the eons of natural history and the millennia of human history. The Bible is God's autobiography, God's story, the record of God's mission."[7] This is God's story that he is directing like a drama unfolding in various scenes and people. In his story, he moves from the particular (Israel) to the universal. I. Howard Marshall explains that the Bible is the result of God's mission. "By this I mean that the documents came into being as the result of a two-part mission, first, the mission of Jesus sent by God to inaugurate his kingdom with the blessings that it brings to people and to call people to respond to it, and then the mission of his followers called to continue his work by proclaiming him as Lord and Savior, and calling people to faith and ongoing commitment to him, as a result of which his church grows."[8]

The Bible, in its entirety, can be summed up in four words: creation, fall, redemption, and consummation. God the Father, Son, and Holy Spirit existed before the creation of the world and enjoyed perfect fellowship, love, and relationship. Hames explains that "when we look at God in the light of Christ, we see that our God is an eternal spring of happiness and goodness, completely and irrepressibly *full*—full of glory, full of life, and full of blessing for the world."[9] God decided to share this fullness with his creation. God decided to create man, share his presence and fullness with him, and appoint him as the caretaker of all his creation. This was Adam's main responsibility: he would exercise dominion over God's creation (Gen 1:26). Missiologists have called this the "cultural mandate." "The creation mandate given to humankind is expressed in Genesis 1:26–31, notably the assignment of 'dominion' (meaning in Hebrew, 'complete

---

7. Wright, *Great Story*, 4.
8. Marshall, *New Testament Theology*, 34.
9. Hames and Reeves, *What Fuels the Mission of the Church*, 35 (emphasis original).

authority') and the subsequent description of plants 'pleasant to the eyes and good for food' (Gen. 2:8)."[10] God created Adam and later he created Eve as Adam's companion in this responsibility. God blessed them and endowed them with the ability to have children also made in the image of God. God gave Adam and Eve the ability to choose to follow his command to eat from any tree in the garden of Eden, with the exception of the tree of the knowledge of good and evil. One day, while looking at this tree, along with her husband, Eve was seduced by Satan, appealing to her lust, her pride, and her physical appetite. She ate the fruit and shared it with her husband, Adam. Adam did not protect his wife from deception, and he willingly decided to rebel against God. Immediately, their relationship with God was severed; they were ashamed of their nakedness and sewed fig leaves to hide their shame. God came looking for them as he regularly visited them. He called them and confronted them with their sin. God distributed punishment to each of them, including the serpent for deceiving them, but gave them the promise of the one who would come and deliver man. God's promise is called the "protoevangelium" (the first announcement of the gospel). "Many have referred to Genesis 3:15 as the first statement (protoevangelium) of God's ultimate answer to sin, anticipating Christ's redemptive work on the cross."[11] Peters explains the significance of this first announcement of the gospel: "The universality of the protoevangelium is basic to Old Testament revelation. It is the soteriological leitmotif . . . and hermeneutical principle governing Old Testament interpretation."[12] Before expelling them from the garden, God sacrificed innocent lambs, took the skins from these animals, and clothed Adam and Eve. The blood that was shed is a picture of the future atonement that Jesus would accomplish on the cross, pictured in the sacrificial system under the Mosaic covenant.

As man fell deeper and deeper into sin and depravity, God destroyed the world through the flood, yet demonstrated his mercy and grace by choosing Noah and instructing him to build an ark. Noah built the ark according to the exact measurements of God's instruction. Later, when Noah's descendants multiplied on the earth, they desired to build a tower, known as a *ziggurat* in those days, so as to make a name for themselves. God punished them by giving them various languages. They gathered with those of the same language and dispersed throughout the world.

10. Moreau, Netland, and Engen, *Evangelical Dictionary of World Missions*, 49.
11. Moreau, Netland, van Engen, *Evangelical Dictionary of World Missions*, 397.
12. Peters, *Biblical Theology of Missions*, 86.

God then called Abram to move to the land of Canaan (Gen 12:1–4). God promised to make Abram a nation, to give him a great name, and to bless all the families of the earth through his seed. We know from Galatians 3:7–18 that the "seed" that God referred to is Christ. God's promise to bless the nations through Abram (later named Abraham) reveals God's plan for the rest of Scripture. God's mission is not a theme only in the New Testament but has its basis in the Old Testament. God's plan is to use Abram and his family as the conduit of God's blessing to the world in order to glorify himself. This plan is further developed through Moses. After the Israelites had multiplied in Egypt, God called Moses to return to Egypt and to deliver them from slavery. He would bring them back to Mount Sinai, where they would worship their creator and redeemer God (Exod 3–4). Here, the ideas of worship and mission are brought together. Repeatedly, God said to Moses that he was "sending" him back to Egypt so that he would display his power and glory to the Egyptians. He would bring Israel to Mount Sinai, where they would worship and offer sacrifices to the Lord (Exod 3:18). The ideas of *sending* (mission) and *worship* (sacrifices) are repeatedly brought together. God sends his people on mission so that there is worship. As this was developed with Moses, God revealed to him that Israel would be a "kingdom of priests and a holy nation" (Exod 19:5–6). Through Israel, God would display his power and glory so that all the nations would see the greatness of God and worship him. This connection of worship and mission is repeated throughout Scripture. Terry, Smith, and Anderson note the reason God chose Israel: "To be sure, Israel was and is his chosen people, but not because he loves them and no others. Rather, he chose them for the sake of the other peoples."[13]

In Psalm 67, the psalmist prays that God would bless "us" (i.e., Israel) and "make his face to shine upon" them (a reference to the high priest's prayer from Num 6:24–26), so that God's ways and his "saving power" would be known among the nations (Ps 67:1–2). Jesus' command in Matthew 28:16–20 is not an afterthought or a last-ditch effort, but it is a major theme running throughout all of the Bible. God is on mission, and he chooses a person, nation, or entity (Adam, who failed; Abraham, later Israel; then Christ) to display his glory so that the nations may "be glad and sing for joy" (67:4). God would bless them so that "all the ends of the earth [would] fear him!" (67:7). The invitation to the world is to

---

13. Terry, Smith, and Anderson, *Missiology*, 54.

"come and see what God has done [in Israel]; he is awesome in his deeds toward the children of man" (66:5).

Israel, however, failed to keep God's covenant with them, as they disobeyed his commandments and worshipped other gods and goddesses. The pinnacle of God's revelation of his glory through Israel was during the time of Solomon (2 Chr 1–9). Solomon received 666 talents of gold every year from the taxes of surrounding countries. The land of Israel had its largest extension during his reign. Solomon imported animals, horses, wood, and all kinds of products from around the world. God endowed him with great wisdom, so much so that people from all over the world came to listen to his wisdom. During the dedication of the temple, fire came down from heaven and consumed all the offerings. The glory of the Lord filled the temple so much so that the priests could not enter it (2 Chr 5:14; 7:1–2). When the people saw the visible manifestation of the glory of God, "they bowed down with their faces to the ground on the pavement and worshiped and gave thanks to the Lord, saying, 'For he is good, for his steadfast love endures forever'" (2 Chr 7:3). However, as the people continued in idolatry and disobedience to the covenant, God removed his glory from the temple (Ezek 1:4–28; 10:1–22) and the people went into exile to Babylon. The sentiment of the people to be God's prized possession and his instrument of his good news to the nations is captured in Jonah's mission to Nineveh. When God called Jonah to Nineveh, he boarded a boat and headed in the opposite direction to Spain (Jon 1:1–3). The Assyrians were the terrorists of that day and Israel greatly disliked them. Jonah, a prophet chosen, called, and sent by God, refused to go until God sent a "great wind" and a "great fish" to swallow Jonah. Inside the belly of the great fish, Jonah repented and came to realize that "salvation belongs to the Lord!" (2:9). Jonah then went to Nineveh and preached repentance. The people repented, but Jonah sulked. He wanted God to destroy them. God taught Jonah that even though they were wicked people, he had compassion for them (4:11). The Jews in Babylon eventually were carried off into exile to Babylon, where their names would be changed to reflect the names of the Babylonian gods. Some of them served in government positions. They faced difficult situations, but God delivered them, even when Haman attempted to lead a genocide against them. God promised to restore Israel one day and promised to send the Messiah, who would purify them "like a refiner's fire and fullers' soap" (Mal 3:2). The Messiah would come, and he would reign, fulfilling all of

God's promises to Israel. Then, the whole world would come to worship the King, the Lord of hosts (Zech 14:16–17).

After four hundred years of silence, of God not speaking through a prophet, Jesus, Emmanuel, was born to the virgin Mary. He came to dwell with his people and reveal God to them and ultimately to us. John stated that Jesus came and "made him [God the Father] known" (John 1:18). "Made him known" is from ἐξηγέομαι (*exēgeomai*) and is used only six times in the New Testament and means to "to set forth in great detail, expound."[14] Jesus *expounded* God the Father to Israel. Everything God wants us to know about him has been displayed in Jesus in his life, death, and resurrection. Jesus fulfilled all God's righteous requirements and demands and died as a perfect atoning sacrifice on the cross. Jesus was raised on the third day. This is the gospel for all nations. Jesus demonstrated during his sinless life love for Jews, for tax collectors, for prostitutes, for gentiles, for women, and for all the outcasts of society.

Just before his return to heaven, Jesus gave his disciples his final command, called the Great Commission. We read this Commission in five passages: Matthew 28:16–20; Mark 16:15; Luke 24:44–45; John 20:21; and Acts 1:8. Each has a different emphasis. In Matthew 28:16–20, Jesus met his disciples on a mountain, and they worshiped him. Based upon his authority, he commanded them to "make disciples" (μαθητεύω, *mathēteuō*, an aorist ingressive imperative emphasizing urgency) of "all nations" (πάντα τὰ ἔθνη, *panta ta ethnē*) by going, baptizing in the name of the Father, the Son, and the Holy Spirit, and teaching them to obey everything he has commanded. The words "going," "baptizing," and "teaching" are all participles that indicate how they were to make disciples.

In Mark 16:15, Jesus' command is to "preach" (κηρύσσω, *kērussō*, also an ingressive aorist with urgency) by going into all the world. They are to preach "the gospel" (εὐαγγέλιον, *euangelion*) to *all* creation (κτίσις, *ktisis*), that is, to all people, not just Jews, but Greeks and gentiles. In Luke 24:45–49, Jesus opened their minds to understand the Old Testament Scripture about himself. Jesus needed to fulfill all the prophecies about his first coming and fulfill all the righteous demands of the Mosaic law. In 24:46, Jesus explained that the Messiah had to suffer and then rise again from the dead. The disciples were to preach this, asking for people to repent so that they would receive forgiveness of sins. This message was to be proclaimed to all nations, beginning with Jerusalem. He

---

14. BDAG, 349.

promised to send the promised Holy Spirit to empower them as his witnesses. The emphasis here in this gospel account is the result of preaching repentance, i.e., forgiveness of sins. In John 20:19–23, Jesus appeared to the disciples and commissioned them. As the Father had "sent" (from ἀποστέλλω, *apostellō*) Jesus, so he now was "sending" (πέμπω, *pempō*) them. In breathing upon them, he temporarily gave them the Holy Spirit until the day of Pentecost arrived, when they would be permanently indwelled by the Holy Spirit. In Acts 1:8, Jesus promised that the Holy Spirit would come upon them, and that they would "be" (from εἰμί, *eimi*, "to be") his witness in Jerusalem, Judea, Samaria, and to the ends of the earth. Here, there is no command, but a statement about the nature of who they would be: his "witnesses" (μάρτυς, *martys*). A witness bears testimony to what he has seen and heard. They would tell what they had seen: Jesus' death, burial, and resurrection. The Holy Spirit would empower them to bear witness to this historical event.

The rest of the book of Acts narrates how they began to do that very thing. They witnessed Jesus' person and work from Jerusalem to Rome. In Acts 1–11, the majority of their witness centered around Jerusalem, Judea, and Samaria. In Acts 11:19–21, we read about the church in Antioch that resulted from the stoning of Stephen. Those who were scattered preached the gospel to other Jews only. But there were some unnamed evangelists from Cyprus and Cyrene (North Africa) who were "speaking" (ἐλάλουν, *elaloun*, from *laleō* in the imperfect tense = continuous activity in the past tense) the gospel to Greeks (Ἑλληνιστὰς, *hellēnistas*, "Hellenists"). "Hellenists" can refer to Greeks or Greek-speaking Jews. Polhill states that it was Hellenist Jews who preached to these gentiles. "The Antioch church, established by Hellenists, those Greek-speaking Jewish Christians who had to flee Jerusalem after the martyrdom of Stephen, began to put this principle into practice and to reach out to the Gentile population."[15] Since there is such a contrast here with 11:19, where they preached the gospel to *Jews only*, Luke is showing how the gospel was now being taken to *gentiles*. Antioch (of Syria) was the third largest city in the Roman Empire, with an estimated population of half a million people, behind Rome and Alexandria. Antioch was founded by Seleucus Nicator in 300 BC, and it was located on the Orontes River, about fifteen miles from the Mediterranean.[16] Antioch was a metropolitan city with temples

---

15. Polhill, *Acts*, 268.
16. Polhill, *Acts*, 268.

to various gods and goddesses and was well known for its immorality. Once the church in Jerusalem heard about this newly established church, they sent Barnabas, once called Joseph, to go and serve this church. He rejoiced in what God was doing and exhorted them to be faithful to the Lord with all their hearts. Barnabas left to find Saul in Tarsus and brought him to Antioch. There they taught great numbers of believers for one whole year. The disciples were called "Christians" here to distinguish them from Jews and those who worshiped idols. After one year (Acts 13:1–4), the church leadership was composed of five prophets and teachers. They too came from multiple ethnic backgrounds: Barnabas (Jewish), Simeon called Niger (African), Lucius (European), Manaen (Palestinian), and Saul (also Jewish). The pastoral team reflected the multi-ethnic makeup of the church. They were worshiping (from λειτουργέω, *leitourgeō*, "to render service," used of priests in the temple). This is translated by the ESV as "worship" and by the NASB as "minister." The idea here is that they were worshiping the Lord. Worship, then, can be seen as service to God. As they were worshiping and fasting, the Holy Spirit spoke and said he had chosen Barnabas and Saul, and the church was to set them aside to preach the gospel to the gentiles. The other leaders and the church laid hands on them, showing their agreement with God and their support of their ministry, and they sent them off (from ἀπολύω, *apoluō*, "to let go" or "send"). This may imply that the church wanted to hold on to these gifted preachers, but they obeyed God and cooperated with the Holy Spirit in sending them off. In verse 4, we read that they were sent (from ἐκπέμπω, *ekpempō*, "to send out") by the Holy Spirit. The church sent them on their mission, and the Holy Spirit empowered them to go. Again, we see the connection between worship and mission. This combination is scattered through the Scriptures: Moses, Isaiah (Isaiah 6), the disciples in Matthew 28:16–20, and now here in Acts 13:1–4. The Scriptures are clear: as God is worshiped, God's people begin to understand who God is and see his love and plan for the whole world.

Barnabas and Saul left on their journey throughout Cyprus, Antioch in Pisidia, Iconium, and Lystra. They preached the gospel, made disciples, organized them into local churches, and equipped elders or pastors to oversee them (Acts 14:21–23). The letters of Paul, James, Peter, John, Jude, and Barnabas (or whoever the author of Hebrews is) are written to local churches and church leaders. They are the result of the disciples fulfilling Jesus' command to make disciples. In the book of Revelation, God completes his plan of taking back the earth. The book begins with a revelation of Jesus to John and a commission to write what he has seen happen and what will happen. Finally, God dwells with his people in the new Jerusalem (Rev 21–22). In Revelation 4–22, we see the activity of worship of God by the twenty-four elders and believers who have been martyred for their faith.

Thus, the entire story of God's unfolding drama is seen in his *creation*, where he created everything by the power of his word. Adam stewarded dominion over God's creation. However, Adam failed and fell into sin (*fall*). God did not abandon them but came looking for them, just as the prodigal's father came looking for him (Luke 15:20–21). God's sacrifice of innocent lambs to clothe Adam and Eve was a picture of his coming *redemption* through Jesus' death on the cross. The church continues Jesus' ministry today by making disciples of all people groups. Finally, after Jesus has destroyed sin and death and has conquered Satan, he will hand over the kingdom to God the Father, when the *consummation* of all things will take place.

MISSIONS AND THE LOCAL CHURCH

Scripture is clear that as we worship God, we will come to learn who he is and see his love and concern for all the peoples of the world. *Worship* will lead to *mission*. Any local church that engages in biblical worship will embrace Christ's mission in the world. Otherwise, worship is only a feel-good exercise and a truncated worship experience. This sentiment is expressed when a person says, "I didn't get anything out of the service today." A worship-focused experience without a focus on Christ's mission clearly misses the mark of Christ's desire. Anyone serious about following Christ will embrace his mission to the world. Jesus' mission in the world today is continued through the church, primarily the local church. Mission is not an option for a select few believers, but it is the mandate of Christ and a primary purpose for the existence of the church. The church exists to worship God, to edify one another, and to carry out Christ's mission in the world.

Since this is true and since this mandate is still vital and commanded by Christ to his church, it should be a part of training for those who would serve him. Christian education or ministry training that does not incorporate Christ's mission to the nations fails to obey Christ's command and fails to see this all-encompassing mandate and story in

Scripture. Training that skips out on Christ's mission to the world is a truncated education.

One morning at a men's Bible study, I was sharing about my upcoming mission trip to the Philippines with a group of men gathered at a local restaurant. I invited a businessman there that morning to come with me and see what God is doing around the world. He responded that God had not yet told him to be involved in mission. I responded that God gave us Matthew, Mark, Luke, John, and Acts, and it is very clear from Jesus' last statements that God desires all his people to be engaged in his mission throughout the world. Many pastors and believers think that they have no role or responsibility in God's mission other than their immediate and surrounding area, or just with their family. In some churches, missions is one or two offerings a year for global missions, or it is what some really committed Christians do, but not the majority. However, Scripture reveals that we are to be on mission through the Holy Spirit to all nations because God deserves their worship.

THE BENEFITS OF INCORPORATING SHORT-TERM MISSIONS INTO MINISTRY EQUIPPING

While there have been critics of the short-term missions movement over the last forty years due to costs, cultural and ministry blunders, and accidents, short-term missions involvement has many benefits.

First, short-term teams or short-term cross-cultural workers can visit partnering ministries to see how God is using the supported missionary and how their investment is being used (accountability). We have seen in a previous chapter the importance of accountability in relationships. Church teams or short-termers can see firsthand how their investment has been used and see the results of their giving and praying. Bud was supporting several of our coordinators in Indochina. An elder of the church approached him and challenged him to see and investigate firsthand if what he was being told was actually true. Bud accompanied us to a teachers' conference in Thailand. On the second day, Bud came to me and said, "David, you've been short-selling me on your ministry. This is much greater than what I imagined." This is not always the donor's response, but it shows the importance of accountability in missions. Are the funds being used in the ways that they were promised? Is the person you are supporting actually doing what they said they would do?

Second, short-term missions allow volunteers to "come and see" the culture, language, and religion of the people group their partner is serving. According to Moreau, "The present generation of missionary candidates tends to make their decisions and commitments based on the knowledge gained through *firsthand experience*."[17] They need to see, taste, and experience the culture and be with the people that they want to serve. The majority of career global workers have been on a short-term mission trip and have experienced missional life in another culture. Charles explains that "Swimming is best learned wet. Before global workers face the pounding surf of full-time ministry, they need a chance to paddle around, flounder and right themselves in shallower waters. The mistakes that knock them down need time to be transformed from failure to insight."[18] Even if a person does not return as a career missionary, experiencing the culture, language, and religion firsthand is an invaluable experience for advocacy for that people group in that person's local church.

Third, the value of short-term missions can be seen in the impact it makes on the life of the volunteer when there is accompanying training before the trip. Being out of one's culture and language results in life change. The volunteer sees his or her life in a different light. Being with people from another language and culture whose lives have been radically changed by the gospel can have an immediate impact on the volunteer's life to show them areas in their life that need changing and the need for the life-changing power of the Holy Spirit. Roger Charles shares the testimony of Dirk, who said, "I have found that my impact on Asians is largely measured by Asia's impact on me."[19]

Fourth, the value of short-term missions can be seen in the ministry involvement of the volunteer once they return to their home church. They have learned how to serve in a cross-cultural ministry and are open and ready to serve in their local church once they return home.

Fifth, volunteers can help the missionary on the field in projects where the impact can be seen immediately. Projects involving construction, medical help, seminars in specialized areas, relief work from disasters, children's ministry during summer breaks, and other short-term needs can have a tremendous impact on the missionary or host's ministry.

---

17. Moreau, Netland, and Engen, *Evangelical Dictionary of World Missions*, 874 (emphasis added).
18. Hoke and Taylor, *Global Mission Handbook*, 212.
19. Hoke and Taylor, *Global Mission Handbook*, 212.

Sixth, volunteers may return as career cross-cultural workers. Once they experience the work of the Holy Spirit in and through them on the field, they may return as a career worker. Cross-cultural workers on the field are often overwhelmed by the scope of their work and need people to come and help them accomplish their ministry. This was true in my life. As my girlfriend (and now wife) and I volunteered in the Philippines for six weeks in 1982, we saw the need, heard the call from God, and later returned there in 1986.

Seventh, involvement in short-term mission opportunities can be a part of ministry training for the volunteer. Training can incorporate the study of the culture, language, and religion before embarking on the trip. Special assignments can be given to the trainee and be a part of their training. The trainee can be required to write up a report afterward of the experience with a self-reflection paper of how it impacted his or her life.

REQUIREMENTS FOR SHORT-TERM OPPORTUNITIES

The first rule in preparing for short-term mission opportunities is to ask the mission partner if they desire a short-term volunteer. Many cross-cultural workers or nationals are not prepared for a volunteer or team or may not desire one to come and help them.

Second, there should be sufficient training prior to the trip. Many failures and accidents have occurred due to the inability to provide adequate training. We have already looked at the training that Culture Link provides. This training is invaluable for the team or volunteer prior to the trip.

Finally, plans for debriefing should be included in the process. Returning to one's culture and home requires preparation and debriefing. The volunteer has had many cultural and ministry experiences. Re-entry requires some training in order to understand the reality of people's responses once the volunteer returns. Debriefing should include reporting to those who gave, and if it is a local church team, they should give their local church a report of all that God did in and through them.

MISSION PARTNERSHIPS

Local churches can partner with a mission organization, a missionary, a national ministry, or a national pastor. In a partnership, both parties have mutual responsibilities to fulfill in the partnership. This is based upon the biblical concept of a covenant. Throughout the Scriptures, we see that God initiated a covenant relationship with Abraham, with Israel through Moses, with David, and with Israel in the new covenant, inaugurated by Jesus, yet to be consummated in his second coming. There are promises made by each party in a partnership. Partnerships can be general or well defined. Generally, there are three levels of partnerships.

First, a local church can financially support and pray for a missionary or missionary family, national ministry, or national pastor. In this partnership, the missionary or pastor promises to serve faithfully. The work of the partner (missionary, national) may be to start a church, translate the Bible or curriculum into a particular language, or other defined ministry. A local church or donor promises by faith to support the missionary or national. Many times, there are no time limits or written expectations from the partner, or the work is not well defined. The church continues to support the partner as long as it is able to give, and the partner continues to serve as long as they are able to faithfully serve. Churches assume that the mission organization is overseeing the missionary or national pastor(s). This is the typical model followed by most local non-denominational churches. In many cases, relationships are highly personality driven. The missionary or missionary family visits the church or donor, and if they like the candidate and what they are planning to do, they will support and pray for them, as long as they are on the field and are serving faithfully. When they leave the field, it is basically up to the mission organization to decide if they want to continue the mission of that people group or ministry.

Denominational churches like the Southern Baptist churches give to the North American Mission Board for North American missions, and they give to the International Mission Board for international missions. Denominational churches may have little to no involvement in what the missionary or staff is doing. Churches trust the mission boards to pursue the mission of the organization.

A second level of partnership is where the ministry supporter and the partner (missionary, national worker) decide to partner together and work together on a project. The church may send volunteers to help with this project. The project may be a construction project, a medical project, or it may be a translation project. The church is able to help the partner elevate their ministry to a new level with the project and the short-term team.

A third level of partnership can be more defined, in terms of time limits, expectations, and outcomes. This is where the church is highly involved in the partner's ministry. This is a strategic partnership. The church and the partner decide to work on a project or projects together over a certain period of time (three to five years), with mutually agreed-upon goals and expected outcomes. They regularly evaluate these expectations and outcomes to see if they are meeting the outlined goals.

The strength of a local church in equipping church leaders, pastors, and cross-cultural workers is that the church will typically be more involved in the lives of their member cross-cultural workers. They will invest more in their projects. They will have a closer relationship with them. This is a strength of developing local church-based training. A relationship is established between the church and those they equip and mobilize.

God's mission is comprehensive and includes creation, fall, redemption, and consummation. Christ's mission for the church today is to continue the ministry Christ started in making disciples of all nations. Ministry training should include God's overarching mission and should focus on the trainees' embracing of Christ's ongoing mission to make disciples of all nations. An equipping ministry that avoids missional involvement is missing out on a robust training experience for the trainee since missions is not just something a few people do, but it is God's plan and desire for the church.

DISCUSSION QUESTIONS

1. Have you ever been on a mission trip? How was your experience?

2. Do you believe that all believers and local churches should be involved in missions? Why or why not?

3. How can you incorporate missions into a ministry training program?

4. Are ministry leaders fully trained if they have never experienced mission work?

5. What would you say about a church that has no mission outreach or program?

PRINCIPLE #8

Empowered by the Holy Spirit

And Jesus, full of the Holy Spirit, returned from the Jordan and was led by the Spirit in the wilderness. (Luke 4:1).

And when they had prayed, the place in which they were gathered together was shaken, and they were all filled with the Holy Spirit and continued to speak the word of God with boldness. (Acts 4:31).

THE FINAL PRINCIPLE FOR having a dynamic equipping ministry is the work and power of the Holy Spirit. Without the Holy Spirit's work in and through us, we can follow the previous principles but not yet see the potential for what God can do through an equipping ministry. Francis Chan laments,

> While no evangelical would deny his existence, I'm willing to bet there are millions of churchgoers across America who cannot confidently say they have experienced his presence or action in their lives over the past year. And many of them do not believe they can. The benchmark of success in church services has become more about attendance than the movement of the Holy Spirit. The "entertainment" model of church was largely adopted in the 1980s and '90s, and while it alleviated some of our boredom for a couple of hours a week, it filled our churches with self-focused consumers rather than self-sacrificing servants attuned to the Holy Spirit.[1]

---

1. Chan and Yankoski, *Forgotten God*, 15.

CHAN IMAGINES A PERSON being on a deserted island with nothing but a Bible to read and then coming to America and attending a church. He would wonder how churches could survive without the Holy Spirit. Well, my family and I did live on an island for fourteen years. We returned to the USA every four years. We saw the Holy Spirit work in incredible ways during our time in the Philippines—how he opened many persons' hearts to the gospel, how he opened evangelistic Bible studies from one village to another village, how he radically changed people from being drunkards and drug addicts to bold witnesses for Christ, how he healed the sick, etc. We organized overnight prayer meetings on the first Friday of every month. We prayed from 9 p.m. to 6 a.m. We witnessed the power of God in our ministry. After teaching an evangelistic Bible study on the life of Abraham one day in a remote village with seventy people in attendance, a man walked up to me and asked us to come to his village and teach the Word of God there.

THE HOLY SPIRIT'S WORK IN THE OLD TESTAMENT

In Genesis 1:2 (cf. Ps 104:30), we read that the Holy Spirit was involved in creation. He imparts and sustains life. "And the Spirit of God was hovering over the face of the waters." The Holy Spirit "contended" with man during the corruption due to sin (Gen 6:3). Walton contends that this word means "to sustain." "This would plausibly yield something like, 'My spirit will not sustain humankind indefinitely' and provides a suitable lead in to the limitations set on human life span."[2] The Holy Spirit imparted the ability to Bezalel to construct the tabernacle and its utensils (Exod 31:3; 35:31). Bezalel was to be "filled him with the Spirit of God, with ability and intelligence, with knowledge and all craftsmanship" (Exod 31:3). The Holy Spirit empowered men for service. Joshua is said to be "a man in whom is the Spirit" (Num 27:18). The Spirit of the Lord is said to have come upon the judges and empower them to lead Israel (Judg 3:10; 6:34; 11:29; 13:25; 14:6, 19; 15:14). The Holy Spirit "rushed upon Saul" and empowered him to lead Israel to battle against the Ammonites (1 Sam 11:6–11). In fact, Samuel prophesied that the Holy Spirit would "rush upon" him and he would "be turned into another man" (10:6; 10). The Holy Spirit was involved in changing a person. The Spirit of the Lord "rushed upon David from this day forward" and enabled

---

2. Walton, *Genesis*, 295.

David to write the songs that he did and lead Israel (1 Sam 16:13). In 2 Peter 1:21, we read that the Holy Spirit carried along the Old Testament prophets who received revelation from God. This is why they were able to declare, "Thus saith the Lord . . ." Thus, the Holy Spirit was involved in imparting life, empowering people for service, revealing truth and future events to prophets and to the writers of the Old Testament, and anointing kings and judges to lead Israel. Jeremiah, Joel, and Ezekiel prophesied of a time when the Holy Spirit would be poured out on all God's people (Joel 2:28–29; Jer 31:31; Ezek 36:26–27). This was fulfilled on the day of Pentecost, when the Holy Spirit was poured out on the believers gathered in Jerusalem, also in fulfillment of Jesus' promise (Acts 1:8).

THE HOLY SPIRIT'S WORK IN THE LIFE OF JESUS

Jesus was conceived through the work of the Holy Spirit (Matt 1:18, 20; Luke 1:35). John prophesied that Jesus would baptize believers in the Holy Spirit and with fire (Luke 3:16–17). The context explains that the "fire" is judgment on those who do not believe. They will face eternal death in the lake of fire ("unquenchable fire"). The Holy Spirit descended upon Jesus in the form of a dove at his baptism (3:21–22). He was led by the Holy Spirit into the wilderness for forty days (4:1–2). Afterward, he was tempted by the devil (4:3–13). Jesus returned "in the power of the Holy Spirit to Galilee" after his temptation and began his ministry of teaching and calling his disciples (4:14–15). Jesus affirmed that "the Spirit of the Lord" was upon him, enabling him to preach the good news, heal the blind, and set free those possessed and oppressed by Satan and his demons (4:18). Jesus taught his disciples about the future work of the Holy Spirit in John 14–16. The Holy Spirit was with them, but he would live (dwell) in them after he left and returned to heaven (14:17).

THE HOLY SPIRIT'S WORK IN THE EARLY CHURCH

Schreiner explains the nature of the book of Acts: "Acts is a model, a prototype, an exemplar for the renewal of the church."[3] Schreiner explains that Acts is transitional and programmatic. "As a transitional book, Acts recounts nonrepeatable events that establish the community of faith . . . Acts also confronts Christians as a programmatic book. It provides

---

3. Schreiner, *Mission of the Triune God*, 20.

guidance for every church in every age."[4] God's messengers in the power of the Holy Spirit testify to Jesus' death, burial, and resurrection. The Spirit works through the messengers to cause the Word to increase and to multiply. In fulfillment of Joel's prophecy, John's prophecy, and Jesus' promise, the Holy Spirit came upon the early disciples on the day of Pentecost (Acts 2:1–13). Each of the disciples were filled with the Holy Spirit and spoke in various languages (2:6–11). This also happened with Cornelius and his household when they heard and believed the gospel (10:44–48; 11:15–18). They received the Holy Spirit just like Peter and the early disciples did (10:47). Through the sign of speaking in various languages they had never studied (tongues), the Jewish believers came to understand that God had also saved and given the Holy Spirit to gentiles (11:18). Otherwise, the early Jewish believers would never have accepted them as equal to them. When Peter returned to Jerusalem, he was criticized and interrogated by those of "the circumcision party" (11:2–3). The Holy Spirit would enable believers to boldly speak the Word of God when he filled them (Acts 4:8). After they prayed, they were filled with the Holy Spirit and preached "the Word of God with boldness" (2:31). Ananias and Sapphira lied to the Holy Spirit, and both died (5:1–11). Candidates who would serve Grecian widows were to be "full of the Holy Spirit" (6:3). Stephen was "full of the Holy Spirit" (6:5). That a person was full of the Holy Spirit was evident to others. People who stubbornly refuse to believe in Jesus are described as resisting the Holy Spirit (7:51). Stephen, while being stoned, was full of the Holy Spirit and was enabled to see Jesus standing to welcome him (7:55–57). The apostles came down to Samaria after men and women had believed the gospel in order to lay hands on them so they could receive the Holy Spirit (8:14–17). Jesus had promised to give the keys to the kingdom to Peter and Peter opened the door for the gospel and the work of the Holy Spirit to Jews (Acts 2), to Samaritans (Acts 8), and to gentiles (Acts 10). Peter's preaching and the Spirit's coming was a fulfillment of Jesus' statement to Peter of the keys to the kingdom. This was a once-and-done ministry that Peter fulfilled. The Holy Spirit directed Philip to go near the Ethiopian eunuch in order to explain the gospel to him (8:29). After baptizing the Ethiopian, the Spirit carried Philip away to Azotus (8:39–40). The Holy Spirit comforted the church throughout all Judea, Galilee, and Samaria (9:31). The Spirit spoke to Peter about the men who had come to visit him (10:19) and

---

4. Schreiner, *Mission of the Triune God*, 21.

the Spirit told Peter to go with them (11:12). Agabus prophesied by the Holy Spirit that there would be a great famine (11:28). The Holy Spirit told the church in Antioch to "set apart for me Barnabas and Saul for the work to which I have called them" (13:2). The Holy Spirit sets apart, and he calls people to the work of preaching the gospel. The Holy Spirit empowered them to go on their first journey (13:4). Saul was filled with the Holy Spirit in talking with Elymas the magician (13:9–10). Those who believed the gospel in Antioch Pisidia were "filled with joy and with the Holy Spirit" (13:52). In the Jerusalem council, Peter testified how the gentiles had believed and God had given them the Holy Spirit (15:8). The Holy Spirit led James and the assembly of apostles and elders to come to a unified decision regarding gentiles and circumcision (15:28). The Holy Spirit is described as forbidding Paul and his team into Bithynia (16:7). Instead, that night, Paul received a vision of a man from Macedonia who urged him to come over and help him. Disciples of John in Ephesus had never heard of the Holy Spirit, but when Paul taught them about Jesus, they believed, received the Holy Spirit, and spoke in tongues and prophesied (19:1–6). The Holy Spirit helped Paul make decisions about his direction as he is said to have "resolved in the Spirit" (19:21). The Holy Spirit constrained Paul to go to Jerusalem and testified to Paul that there would be hardships ahead of him (20:22–23). The Holy Spirit made the elders in Ephesus overseers of the church there (20:28). In Tyre, believers through the Spirit told Paul not to go to Jerusalem (21:4). In other words, the Spirit revealed to them that Paul would face hardships in Jerusalem, and they tried to persuade him not to go there. The Holy Spirit also revealed to Agabus that Paul would face hardships (21:11). While Paul was in Rome, he met with Jewish leaders and shared with them about Jesus, but they would not believe. Paul told them (as said through Isaiah) that they would not understand because of their hard hearts (28:26–27).

THE WORK OF THE HOLY SPIRIT AND THE TEACHING ABOUT THE HOLY SPIRIT IN THE LETTERS

In the letters, we learn that the Holy Spirit indwells the gathered local church (1 Cor 3:16). He also indwells believers individually (Rom 8:9; 1 Cor 6:19–20). A person who does not have the Spirit does not have Christ. True believers are indwelled by the Holy Spirit. Every believer has been baptized by the Holy Spirit (1 Cor 12:13) and has been given spiritual gifts (1 Cor 12:4–11; 1 Pet 4:10–12). The Spirit bears witness with our spirit that we are God's children (Rom 8:16). The Spirit empowers and sanctifies (Rom 15:13, 16, 19). The Holy Spirit teaches us the things of God (1 Cor 2:13). The Holy Spirit washes, justifies, and sanctifies (1 Cor 6:11). The Spirit is a guarantee until Christ returns (2 Cor 1:22; 5:5; Eph 1:13–14). The ministry of the Spirit is glorious and transforms us from glory to glory (2 Cor 3:3–18). Through the Spirit, God works wonders and miracles to authenticate his message and his messengers (Gal 3:5; Heb 2:4). God's Spirit lives in our hearts and cries out, "Abba, Father" (Gal 4:6). We are commanded to walk in the Spirit (Gal 5:16). The Spirit bears fruit in our lives (Gal 5:21–22). We are to keep in step with the Spirit (Gal 5:25). The Spirit imparts wisdom (Eph 1:17). We are to endeavor to maintain the unity of the Spirit through the bond of peace (Eph 4:1). This means that through the Holy Spirit's work, we can have good, meaningful relationships with other believers and work together for the glory of God. We are to be filled with the Spirit (Eph 5:18). Being filled with the Spirit will lead to worship, giving thanks, and mutual submission (Eph 5:19–20). A Spirit-filled wife will submit to her husband. A Spirit-filled husband will love his wife as Christ loves the church. Spirit-filled children will obey and honor their parents. Spirit-filled fathers will instruct their children in the Lord and not provoke them to anger (Eph 5:22–6:4). Spirit-filled workers will obey their employers and Spirit-filled employers will treat employees with respect (Eph 6:5–9). The sword of the Spirit is the "Word" (ῥῆμα, *rhēma*) of God (Eph 6:17). *Rhēma* is a synonym of *logos* but has a much smaller range of meaning than *logos*. When we speak God's written Word, we are wielding the Spirit's sword in spiritual battle. We are to pray at all times in the Spirit with all kinds of prayers and supplications, which means that we pray in the realm of the Spirit. The preposition ἐν (*en*) can mean "with the help of" and refer to agency.[5] In other words, the Holy Spirit guides our prayers. We are to be sensitive to the leading of the Holy Spirit as we are praying. In 1 Thessalonians 1:5, Paul and his team's preaching was "in power and in the Spirit," which means that his preaching was through the power of the Holy Spirit and directed by the Holy Spirit. In 1 Thessalonians 5:19, the church is commanded not to "quench the Holy Spirit" or to put out the fire of the Holy Spirit. Here, it refers to stifling or suppressing the work of the Holy Spirit. The following verses explain in what way the church could

---

5. BDAG, 329.

suppress the work of the Spirit, i.e., by rejecting prophetic revelation. God revealed truth to the apostles and prophets prior to the completion of the New Testament. Paul, as an apostle, received revelation from God that was considered inspired when written down (2 Pet 1:20–21; 2 Tim 3:16–17; Eph 3:5). In Ephesians 3:5, we read that God revealed the truth of the mystery of Christ through his holy prophets and apostles. We see God the Father and God the Spirit's role in salvation in 2 Thessalonians 2:13—God chose us to be saved, the Holy Spirit sanctified us, and we believed in the truth of the gospel (see also 1 Pet 1:2). The Holy Spirit vindicated Christ's incarnation, which is a reference to his resurrection (cf. Rom 1:4; 8:11). The vindication of Christ's claim as Messiah and Son of Man is that the Holy Spirit raised him from the dead. The Spirit clearly revealed the future of people falling away from the truth (1 Tim 4:1). We are indwelt by the Holy Spirit (2 Tim 1:14). The Holy Spirit regenerated and renewed us at salvation (Titus 3:5). God bore witness to the gospel through the signs and wonders produced by the Holy Spirit (Heb 2:4). When the prophets wrote in the Old Testament, it is the same as the Holy Spirit speaking (Heb 3:7; 1 Pet 1:10–12). It is possible to taste the work of the Holy Spirit (Heb 6:4). Jesus offered himself as a sin sacrifice to God through the Holy Spirit (Heb 9:14). It is possible for a person to outrage the Holy Spirit (Heb 10:29). We can be sure that a preacher is preaching by the Holy Spirit if he confirms the incarnation and deity of Christ (1 John 4:2). The Holy Spirit leads people into truth (1 John 4:6), not false doctrine.

THE WORK OF THE HOLY SPIRIT IN REVELATION

The Spirit speaks through the revealed word to the churches (Rev 2:2, 11, 17, 29; 3:1, 6, 13, 22). Through the Holy Spirit, John saw visions and was led to see the future things (Rev 1:10; 17:3; 21:10. Jesus and the Holy Spirit are inviting people to come and drink the water of eternal life (Rev 22:17).

CONCLUSION

From this list, it is evident that the work of the Holy Spirit is robust in the life of the believer. We are commanded to "walk" (περιπατεῖτε, *peripateite*, from *peripateō*, present active imperative) in the Spirit (Gal 5:16), to "keep in step" (στοιχῶμεν, *stoichōmen*, present active subjunctive) with the Spirit, "be filled" (πληροῦσθε, *plērousthe*, present passive imperative) with the Holy Spirit (Eph 5:18), to not "quench" (σβέννυτε, *sbennute*, present active imperative) the work of the Holy Spirit (1 Thess 5:19), and to not "grieve" (λυπεῖτε, *lupeite*, present, active imperative) the Holy Spirit (Eph 4:30). Believers are not commanded to be baptized by the Holy Spirit, nor to be indwelt by the Holy Spirit, nor to receive the Holy Spirit. The Holy Spirit is a "gift" (Gal 3:2; 1 John 3:24—ἔδωκεν, *edōken*, from *didōmi*). The Holy Spirit revealed truth to the apostles and to the prophets. The Holy Spirit imparts spiritual gifts to every believer for the benefit of others as he decides (1 Cor 12:7). Through the Spirit, God works wonders and miracles (Gal 3:5). The Spirit guides us and opens our minds to understand God's truth (1 Cor 2:10-16).

THE HOLY SPIRIT'S WORK IN OUR TRAINING

Since there is so much emphasis on the work of the Holy Spirit, we should not only train our trainees in the doctrine of the Holy Spirit, but we must also model serving in the power of the Holy Spirit. Much of the Evangelical expression of the work of the Holy Spirit either focuses on intellectual study or borders on sensationalism and entertainment. The Spirit transforms a person into a bold witness, not as an actor on a stage wowing the audience. Our study must be heartfelt and sincere, avoiding intellectualism or sensationalism. His empowering presence through the gospel, which has the power to change lives, grow, increase, and multiply, must be modeled. In much education and training today, doctrine, including the doctrine of the Holy Spirit, is only an intellectual exercise, rather than a heart exercise and experience. We are to model the working and empowering of the Holy Spirit with our trainees. We are to teach them how to serve in the power of the Holy Spirit. We need to train them in the gifts of the Holy Spirit and the working of the Holy Spirit. This is not only a teaching exercise; it is not only a modeling exercise, but it is also an intentional training exercise. In American culture, which is a culture of rugged individualism, pulling yourself up by your own bootstraps, and vertical mobility, we must not use the working of the Spirit to elevate ourselves into higher positions or to miss the work of the Holy Spirit altogether. In any culture, in our flesh, we depend upon ourselves. We must train ourselves and our students to learn to depend upon and be empowered by the Holy Spirit.

The Holy Spirit brings together all the principles of this book. Through the Holy Spirit, we model to our trainees how to serve the Lord. Through the Holy Spirit, we develop close relationships with our trainees, and the Spirit guides us with insights into the trainees' lives. Through the Holy Spirit, we impart sound doctrine to our trainees. Through the Holy Spirit, we give our trainees guided opportunities. Through the Holy Spirit, we entrust ministry to faithful men and women as they prove faithfulness. Through the Holy Spirit, we serve in local church ministry together. Through the Holy Spirit, we serve in cross-cultural ministry together and use this as an opportunity for discipleship and training. The Holy Spirit is the one who makes our ministry effective and brings together all the ideas of this book.

DISCUSSION QUESTIONS

1. How have you experienced the empowering work of the Holy Spirit in your life and ministry?

2. What do you see as the greatest work of the Holy Spirit in a person's life and ministry?

3. How could a trainer model the Holy Spirit's empowering work to his trainees?

4. How do you think a trainer could train someone not only in the content of the doctrine of the Holy Spirit but also in the work of the Holy Spirit in their lives and ministry?

The Biblical Pattern for Equipping and Multiplying Leaders

IN THIS FINAL CHAPTER, we will look at the biblical examples for equipping and multiplying leaders. What examples in the Old and New Testaments guide us and give us principles today that we can follow and implement?

INTRODUCTION

A study of the Old and New Testaments reveals life-on-life training in the context of actual ministry activity. As relationships developed, leaders were equipped for ministry through modeling. The context of the training was the real day-to-day life problems and situations that prophets and leaders faced. The New Testament reveals training in the context of missional church activity, where churches were planted and nurtured. Leaders were trained through deepening relationships, modeled from one life to another, in the context of ministry assignments, which were entrusted to the trainee. These examples provide one with a basis for training and equipping for tomorrow's leaders. The genre of the literature examined in this paper is mostly narrative, which is descriptive of events and models. As narrative, it does provide excellent examples and derivative principles for the leaders in training and for equipping the next generation of leaders. Some passages, however, are discourse and are prescriptive outlining of what God's expectations are for godly, Christlike leaders.

EQUIPPING LEADERS IN THE OLD TESTAMENT

Moses and Joshua

Prior to the book of Joshua, Joshua is referenced twenty-eight times (Exod 17:9, 10, 13, 14; 24:13; 32:17; 33:11; Num 11:28; 13:16; 14:6, 30, 38; 26:65; 27:18, 22; 32:12; 32:28; 34:17; Deut 1:38; 3:21, 28; 31:3, 7, 14, 23; 32:44; 34:9). Four times Joshua is called Moses' "assistant" (Exod 24:13; 33:11; Num 11:28; Josh 1:1). "Assistant" is from the Hebrew verb שָׁרַת (*sharath*), which occurs ninety-six times the Old Testament and is translated five times as "assistant" or "aide" (Exod 24:13; 33:11; Num 11:28; Josa 1:1; and 1 Kgs 19:21). It was used of Joseph as Potiphar's servant (Gen 39:4) and other personal servants (2 Sam 13:17, 18). Aaron and his descendants are said to have served or ministered in the tent of meeting (Exod 28:35). This is the most common use, where the Levitical priests and workers serve God in the tent of meeting or later in the temple. Eunuchs served King Xerxes (Esth 1:10). Angels are referred to as God's "messengers (Ps 104:4). David was called God's "servant" (Jer 33:21). Joshua is said to have been Moses' "assistant" since his youth (Num 11:28). As his aide for forty years, Joshua accompanied Moses through the difficulties and triumphs of Israel's journey from slavery in Egypt to the conquest in Canaan. The togetherness of Moses and Joshua is a pattern that is found throughout Scripture, showing the importance of a modeling relationship. The following is a list of what Joshua learned from Moses during their forty years together, from Egypt to the Jordan River.

The Battle with the Amalekites (Exodus 17:8–16)

In the context, the Lord had taught Israel that he is the one who meets their needs for food and drink (see Exod 16–17). In this pericope, God taught Israel that he would protect them from their enemies.[1] While Joshua was leading the battle against the Amalekites, who attacked the Israelites at Rephidim, Moses lifted the staff of God towards heaven. As Moses continued to hold up the staff, Joshua and the Israelites were winning the battle, but as Moses grew tired, he lowered the staff, resulting in defeat. Aaron and Hur, who accompanied Moses on the hill, placed a stone under Moses and held up his arms, holding the staff, with Aaron on one side and Hur on the other. The staff in Moses' hands revealed

---

1. Cole, *Exodus*, 136.

his human weakness, i.e., that he could not lead Israel alone. Joshua was unaware of what was transpiring on the hill; he was aware, however, that at one point they prevailed and at another point they experienced defeat. The Lord instructed Moses to write this for the benefit of Joshua (17:14) so that he might know God's judgment against the Amalekites. In addition, the lifting of hands has been interpreted by some as a military signal, an oath against the Amalekites and as symbolic for dependence upon God in prayer.[2] Jamieson points out, however, that the staff of God "was given to Moses for the express purpose of working wonders (ch. iv. 17), and that it never seems to have been used in a season of prayer."[3] With the sword in Joshua's hands and the staff in Moses' hands, one can recognize God's sovereignty and human responsibility.[4] While noting God's sovereignty in the staff, Moses, with the help of Aaron and Hur, had to hold it up while the battle was raging below. "Moses' outstretched arms primarily symbolized his appeal to God."[5] Furthermore, it was a lesson on godly men working together; God did not intend for Moses to lead Israel by himself, and in and of himself, he was inadequate for the work of leading Israel effectively, as Jethro would so succinctly communicate in the next chapter.

Jethro's visit to Moses

In the following chapter (Exodus 18), Jethro, Moses' father-in-law, visited Moses. Jethro was shocked to see Moses making all the decisions while everyone stood around him. Jethro's question was poignant: "What is this that you are doing for the people? Why do you sit alone, and all the people stand around you from morning till evening?" Jethro rebuked Moses for what he was doing because it would only wear him and the people out (18:18). "Like many a Christian leader, Moses was wearing himself out unnecessarily (verse 18) by trying to do everything single-handed. This is not always a mark of ambition; it is sometimes the mark of the over-conscientious and over-anxious."[6] The work was "too heavy" to do it "alone" (18:18). Jethro then instructed Moses to teach the people God's

---

2. Cole, *Exodus*, 136.
3. Jamison, *Commentary*, 345.
4. Gaebelien, *Expositor's Bible Commentary*, 2:408.
5. Gaebelien, *Expositor's Bible Commentary*, 2:408.
6. Cole, *Exodus*, 140.

laws and the "way to live" (18:19). He would choose capable, trustworthy men who had a healthy relationship with God ("men who fear God") and were trustworthy in making decisions involving finances ("who hate a bribe") (18:21). In Deuteronomy 1:9, 13, Moses involved Israel by having them choose these men. The result would be that he would not be overwhelmed by the work and the people would "go to their place in peace" (Exod 18:23).

Although Joshua's name was not mentioned in this story, it is an appropriate story to mention because of its relevance to the topic. Most likely, since Joshua was Moses' aide, he was present during Jethro's visit.

Other Significant Events

Receiving the Ten Commandments (Exod 24:13). When Moses ascended Mt. Sinai to receive the Decalogue from God, Joshua accompanied him. Moses and Joshua together saw the glory of God.

The Golden Calf story (Exod 32:17). Joshua wrongly observed that there was war in the camp below and was corrected by Moses. Joshua witnessed Moses' righteous anger at Israel's idolatry and witnessed God's judgment against Israel.

The tent of meeting and the glory of God (Exod 33:11). Joshua witnessed the building of the tent of meeting (the tabernacle) and the subsequent descent of God's glory. He and Moses entered the tent and spoke with God "as a man speaks to his friend" (33:11). When Moses exited the tent, Joshua remained inside, worshipping the Lord. Thus, Joshua learned the importance of worship and prayer under Moses' leadership, something that he would still need to learn in his failure at Ai.

The seventy elders prophesying (Num 11:28). Joshua witnessed the seventy elders prophesying and foolishly admonished Moses to forbid Eldad and Medad from prophesying since they were not in the company of the elders but remained in the camp.

Spying out the land and subsequent judgment (Num 13:16; 14:6, 30, 38; 34:17; Deut 1:38). Joshua was the head of the tribe of Ephraim, and it was at this point that his name was changed from Hoshea to Joshua (Num 13:8). Joshua and Caleb returned and encouraged the people to take possession of the land. Joshua was a man of courage and faith and learned through this occurrence to trust and obey God. Only he and Caleb from that generation were allowed to enter Canaan.

The commissioning of Joshua (Num 27:18, 22; 32:28; Deut 3:21, 28; 31:3; 31:7, 14, 23). God commanded Moses to commission Joshua. Moses laid his hands on Joshua and gave him his authority.

Conclusion

For a period of forty years, Joshua, as the aide of Moses, accompanied him from Egypt to Canaan. He witnessed significant events in the history of Israel. Moses instructed him along the way through the successes and failures of the deliverance from Egypt and the wandering through the wilderness. God used these experiences under the guidance and modeling of Moses to prepare Joshua to lead Israel into Canaan. Moses commissioned Joshua and entrusted him with the responsibility of leading Israel to the conquest. Joshua's preparation was not in a classroom divorced from real-life situations but was in the muck and mire of everyday life, led by a growing leader (Moses) who had been appointed and equipped by God to lead Israel. Joshua's training was accomplished in the context of a dynamic model and teaching relationship between him and Moses. The point of the study is that God uses maturing leaders to train new leaders in the ebb and flow of life. Joshua was prepared for leadership by a maturing leader in the context of real-life situations.

Elijah and Elisha

Elisha is not mentioned in the Bible until Elijah was discouraged and asked God to take his life (1 Kgs 19:16). Elijah had defeated the prophets of Baal at Mt. Carmel and outran Ahab's chariot. When Jezebel learned of all that Elijah did through King Ahab, she gave the command to have Elijah's life taken. When Elijah learned of her plans, he fled to a cave at Mt. Horeb (Sinai) for a period of forty days and forty nights (much like Moses and Jesus). God caused miraculous signs to occur in front of Elijah through a terrible wind, earthquake, and fire. Nevertheless, the Lord was not in any of those. God then spoke to Elijah through a quiet voice at the mouth of the cave, and Elijah hid his face, as Moses had years before. The cave is designated as "the cave" and thus may have been the place where God revealed himself and his glory to Moses (Exod 33:22).[7] God ordered him to anoint Hazael as king of Aram, Jehu as king of Israel, and Elisha as

---

7. Wiseman, *1 and 2 Kings*, 256.

the prophet to take his place. Elijah's perception was that he was the "only one left" among the prophets who served the Lord (1 Kgs 19:14). God answered by saying that there were another seven thousand (presumably prophets) who faithfully followed him (1 Kgs 19:18). Elijah's perception was completely wrong; while he thought he was the only one left, there were many more who were faithful to God's covenant. While Elijah obeyed the Lord's command to anoint Elisha, had he understood the value of shared leadership, this low point in his life may have never happened. He did obey the Lord's command and learned from the situation.

Elijah obeyed the Lord's command and left to anoint Elisha. Elisha came from an affluent family since he was plowing with twelve pairs of oxen. Upon arrival, Elijah threw his cloak upon Elisha, symbolizing the prophetic call. Elijah's act was an "act of investiture denoting authority rather than contractual magic."[8] The cloak denoted "divine and consecration to the regal and prophetic offices."[9] Elijah "would take him under his care and tuition as he did under his mantle."[10] Elisha's response was to say goodbye to his family. Elijah's response was a reminder of what he did in calling him. Elisha's response was not like the response of a would-be disciple who would follow Jesus (Matt 8:21–22), but one ready to follow but first must bid farewell. Much like Matthew after he left all to follow Jesus by throwing a party for his friends, Elisha did so by sacrificing the oxen, feeding his family and friends, and then following Elijah. His slaughter of the oxen was symbolic of his acceptance of the prophetic call. There was nowhere to turn except to follow the prophet and become his "attendant." The word "attendant" is from the same Hebrew word (*sharath*) used of Joshua. It was well known later that Elisha served Elijah, he "who poured water on the hands of Elijah" (2 Kgs 3:11). Elisha became Elijah's servant until Elijah was translated to heaven, a period of about ten years.[11] Elisha was the one who carried out the first two commands of the Lord to anoint Hazael and Jehu (see 2 Kgs 8:7–13; 9:1–10).

The lesson Elijah learned through all this was that he needed an Elisha to be with him, to train, to mentor, and to encourage, and in doing so he himself would have been encouraged to stand courageously. "It may

---

8. Wiseman, *1 and 2 Kings*, 174.

9. Keil and Delitzsch, *Biblical Commentary on the Old Testament*, 260. Gaebelein, *Expositor's Bible Commentary*, 151.

10. Henry, *Matthew Henry's Commentary*, 330.

11. Wood, *Prophets of Israel*, 67.

be that God was saying Elijah had needed an Elisha with him that night to help him decide aright."[12]

In 2 Kings 2, Elijah was translated to heaven. Here in this chapter that we learn about the "sons of the prophets" (2 Kgs 2:3, 5, 7, 15; also in 4:1, 38; 5:22; 6:1; 9:1) (בְּנֵי־הַנְּבִיאִים, *bene-hannebi'im*). The phrase also means "disciples of the prophets." Disciples were called "sons," and their teachers were called "fathers" (in Elijah's translation to heaven, Elisha calls him "father"; 2 Kgs 2:12). Teachers were respected as a son respected his father and thus were called "father."[13] Some scholars interpret this phrase as "students of the prophets."[14] During Elijah and Elisha's time, companies of prophets were located at Bethel (2:3), Jericho (2:5) and Gilgal (4:38). Evidently, since the time of Elijah's despondency, he formed companies or schools of prophets. If this is the case, Elijah grew from his experience as a "Lone Ranger" prophet to meeting with, teaching, developing, and mentoring others. During Samuel's time, a group of prophets prophesied, among whom was Saul (1 Sam 10:5–10; 19:20). Leon Wood observes that "these texts connote a group of which could well have constituted a type of school. In both passages the companies were clearly groups approved by Samuel, and in the second Samuel is pictured serving as their leader."[15] Furthermore, he makes the following observation about Samuel's "school."

> He probably gathered his students from concerned young men of the day, perhaps many of them Levites like himself. He knew they would need training in what they were to do, which called for the idea of a school, and Samuel was the logical one to serve as teacher. It would have taken some of Samuel's valuable time to do this, but apparently, he saw wisdom in taking that time so that the total task could be accomplished in a shorter period. It is possible, too, that Samuel did much of his instructing as he walked from one city to another. This would have saved time and the young trainees could have profited from seeing Samuel directly in action.[16]

---

12. Wood, *Prophets of Israel*, 224.

13. "בֵּן," http://www.blueletterbible.org/lang/lexicon/lexicon.cfm?Strongs=H1121&t=NIV.

14. Lewis, "Schools of the Prophets," 3.

15. Wood, *Prophets of Israel*, 164.

16. Wood, *Prophets of Israel*, 164.

It is unclear whether this was a formal school, but in 2 Kings, they in some ways were connected to Elijah and Elisha.[17] In the following chapters (2 Kings 2ff.), the life and ministry of Elisha, especially his miraculous deeds, are described. Again, the sons of the prophets are referenced, one numbering around one hundred men (4:38–43). Garrett states that "Members of this prophetic guild were social, religious, and political reformers."[18] During a communal meal, Elisha met with the company (4:38). Apparently, Elisha continued the ministry of the training of these schools after Elijah's translation to heaven. Upon Elijah's return from his encounter with God, he apparently saw the need to revive these companies or schools because God did not intend for one to lead ministry alone but in concert with others. However, one cannot extrapolate current institutional thinking upon the text as if a formal school existed. Groups of prophets did exist, and in some way, Elisha was their mentor as they called him "man of God" (2 Kgs 4:40) and "lord" (6:5). In 2 Kings 6:1, the meeting hall for their instruction was much too small for their number, so they began a building project for a larger building. This passage implies that instruction and training occurred, but no details are given. One can only speculate as to the details. These occurrences demonstrate that Elisha spent time with the men he was training and performed miracles in their presence (multiplying the bread and making the axe float). The Targum, Josephus, and others saw them as disciples of the prophets.[19]

The principles taught in these passages are the following. First, God uses mature men in his calling of other men. Elijah was instrumental in passing the mantle of God's call to Elisha. Second, God designed his people to minister together (Elijah and Elisha), and not alone as Elijah did for many years. Third, mature leaders are to train growing leaders. Apparently, Elijah learned his lesson. After his encounter with God on Mt. Sinai, he obeyed the Lord and assembled three companies of the prophets. Fourth, training is best accomplished in the context of growing relationships. Fifth, training is best accomplished in the context of ministry itself. The building project was a spiritual project. Ministry is caught as much as it is taught. Elijah's modeling for Elisha can be seen in the response of the company of the prophets. They watched Elisha after Elijah was taken to heaven. Second Kings 2:15 reads, "The company of the prophets from Jericho, *who were watching*, said, 'The spirit of Elijah is

---

17. Gaebelein, *Expositor's Bible Commentary*, 2:177 n. 2.
18. Garrett, "Sons of the Prophets," n.p.
19. Lewis, "Schools of the Prophets," 8.

resting on Elisha.' And they went to meet him and bowed to the ground before him" (emphasis added). American culture tends to individualistic, while these examples from Scripture demonstrate community and the value of togetherness and modeling. The truth is that the one who is new and growing learns from someone else who is already experienced and mature.

EQUIPPING LEADERS IN THE NEW TESTAMENT

Jesus and the Twelve Disciples

Much has been written on Jesus and his training of the Twelve. Of notable value are *The Training of the Twelve* by A. A. Bruce, *The Master Plan of Evangelism and Discipleship* by Robert E. Coleman, *Jesus Christ Disciplemaker* by Bill Hull, *The Lost Art of Disciple Making* by LeRoy Eims, *All the Apostles of the Bible* by Herbert Lockyer, and more recently *Twelve Ordinary Men* by John MacArthur. A. A. Bruce recognized three stages in their training: believers who occasionally accompanied him, fellowship with Christ, leading into discipleship and apostleship.[20] In regards to training, Bruce notes the following: "Both from His words and from His actions we can see that He attached supreme importance to that part of His work which consisted in training the twelve."[21] Even in his high priestly prayer, Christ alluded to his training of the twelve. "The careful, painstaking education of the disciples secured that the Teacher's influence on the world should be permanent . . ."[22]

Eims recognizes four stages of discipleship: convert, disciple, worker, and leader.[23] Hull recognizes four stages of Jesus' training of the disciples: come and see, come and follow me, come and be with me, and come and abide in me.[24]

MacArthur also recognizes four "distinct stages."[25] There was a calling to *conversion*, where they came to know Christ for salvation. Second, they were called to *ministry* when they left their professions to follow Christ. Third, they were called to *apostleship* (Mark 3; Luke 6), and Jesus

---

20. Bruce, *Training of the Twelve*, 11–12.
21. Bruce, *Training of the Twelve*, 13.
22. Bruce, *Training of the Twelve*, 13.
23. Eims, *Lost Art of Disciple Making*, 184ff.
24. Hull, *Jesus Christ Disciplemaker*, 29ff. (essentially the whole book).
25. MacArthur, *Twelve Ordinary Men*, 3–5.

sent them on missions to various places. Fourth, they were called to *martyrdom* (after the resurrection).

Harold Longenecker, in *Growing Leaders by Design*, also recognizes four dynamic elements of their training based upon the book of Mark.[26] They include servant leadership, relationships, the group, and discipleship. According to Longenecker, "the planting of His church in the world required the training of this group for leadership in that church." Thus, the focus of Jesus' training was the disciples, not the crowds.[27] From these four elements, the disciples emerged as leaders. They transitioned from belief (converts) to growth (disciples), to proper relationships (leaders), and to aspirations (visionaries). "Their unique pilgrimage—from impotence to influence, from mediocrity to excellence, from obscurity to prominence—began when they were touched *by the training ministry of Jesus*."[28]

Lockyer observes three stages of the disciples training: discipleship, ambassadorship, and apostleship.[29]

Aubrey Malphurs and Will Mancini recognize "at least three stages"[30] or phases. Jesus' disciples grew from seekers to believers, from believers to full-time followers, and from followers to leaders. Malphurs and Mancini see Jesus' development as descriptive for the church today and not prescriptive.[31] From these three steps, they recognized four principles of leadership development: recruitment, selection, training, and deployment. Because Jesus focused on the "core" and not the crowd, pastors and leaders today should focus on developing core leaders. "Jesus' example teaches us that the size of our *core*, not the *crowd*, is what ultimately counts in ministry and will honor him over the long haul. We can measure our success not by the numbers of people we attract but by our relating to and training a competent, godly core of leaders who will have significant ministries long after we have been forgotten."[32]

Malphurs and Mancini see training as a separate step in the development of the disciples. Yet, the entire time Jesus spent with the disciples could be considered training. Developing his relationship with

26. Longenecker, *Growing Leaders by Design*, 27–37.
27. MacArthur, *Twelve Ordinary Men*, 22.
28. Longenecker, *Growing Leaders by Design*, 41 (emphasis added).
29. Lockyer, *All the Apostles of the Bible*, 20–23.
30. Malphurs and Mancini, *Building Leaders*, 63–67.
31. Malphurs and Mancini, *Building Leaders*, 63.
32. Malphurs and Mancini, *Building Leaders*, 71 (emphasis added).

the disciples was an integral part of the training because the relationship became the foundation and catalyst for their development. Second, Jesus' modeling for the disciples was as much training as was their "classroom" experience, where he specifically taught them in groups and in one-on-one situations. Even then, in many of these contexts, the crowds were present during Jesus' instruction.

Based upon these recognized steps in Jesus' training of the Twelve, the following stages of training can be identified.

New Believers Growing in Relationship to Christ (John 1–3) ("Come and See")

Upon Jesus' return from the temptation in the desert, John the Baptist saw Jesus and proclaimed, "Look the Lamb of God" (John 1:36). Immediately, two of John's disciples left John to follow Jesus and spent the day with him (1:39). At this point, they did not leave all to follow Jesus, but simply followed him from time to time.[33] However, the event left such an indelible mark in John's mind that he remembered the time they accompanied Jesus to his home.[34] Jesus' presence with the disciples and the time he gave them made an incredible impact on their lives. This truth illustrates the impact that a Christlike example can leave on a person's life. The truth of human behavior is that one learns more from watching others—especially a Christlike leader—than from just simply reading it in a book or hearing a message. Jesus' choice of the Twelve was not based upon them or their gifts and abilities, but "because of what, under His tuition, and by His power they would become . . . But the whole world would come to know what the example and equipment of Christ made them—twelve of the strongest, noblest, and most fearless and serviceable men (except for Judas Iscariot) who have appeared in human history. The transformation of the twelve was the not the least; it was almost the greatest of Christ's miracles."[35]

In John 2:1, his disciples accompanied Jesus to a wedding in Cana. After the wedding, he stayed a few days with his disciples in Capernaum (2:12) before returning to Jerusalem when he drove out the moneychangers (2:13f.). In 3:22, after his visit with Nicodemus, he spent some time

---

33. Alford, *Greek Testament*, 699.
34. Nicoll, *Expositor's Greek Testament*, 699.
35. Lockyer, *All the Apostles of the Bible*, 11.

with his disciples and baptized. The point of these first few months of Jesus' time with his disciples is that Jesus developed a close relationship with his disciples. They were curious converts. They were intrigued with Jesus, saw his miracles, listened to his teachings, and observed his interaction with others, like Nicodemus. In his training of the disciples for the future entrusting of ministry, Jesus got to know them and allowed them to be able to know him. The relationship with the disciples became the catalyst and basis for the training of the disciples during the next stage.

Growing Disciples Who Embraced Leadership (Matt 4–9; Mark 1–3; Luke 5–9; John 4–11)
("Come and Follow Me")

As Jesus was teaching from a boat on the Sea of Galilee, he told Peter to throw out their nets in the deep (Luke 5:1–4). Upon catching a large catch of fish, Peter realized his sinfulness and asked Jesus to depart from him because of his sinfulness (5:8). Jesus then called them to follow him, and he would make them fishers of men (Matt 4:19; Mark 1:17). Jesus began to teach them in the spiritual disciplines: prayer, fellowship, evangelism, and the Word of God.[36] As the relationships deepened, the commitment of the disciples increased. During this time, the disciples grew from being curious converts to committed disciples who followed Jesus at any cost.

Commissioned Leaders Appointed and Endowed with Authority and Power
("Come and Be with Me")

Over a year later, after spending the night in prayer, Jesus appointed twelve men as his apostles. He called them that "they might be with him and that he might send them out to preach" (Mark 3:14). Jesus' choice of the twelve disciples was for the purpose of relationship and ministry. Again, Jesus continued to deepen his relationship with his disciples ("that they might be with him"). The deepening relationship provided the catalyst for their development and equipping, now as his "apostles." This principle is consistent throughout Scripture. In 2 Timothy 2:1–2, Paul exhorted Timothy to be strengthened by the grace of God in his relationship with Jesus Christ. Upon the basis of this growing relationship with

---

36. Hull, *Jesus Christ Disciplemaker*, 79–142, esp. 140.

Christ, would Timothy be able to "entrust to faithful men" the good deposit, which he had heard from Paul "in the presence of many witnesses" (2 Tim 2:1–2). Jesus chose the Twelve also in order to send them out "to preach and to have authority to drive out demons" (Mark 3:15). At this point in Jesus' ministry, he began to send them out; thus, they were appointed as "apostles" or "sent ones" (from ἀποστέλλω, *apostellō*, "to send out" or "to dispatch someone for the achievement of some objective, *send away/out*"[37]) (cf. Matt 10; Luke 10). Before entrusting them with ministry, Jesus concentrated on relationship development, teaching, and modeling for the newly appointed apostles. He then sent them out, two by two, to the "lost sheep of the house of Israel" (Matt 10:6). The disciples then experienced the power of the authority Jesus had entrusted to them as they saw demons leave in Jesus' name. At this point, the committed disciples became competent leaders who began to imitate their Master and do the same as he had demonstrated to them. Most of the material in the Synoptic Gospels concentrates on this period (Matt 10–25; Mark 3–13; Luke 10–21). Ministry involvement exposed weaknesses in the lives and character of the disciples, which afforded their Master Teacher the opportunity to correct and rebuke them (e.g., Matt 16:23–28).

Entrusted Christlike Reproducers Who Impacted the World ("Come and Abide in Me")

This final stage began during the final hours of Jesus' life before his death (John 15). Jesus' desire was that they would bear much fruit, but they could only do so by abiding in him (15:5–8). Again, Jesus emphasized the relationship of his disciples with him. Even though he would be leaving this world and returning to his Father, he desired that they continue to depend upon him and allow them to live his life through them. He would not leave them alone but would send the Holy Spirit, who would enable them to do more than he had (John 16:7ff.). Before this, Jesus had modeled the importance of servant leadership for his disciples (John 13:1–17). Even in his sufferings, Jesus continued to model for the disciples what many of them would later undergo themselves. Finally, in his post-resurrection appearances, Jesus entrusted his ministry to them (Matt 28:16–20; Mark 16:15; Luke 24:44–45; John 20:21; Acts 1:8). Their job was to "make disciples of all nations" (Matt 28:18) by going, preaching the gospel to all

---

37. BDAG, 121.

creation, and preaching repentance to all nations. They were to make disciples in Jerusalem, Judea, Samaria, and to the ends of the earth. Jesus thus entrusted his whole plan and purpose into the hands of eleven ordinary men, who would later turn the world upside down. The disciples did not fully understand Jesus' message and mandate to the nations. The gospel would encompass every people group, including Greeks, Barbarians, and peoples from all over the globe. At first, they remained in Jerusalem, but persecution drove them to Antioch and beyond (Acts 8; 11:19ff.). The church was born on the day of Pentecost (Acts 2:42–47) and expanded through the apostles and disciples. Even the religious leaders recognized that these men had been with Jesus, even though they were ordinary men (Acts 4:13). At this point, the once curious converts who had become committed disciples and competent leaders now became Christlike reproducers. As Christ lived his life through them through the Holy Spirit, they touched the world through word and deed.

The lessons one can learn from Jesus' training of the Twelve are numerous.

Relationship Development

Jesus developed a relationship with these curious converts before entrusting responsibility to them. The deepening relationship with these up-and-coming leaders became the catalyst and foundation for their growth.

Modeling

Jesus modeled to the disciples what a leader should be and how one should lead. For over a year, the disciples followed Jesus and observed as he healed the sick, taught the crowds, and cast out demons. His model became the visual example for them that they would later follow. Lockyer observes, "They could not function as apostles until they had studied with Christ."[38]

---

38. Lockyer, *All the Apostles of the Bible*, 21.

Entrusting Ministry

Jesus entrusted ministry to the disciples and gave them the authority to be effective as leaders. During their ministry activity, Jesus shaped their character and continued their training. Jesus entrusted his whole franchise and vision to them for them to take and lead. This is the most amazing truth about Jesus' training of the Twelve, i.e., he placed his entire enterprise, plan, and purpose in the hands of these ragamuffin men who were unknown, ordinary, common, and unschooled. "He didn't choose a single rabbi. He didn't choose a scribe. He didn't choose a priest. Not one of the men He chose came from the religious establishment."[39] Yet, when endowed with the power of the Holy Spirit, they turned the world upside down.

Ministry Involvement during Training

The disciples were involved in ministry as they were being trained and as they developed into Christlike leaders. "Instead, Jesus taught them in the context of ministry. They learned while doing."[40]

Leaders Are Made and Shaped.

This is a point that Lockyer succinctly makes in his book *All the Apostles of the Bible*. He aptly says, "There are no self-made Christians in his service; they are all Christ-made. Self-made men are usually not made up of good material, and they can be wrapped in a very small parcel. But those whom the Lord wants and wins, are those He is able to fashion into human books to tell the story of His love and grace."[41] The point here is that Christlike, mature, effective leaders are made and shaped. In American Christianity, typically, one is on his own to chart his own course, unless he or she seeks out a mentor. Christlike, mature leaders in following the Master's example are to seek out others to train as did Jesus. Jesus' choice of the Twelve was a sovereign choice, based upon a night of prayer, limited to twelve typical men, which resulted in their becoming apostles and

---

39. MacArthur, *Twelve Ordinary Men*, 7.
40. Malphurs and Mancini, *Building Leaders*, 67.
41. Lockeyer, *All the Apostles of the Bible*, 12.

had clear objectives.[42] In other words, Jesus' choice was intentional and spiritual, as training today should be.

The thesis here is this very truth that one can follow the example and pattern of our Lord and see similar results. By modeling, developing relationships, training, and empowering with authority and responsibility, the world can be turned upside down again in the twenty-first century.

Barnabas and Saul

One of the greatest examples of an encourager is Barnabas. In fact, his name was changed from Joseph to Barnabas to demonstrate this character trait (Acts 4:36). Later after Saul's conversion on the road to Damascus, Barnabas is the one who introduced him to the apostles (9:36–40). After persecution scattered the disciples throughout the surrounding areas of Jerusalem and Judea, a church was birthed in Antioch, which would later become the base of the missionary journeys of the apostle Paul (11:19ff.). After the church was started in Antioch by Jews from Cyprus and Cyrene who dared to preach the gospel to Greeks, the church in Jerusalem sent Barnabas to strengthen the church (11:22–24). This was the first instance of a wide-scale outreach to gentiles in the early church. It was in this environment that Barnabas was commissioned.

Barnabas saw the evidence of the grace of God and encouraged them to stay true to the Lord (11:23). Barnabas, however, realized that he could not lead the church alone, so he searched intensely for Saul (11:25).[43] With the invitation of Barnabas, Paul "made his debut as a teacher of Gentile Christians."[44] For one whole year, they taught great numbers of people and there the disciples were called "Christians" (11:26), either out of derision or as descriptive term they themselves chose.[45] About a year later, there were not two leaders leading the Antioch church, but at least five (13:1–4). Simeon, called Niger, was probably an African since the word "Niger" is Latin for "black-skinned."[46] Lucius was from Cyrene;

---

42. Lockyer, *All the Apostles of the Bible*, 14–26.

43. The Greek word *anazateō* implies an intense search for Saul. Bruce believes that Saul by this time had been disinherited and was difficult to find (Bruce, *Commentary on Acts*, 240). Harrison notes that the "language suggests uncertainty as to Saul's whereabouts" (*Interpreting Acts*, 194).

44. Kistemaker, *New Testament Commentary: Acts*, 402.

45. Kistemaker, *New Testament Commentary: Acts*, 403.

46. Bruce, *Commentary on Acts*, 260; Harrison, *Interpreting Acts*, 215. Kistemaker,

his name is Latin, and he was probably Roman. It is ironic that Manaen is listed with this leadership team. He had grown up with Herod, the one who killed John the Baptist and tried Jesus before his crucifixion. Manaen, because he grew up with Herod, was of royal descent and influence.[47] Several observations can be made from this text. Antioch was a multi-cultural, cosmopolitan city and was the third largest in the Roman Empire, with an estimated population of half a million, behind only Rome and Alexandria.[48] Not only was the church multi-cultural, but also so was the leadership team of the church. Antioch was situated fifteen miles from the Mediterranean Ocean on the Orontes River, and had a large Jewish population.[49] Because the cult worship of Artemis, Apollo, and Astarte was centered just a few miles away at Daphne, prostitution was widespread as a part of cultic worship.[50] "Antioch was a cosmopolitan city, where Jew and Gentile, Greek and barbarian rubbed shoulders, where Mediterranean civilization met the Syrian desert; racial and religious differences which loomed so large in Judea seemed much less important here."[51] Harrison notes that "in such a cosmopolitan atmosphere people learned to live with one another in a spirit of toleration, a fact that is borne out by the fact that Luke recorded no persecution of the church there, either by Jews or pagans."[52] Christianity made such an impact on the city that the believers were first called "Christians" there.

Second, they were worshiping the Lord together; worshiping together enabled them to work together and overcome their cultural differences. Typically, Jews did not associate with gentiles for ceremonial reasons. Third, out of this worship experience as a multi-cultural leadership team of prophets and teachers, the Holy Spirit called the first cross-cultural workers, Barnabas and Saul, to proclaim the gospel among the gentiles. Fourth, the church cooperated with the Holy Spirit in sending out the first cross-cultural workers (13:3, 4).[53] While the Holy Spirit *sent*

New Testament Commentary: Acts, 454.

47. Kistemaker, *New Testament Commentary: Acts*, 454.
48. Marshall, *Acts of the Apostles*, 200–201.
49. Bruce, *Commentary on Acts*, 238.
50. Bruce, *Commentary on Acts*, 238.
51. Bruce, *Commentary on Acts*, 241.
52. Harrison, *Interpreting Acts*, 192.
53. Interestingly, Luke uses two different words in 13:3 and 13:4 for "send," namely *apoluo* and *ekpempo*. *Apoluō* is used of "setting free" (Luke 13:12), "letting go" or "dismissing" (Matt 15:23) and even divorce (Matt 1:19). The possible implication is that the

them, the church *released* them for the work that God had called them. The Antioch church had learned generosity with their resources when prophets indicated that there would be a famine in Judea. As a result, they had given for this project by sending the offering by the hand of Barnabas and Saul, showing their love and concern for the believers in Judea (11:27–30). They now learned generosity with their leadership by releasing these men to the Holy Spirit to the work for which he had called them.

In this environment of a growing, impacting mega-church of Antioch, Saul, later known as Paul, was allowed to grow and develop his ministry and skills as a teacher and multiplier. Under Barnabas's encouragement and mentoring, Paul grew as a leader. The skills, experience, and maturity afforded by this time enabled Paul to become the leader he would eventually become. Under maturing leaders such as Barnabas, aspiring leaders such as Paul can grow and flourish, when given the authority and freedom to lead. Barnabas was an encourager and a servant leader and allowed a potentially threatening leader like Saul to gain valuable experience.

Several principles emerge from this account of Barnabas and Saul's ministry at the church of Antioch.

Local Church-Based Training

The training of Saul and the emerging leaders of the Antioch church was based in the local church. In this growing, impacting church, emerging leaders were trained and empowered to serve. Training in local churches like the Antioch church allows for immediate ministry application and experience and, coupled with structured training, emerging leaders grow into capable, Christlike leaders.

---

church in Antioch released the newly called even though they really did not want to. See also Harrison, *Interpreting Acts*, 217: "Notable is the change in terminology denoting the relation of the missionaries to the Holy Spirit. Whereas the church 'sent them off' (v. 3), or 'let them go' (indicating that the parting was not altogether easy), the two men were 'sent on their way by the Holy Spirit.' It was by His authority and designation that they went forth."

Mentoring Relationships

Training best takes place under the mentoring of Christlike leaders, like Barnabas, a man full of faith and the Holy Spirit who was an encourager and servant-leader. Leaders who are servant-leaders like Barnabas should give significant consideration and time to concentrating their ministries on emerging leaders like Saul, Simeon, Lucius, and Manaen.

Local Church Ministry Experience

Those called by God, like Saul, should gain valuable church ministry experience before launching out on a mission. The time in Antioch allowed Saul to grow in his skills and allowed the church to get to know him and send him out as they heard through prophecy that the Holy Spirit had called Barnabas and Saul. God's call to Saul was thus a call to the whole church, as the whole church released Barnabas and Saul to the work for which God the Holy Spirit had called them.[54] Thus, God's call to Paul was confirmed to the church.

Multi-Cultural Contexts

Training in multi-cultural contexts allows emerging leaders to learn and grow, developing skills for practical understanding of various cultural differences and nuances, possibly eliminating cultural bias and prejudice.

Spiritual Disciplines

Training in the context of a highly spiritual atmosphere, where prayer and fasting are emphasized, shapes the leader's heart and trains in the disciplines of the spiritual life, emphasizing the *being* aspects of godly leaders and not just action and ministry activity.

---

54. Kistemaker, *New Testament Commentary: Acts*, 455. Harrison aptly states that the laying on of hands signified "that the whole group was going with them in spirit, committed to faithful prayer on their behalf" (*Commentary on Acts*, 216).

Missional Contexts

Training in missional contexts, such as the Antioch church, shapes the vision of emerging leaders for cross-cultural ministry and for God's heart for the nations.

Paul and Timothy

Timothy joined Paul and his missionary team after the controversy over John Mark (Acts 15:36–41). Timothy was well spoken of by the church in Lystra and in Iconium (Acts 16:2), where Paul and Barnabas had first preached the gospel and planted churches. Since Timothy's mother was Jewish and there were many Jews in that area (16:1–3), Paul had Timothy circumcised as a strategic step for their mission to the Jews who lived in the urban areas throughout the Roman Empire. Timothy's training for the next fifteen years took place on the road along with Paul. From Asia Minor to Macedonia to Greece, they, along with Silas, traveled, preaching the gospel and planting churches. Paul discipled Timothy along the way, from "house to house," from city to city, and from province to province. As Jesus had discipled the Twelve, so now Paul discipled and trained Timothy, along with Silas and other numerous converts from the areas they planted churches (cf. Acts 20:4). As leaders were trained, some joined Paul's missionary team to the next place. Significant passages have emerged from Paul's writings of his training of Timothy and others.

First, the training was *relationally based*. In 2 Timothy, it is evident that Paul knew Timothy's family (2 Tim 1:5). He knew his mother and grandmother and their names. He knew Timothy's weaknesses (1:6–8), his appointment to ministry ("fan into flame the gift of God"), and the difficulties he faced in Ephesus in establishing the church. Paul exhorted Timothy to join with him in suffering for the gospel (1:8), that he was not to be ashamed of him nor the gospel message. In 2 Timothy 3:10ff., the implication is that Timothy and Paul had a long history. Timothy knew about Paul's way of living (3:10). He knew about his faith and vision. He knew about the persecutions he encountered in Lystra, Iconium, and Derbe. No one could say these things about someone unless there is a close personal relationship. Paul's mentoring and training of Timothy occurred in the context of a close personal relationship.

Second, in Paul's training of Timothy, he *entrusted* ministry to him. He sent him to Philippi, Thessalonica, and Berea to follow up on the fledgling churches (e.g., Acts 18:5). Timothy met Paul in Corinth and brought an offering from the Philippian church (Phil 1:5; 4:15–20). Ministry was entrusted to Timothy because he had been spoken well of by his local church, which Paul also started, and because Timothy had proved to be trustworthy, as a son to Paul (Phil 2:22). Paul had no one else like him because he was genuinely concerned for the welfare of others (2:20). He had served with Paul in furthering the gospel (2:22). In fact, while writing Philippians, he planned to send Timothy to them (2:19). A perusal of Acts and Paul's letters reveals that Paul looked for faithful men to enroll in his missionary team and to train them for the furtherance of his mission to the gentiles. This reveals a third characteristic of Paul's training of Timothy.

Third, he trained him (and others) *in the context of God's mission to the nations* that had been entrusted to him in bringing the gospel to the gentiles. As these men were exposed to church-planting efforts in urban areas among various ethnic groups, their vision and horizons were broadened to see that the gospel is for *all the nations* and not just Israel, and that in the church Jew and gentile alike could be part of this new society that God was building (see Eph 2:11–20). This truth had been difficult for Peter to learn (see Acts 10; Gal 2:11–15). Their training was not divorced from the mission of God to the nations, as revealed in Scripture (e.g., Gen 12:1–4).

In "Recovering Missional Ecclesiology in Theological Education," Mark Laing maintains that the Protestant missionary movement has "exported this defective ecclesiology," one that has focused more on abstract theology than on God's mission to the world.[55] The result has been an introspective Christianity unaware of its apostolic nature as seminaries have tacked on missiology to their curriculum. This (Paul's mission to the nations) was no different than Jesus had modeled, as he served Jew and gentile alike. In John 4, burdened, Jesus intentionally traveled through Samaria to meet the Samaritan woman at Jacob's Well in Sychar.

Fourth, he expected them to train *the next generation* of leaders. Three significant passages are noteworthy of mention.

---

55. Laing, "Recovering Missional Ecclesiology," 11.

Ephesians 4:11–16

Understanding the context of Ephesians 4:11–16 is significant in accurately interpreting this text. Paul's theme here is the unity of the church. He exhorted them to unity in 4:1–3. He emphasized diversity and unity with the Godhead (4:4–6). Each person in the triune God has various roles in God's economy. He emphasized the spiritual gifting of all believers in 4:7–10. Each believer has a unique gifting from Christ. In Ephesians 4:11–16, Paul outlined the gifted leaders of the church, namely, apostles, prophets, evangelists, pastors, and teachers. "The gifts are the people."[56] "The gift was a double gift. Christ first endowed the men, and then He gave them, so endowed, to the Church."[57] Literally, Paul said that Christ has given apostles, prophets, evangelists, pastors, and teachers.[58] These men are gifts to the church for certain purposes (vv. 4:12ff.).

Paul defined the role of the gifted individuals as consisting in preparing "to equip the saints for the work of ministry, for building up the body of Christ." Verse 12 has a unique construction, resulting in various interpretations. Literally, Paul said, "for the equipping of the saints [πρὸς τὸν καταρτισμὸν τῶν ἁγίων, *pros katartismon ton hagion*], for works of service [εἰς ἔργον διακονίας, *eis ergon diakonias*], for the building up of the body of Christ [εἰς οἰκοδομὴν τοῦ σώματος τοῦ Χριστοῦ, *eis oikodomen tou somatos tou christou*]." The three prepositions Paul used are *pros*, *eis*, and *eis*, which are all translated "for." The question in interpreting these phrases is this: are they parallel constructions or are the last two phrases dependent on the first? Some have interpreted this as parallel constructs where *pros . . . eis . . . eis* delineate the functions of the officers of verse 11.[59] They have interpreted the three phrases with the variation in prepositions as stylistic variations of Paul. Stylistic variations are common in Paul's writings;[60] however, it should be observed that the first phrase is preceded

---

56. Foulkes, *Epistle of Paul to the Ephesians*, 125. Abbott, *Critical and Exegetical Commentary on Ephesians and Colossians*, 117.

57. Westcott, *Saint Paul's Epistle to the Ephesians*, 62.

58. The "some" of the New International Version (NIV) is not part of the original text. The emphasis is on the fact that "he himself gave" when he was exalted to heaven (4:11). The personal pronoun *autos* is emphatic in the verse with a reflexive sense. In the context of 4:10's purpose of Christ's filling all things (with himself), the way he fills all things is by giving these offices to the church. Salmond, " Epistle to the Ephesians," 329.

59. Gordon, "'Equipping' Ministry in Ephesians 4?," 70. The KJV also supports this idea of a parallel construction.

60. Abbott, *Critical and Exegetical Commentary on Ephesians and Colossians*, 330.

by the definite article, while the last two are not, and the last two are *eis* instead of *pros*. Thus, the second phrase is the object of the first and the third phrase is the object of the second. Salmond succinctly observes that the interpretation of the three phrases as parallel "gives a somewhat awkward and involved construction, and reduces the force of the third clause, which would naturally be expected to bring us to the larger, ultimate purpose of Christ's giving. The proper construction . . . is the simplest. It . . . understands the three clauses as successive, the first looking to the second, the second to the third, the third forming the climax and expressing the ultimate object of the giving on the part of the ascended Christ."[61] Foulkes also interprets the three in the same way: "The difference of the prepositions in the Greek is against this [i.e., as parallel constructs], and at least implies that the latter two are dependent on the first."[62] Westcott notes that the three prepositions are not coordinate.[63] In the following verses, this makes the best sense, with every believer doing his or her part, thus building up the body of Christ. F. F. Bruce also notes that three prepositional phrases in Ephesians 4:12 are "not coordinate with another. . .the second and third phrases are dependent on the first, as is indicated by their being introduced by a different preposition from the first."[64]

The word καταρτισμὸν (*katartismon*), even though it is a noun, in the context, has a verbal idea. The purpose of these officers—i.e., apostles, prophets, evangelists, pastors, and teachers—is to *equip* the saints. Gordon rejected the idea that καταρτισμὸν (*katartismon*) is to be translated as "equip" and agreed with the KJV's translation of "perfect."[65] However, others have noted that καταρτισμὸν (*katartismon*) in 4:12 is to be translated "equip" and that it denoted the "equipment of the saints for the work of the ministry."[66] Bauer defines καταρτισμός (*katartismos*) as "equipment": "*equipping* . . . through *training, discipline.*"[67] It was a medi-

---

61. Salmond, "Epistle to the Ephesians," 331. A .T. Robertson also sees the ultimate purpose of the building up of the body of Christ. Robertson, *Word Pictures in the New Testament*, 4:537.

62. Foulkes, *Epistle of Paul to the Ephesians*, 128.

63. Westcott, *Saint Paul's Epistle to the Ephesians*, 63.

64. Bruce, *Epistles to the Colossians, Philemon, and Ephesians*, 349. Bruce also notes in footnote 77 that the variation in the construction "suggests that the three phrases are not coordinate, and this is borne out by the sense of the sentence."

65. Gordon, "'Equipping' Ministry in Ephesians 4?," 72–73.

66. Kittel, *Theological Dictionary of the New Testament*, 1:476–477. Salmond, "Epistle to the Ephesians," 331. Gaebelein, *Expositor's Bible Commentary*, 11:58.

67. BDAG, 526.

cal technical term for setting bones in place.⁶⁸ Καταρτισμός (*Katartismos*) is a *hapax legomenon*, yet the verb καταρτίζω (*katartizō*) occurs in various texts for mending nets (Matt 4:21) and restoring a sinning believer (Gal 6:1). From the usage of the verb, Gordon wrongly concludes that καταρτισμός (*katartismos*) could not mean "equipping." Salmond succinctly demonstrates that καταρτισμός (*katartismon*) can mean "*preparing, furnishing,* [or] *equipping*" based upon extra-biblical texts and Luke 6:40, where a fully equipped disciple will be like his teacher.⁶⁹ Phillips also notes that the "thought, then, behind the word *katartismos* is that of making something fully ready, of perfectly equipping someone, of fully preparing something. The proper use of the gifts is to bring the body of Christ to its full potential."⁷⁰

The ESV correctly emphasizes the goal of the training, i.e., "for building up the body of Christ." Thus, the building up of the body is a direct result of the equipping role of leadership. Equipping the saints also has a preventative result. Believers will not be deceived by false teachers and false teaching (Eph 4:14). The sea image Paul painted denotes instability, literally of a boat in a storm surge where it is violently swinging and passengers are seasick.⁷¹ Thus, an equipping ministry will prevent such a state in the church. In 4:14, Paul used the word μεθοδείαν (*methodian*) in referring to the deception of false teachers. It was also used in 6:11, of Satan, whose plan or method is to deceive believers. False teachers, then, are instruments in the hand of the enemy to prevent the church from attaining doctrinal and spiritual maturity.

Thus, Paul expected the leaders that Christ gifted to the church would prepare and equip God's people (i.e., "saints" in 4:12) for works of service. The whole body grows as each person does his or her part (4:16). Thus, the purpose of Christ giving gifted leaders to the church is to prepare each to do his part so that the whole body grows and becomes more like Jesus Christ. "The responsible officers of the congregation work through others and find no rest till everyone fulfils his function."⁷² This ministry orientation implies an exerted effort on the part of gifted leadership to focus on the equipping of the saints, thus a training effort so that each part does its work. It also implies that the role of gifted leaders is not to monopolize all

68. BDAG, 526.
69. Salmond, "Epistle to the Ephesians," 331.
70. Phillips, *Exploring Ephesians & Philippians*, 119.
71. Cf. Foulkes, *Epistle of Paul to the Ephesians*, 131.
72. Westcott, *Saint Paul's Epistle to the Ephesians*, 63.

the work of the ministry, while members occupy the pew. "Gifted people should help equip others to carry out the work of winning people to Christ, shepherding the flock, and teaching God's Word."[73]

The desired result of the *equipping role* is that there be doctrinal unity and Christlikeness. The definite article with "faith" points to the fact that Paul had in mind a body of beliefs.[74] In the context, he was most likely referring to Ephesians 4:4–6.[75] In 4:4–6, Paul explained the basis of spiritual unity, exhorted in 4:1–3. The theological foundation of unity is founded upon the biblical teaching of the Holy Spirit, Jesus Christ, and God the Father. The Spirit called believers to salvation into one body (4:4). Belief in Christ is evidenced by baptism (4:5). The Father is the Creator of all; he is transcendent, imminent, and sustains all things. Doctrinal unity provides stability (the lack of which was illustrated by Paul through an image of a ship without proper steering). The image of the body communicates the idea of maturity, which Paul explicitly touched on in 4:13. Also, to be noted, the goal of this equipping is the *attaining of unity*. The word "attaining" is used nine times in Acts (16:1; 18:19, 24; 20:15; 21:7; 25:13; 26:7; 27:12; 28:13) for reaching a destination.[76] It is used metaphorically here and in Philippians 3:11.

The goal of equipping the saints is unity and Christlikeness. This unity is not only doctrinal but also relational, i.e., unity in the "knowledge of the Son of God" (Eph 4:13). The word translated "knowledge" is ἐπιγνώσεως (*epignoseōs*), not a conceptual knowledge but an experiential knowledge, i.e., an intimate relationship with Jesus Christ. The same idea is also conveyed in Philippians ns 3:9–11, where καταντάω (*katantaō*) was also used.

Since spiritual gifts have been given to each believer (Eph 4:7), each believer is to discover his or her gift, using their gifts so that the whole body may be built upon to resemble Christ (4:16). As Foulkes succinctly notes, "it is thus implied that every Christian has a work of ministry, a spiritual task and function in the body."[77] The results of Christlikeness

---

73. Phillips, *Exploring Ephesians & Philippians*, 119.

74. This is in contrast to F. F. Bruce's opinion (Bruce, *Epistles to the Colossians, Philemon, and Ephesians*, 350) that a body of belief is not in mind; however, in Paul's letters, when *pistis* is preceded by the definite article, it usually refers to a body of belief (cf. 2 Cor 13:5; Gal 1:23; 1 Tim 4:1, 6; 5:8; 6:10, 21; 2 Tim 2:18; 3:8; 4:7; Titus 1:1, 13; 2:2).

75. Foulkes, *Epistle of Paul to the Ephesians*, 129.

76. Foulkes, *Epistle of Paul to the Ephesians*, 129.

77. Foulkes, *Epistle of Paul to the Ephesians*, 128.

and "unity in the faith" is conditional upon gifted leaders equipping the saints for the work of ministry, literally εἰς ἔργον διακονίας (*eis ergon diakonias*). Διακονίας (*diakonias*) referred to an *office* (1 Tim 1:12; Acts 1:17), meal preparation (Luke 10:40), financial *support* (Acts 6:1), the *office of a deacon* (Rom 12:7), or service in general (Heb 1:14).[78] It is closely related to διακονέω (*diakoneō*, verb) and διάκονος (*diakonos*, noun). It refers not only to an official office, but also to service in general by believers to one another (1 Pet 4:10).[79] Thus, each believer is to serve, using his or her spiritual gifts ("grace") to build up others. The connection between gifted leaders gifted by Christ to the church and to believers in general is the equipping role of the leaders in office. The body's resemblance of Christ ("we will in all things grow up into him who is the Head, that is, Christ"; 4:15) is contingent upon the officers embracing their role as equippers and members responding to the equipping. Thus, the equipping of individual believers is directly related to the overall health of the body. As believers are equipped with their spiritual gift to serve one another, the body "builds itself up in love" (4:16). This again highlights the importance of the equipping ministry in the local church. A. T. Robertson notes that "no pastor has finished his work when the sheep fall so short of the goal" (i.e., maturity in Christ).[80]

The passage also highlights the importance of the *community* of believers. The image of a body shows that each believer has a vital role and is not alone but grows in relationship with other believers. In other words, God has given the church, i.e., the body of Christ, as a means of growth to individual believers. Believers do not grow in isolation but in community with others. This truth highlights the importance of *training in community* and the *benefit of local church-based training*. "No one can attain full spiritual maturity apart from the give-and-take of a local church fellowship."[81] In the setting of a local church, training that is communal facilitates the growth of each believer. God uses the relationship each believer has with others to stimulate personal growth. The body image also highlights the importance of *growth together*. Individual growth

---

78. BDAG, 230.

79. Abbott wrongly interprets "works of service" as the work of an official office (*Critical and Exegetical Commentary on Ephesians and Colossians*, 119). Since the phrase follows the "equipping" role of gifted leaders, "works of service" most naturally designates the function of "the saints."

80. Robertson, *Word Pictures in the New Testament*, 4:538.

81. Phillips, *Exploring Ephesians & Philippians*, 120.

is like a body part outgrowing another body part. Stunted growth in one part affects the appearance of the whole body; thus, the growth of each person is equally important. This growth is facilitated by equipping.

2 Timothy 2:1–2

In his final letter, which was also his second letter to Timothy, Paul gave instructions to Timothy in regard to sound doctrine (1:14) and godly leadership (ch. 2). His tone was one of deep concern as many had deserted him (1:15) and he was facing death (4:6f.). In contrast to those who had deserted him, Timothy was to continue to live a life that reflected and was empowered by the grace of God (2:1). Timothy had already been a believer for many years and Paul exhorted him to be empowered by God's grace in facing difficulties of various kinds and in completing the task God had entrusted to him. The grace Paul exhorted Timothy to be empowered by was not grace for salvation but grace for service and suffering. Indeed, he faced a difficult situation at Ephesus as he continued to establish and organize the church. As Christ selected his disciples so that they might be with him, Timothy needed to continue (present tense) to be empowered (passive voice) and nurtured by means of or in the grace of Christ.[82] This power would be found in his relationship with the Lord Jesus Christ.[83] Timothy in his inner man needed to be nourished by the power of the Holy Spirit. This verse reveals another principle of leadership training: *growing leaders need the continuing grace of God for life and ministry through their relationship with Jesus Christ.* "Christ is the dynamo for power only when and while we keep in touch with him."[84]

In addition (2:2), Paul expected Timothy to train the next generation with the sound teaching he himself had heard. Timothy would need God's unmerited empowerment (2:1) in accomplishing the exhortation Paul gave in 2:2. Timothy had heard the "good deposit" (1:14) in the "presence of many witnesses" (2:2) as he and Paul itinerantly traveled from one place to another planting churches.[85] Timothy had heard "sound teaching" from Paul himself, ἤκουσας παρ' ἐμοῦ (*ēkousaspar' emou*).

---

82. Kelly, *Commentary on the Pastoral Epistles*, 172. MacArthur, *MacArthur New Testament Commentary: 2 Timothy*, 38. MacArthur interprets "in the grace" as being instrumental, i.e., "by *means of the grace that is in Christ Jesus*" (italics original).

83. Robertson, *Word Pictures in the New Testament*, 4:616.

84. Robertson, *Word Pictures in the New Testament*, 4:616.

85. Stott, *Message of 2 Timothy*, 50.

Timothy had heard Paul preaching the gospel in Philippi, Thessalonica, Berea, Corinth, Ephesus, Miletus, Jerusalem, Caesarea, and Rome, to mention a few places. He had witnessed riots, revivals, and Paul going from door to door teaching the Word of God and preaching the gospel. Another principle of training this communicates is that *training is passed from one person to another*. It is *relational*, as seen in the life of Christ in training the Twelve.

Timothy's assignment was to entrust to qualified men what he had heard so that they could train others also. The word translated "entrust" is from παράθου (*parathou*), meaning to "set beside," "entrust," "commend," or "deposit."[86] In Hellenistic writings, it was used of a deposit, entrusted goods, and "a trust agreement."[87] "The trustworthiness of the trustee was thus most important."[88] It was used twenty-six times in eighteen verses and only three times by Paul. In the LXX, it was used of a man entrusting goods to a neighbor (cf. Exod 22:7–13). In Acts 14:23 and 20:32, the leaders of the churches Paul appointed were committed to the Lord "in whom they had believed." In the middle voice, it was used as a commercial term, meaning "to commit" or "to deposit."[89] In 1 Timothy 1:18 and here Paul's usage has the idea of committing an assignment or responsibility to Timothy. It has the same idea as 2 Timothy 1:12 and 1:14. In 1 Timothy 6:20, Paul communicated the same idea with φύλαξον *phylaxon* ("to guard") and τὴν παραθήκην (*tēn paratheēkēn*). "The idea is clearly to entrust something to another for safe keeping, and in the present context this notion is of great significance. The transmission of Christian truth must never be left to chance . . ."[90] Lock notes that the noun τὴν παραθήκην (*paratheēkēn*) "always implies the situation of one who has to take a long journey and who deposits the money and other valuables with a friend, trusting him to restore it on his return . . ."[91]

From this verse, a second principle of leadership training can be derived: *ministry is an entrustment*. God commits to his gifted, called leaders an assignment and he commits these many times through others, as did Paul to Timothy. It is important to understand from this passage that ministry assignment is committed from one person to another

---

86. "παρατίθημι," *Blue Letter Bible*.
87. Friedrich, *Theological Dictionary of the New Testament*, 162–63.
88. Friedrich, *Theological Dictionary of the New Testament*, 162.
89. Friedrich, *Theological Dictionary of the New Testament*, 163.
90. Guthrie, *Pastoral Epistles*, 151.
91. Lock, *Critical and Exegetical Commentary on the Pastoral Epistles*, 90.

and ultimately from Jesus Christ. The exercise of ministry assignment is not isolated from others, but many times mediated through others, as was through Moses to Joshua, Elijah to Elisha, and the Lord Jesus to the twelve disciples.

The men Timothy was to entrust this good deposit to were *"faithful men."* "Faithful men" (πιστοῖς ἀνθρώποις, *pistois anthropois*) are men who are trustworthy men of character. The relative pronoun that follows (οἵτινες, *hoitines*) and the adjective ἱκανοὶ (*hikanoi*) emphasize the character of these men.[92] These men would be able to teach others as well. Thus, Paul emphasized the continual passing on of the baton of sound doctrine and the gospel to other qualified men.

Another principle this passage teaches is that *faithful men are to pass on to the next generation through training and equipping*. "Here, then, are the four stages in the handing on of the truth, which Paul envisages: from Christ to Paul, from Paul to Timothy, from Timothy to 'faithful men', and from 'faithful men' to 'others also'. This is the true 'apostolic succession' . . . the succession from the apostles is to be more in the message itself than in the men who teach it."[93] "The Christian Church is dependent on an unbroken chain of teachers . . . The teacher is a link in the living chain which stretches unbroken from this present moment back to Jesus Christ."[94]

This also highlights a final principle, i.e., that *the Christian message of the gospel is to be passed on from generation to generation*. In other words, *the training itself centers on the Word of God* (τὴν παραθήκην, *tēn parathēkēn*) that was entrusted by God's prophets and apostles to the church today.

2 Timothy 3:10-17

In this passage, Paul opened his heart to Timothy to remind him of his responsibility to continue in what he had taught him, i.e., all Scripture, which is God breathed, and from whom he had learned the gospel, i.e., Paul himself. This passage, probably more than any other, demonstrates Paul's relationship with Timothy, specifically in how Timothy was trained.

---

92. Stott, *Message of 2 Timothy*, 51.

93. Stott, *Message of 2 Timothy*, 51–52. MacArthur, *MacArthur New Testament Commentary: 2 Timothy*, 39: "The New Testament neither teaches nor supports the idea of apostolic succession. But it does clearly teach, in this passage and elsewhere that the gospel is to be promulgated from *generation to generation*" (emphasis added).

94. Barclay, *Letters to Timothy, Titus, and Philemon*, 158.

Paul exhorted Timothy, in contrast to false teachers (3:1–9), to continue to grow and remain in the Scriptures.

For a period of almost twenty years, Paul trained Timothy in much the same environment as Jesus had trained the Twelve, i.e., on-the-job training. During Paul's second missionary journey, Timothy accompanied Paul. Most likely, Timothy believed in Jesus Christ during Paul's first visit to the province of Galatia (Acts 14). The emphasis of the passage is on the relational aspect of Timothy's training.

"You" (Σὺ δὲ, *su dè*) is emphatic (also in 2 Tim 3:14) and contrasts with false teachers Paul had warned about in 3:1–9.[95] Timothy had followed (from παρακολουθέω, *parakoloutheō*, "to follow faithfully")[96] Paul's teaching. Timothy was a follower of Paul, who was a follower of Jesus Christ. Timothy was a disciple of Paul. The verb is a "technical term defining the relation of a disciple to his master..."[97] He was well acquainted with his "way of life" (τῇ ἀγωγῇ, *tēagōgē*). This noun, only occurring here, is from αγω (*agō*, "to lead").[98] The idea is how one leads one's life. Timothy was intimately knowledgeable of Paul's lifestyle since the two had traveled and served together throughout many years and in many places. In addition, Timothy followed Paul's "my aim in life, my faith, my patience, my love, my steadfastness, my persecutions and sufferings." Paul's selfless service stood in stark contrast to the self-serving false teachers in 3:1–9. His own example was to be an encouragement and pattern for Timothy. Paul referenced the persecutions he endured (in contrast to the lifestyle of the false teachers) because Timothy was a witness to these persecutions and they may have been instrumental in Timothy's conversion.[99] In 3:14–15, Paul reminded Timothy to continue in what he had learned (μανθανω, *manthanō*, closely related to μαθητεύω, *mathēteuō*, "to make a disciple," which is used in Matt 28:19) and had believed in. The reason for Paul's exhortation was that he knew from whom he had learned these

---

95. Guthrie, *Pastoral Epistles*, 172.

96. Barclay points out that the verb "is indeed *the word for the disciple*, for it includes the unwavering loyalty of the true comrade, the full understanding of the true scholar and the true scholar and the complete obedience of the dedicated servant" (*Letters to Timothy, Titus, and Philemon*, 195, emphasis added).

97. Kelly, *Commentary on the Pastoral Epistles*, 198.

98. ἄγω," http://www.blueletterbible.org/lang/lexicon/Lexicon.cfm?Strongs=G71&t=NIV.

99. Stott, *Message of 2 Timothy*, 95–96; Guthrie, *Pastoral Epistles*, 173.

things and could be confident in this training because of the integrity of those whom he heard it from.[100]

Thus, a strategic element of Timothy's training was based upon the relationship between him and his mentor Paul. This principle of *the relational aspect of training* and equipping has been stressed throughout this book in the various examples of Scripture but is probably most clearly seen here. Paul's exhortations to Timothy were based upon their close relationship. In other words, the environment and catalyst for Paul's training of Timothy was the close relationship. Without Paul's close relationship with Timothy, it would have been difficult to exhort him on a personal level as seen repeatedly throughout this book. Thus, the environment and catalyst for effective training and equipping is the close relationship between the teacher-trainer and the student-disciple. As Barclay notes, "Real teaching is always born of real experience. There is *training.*"[101] Through such relationships, greater personal responsibility is given to the training. When personal relationships exist, the mentor is more likely to give greater emphasis and involvement in the life and equipping of the trainee. Conversely, where training is impersonal, there is little felt responsibility on the part of the trainer in the life of the trainee and much of the training centers on the acquisition of information and the intellectual aspects of the training. Relationally based training facilitates the Christlikeness that a trainee needs in living out the gospel. Paul took responsibility for the effectual training of Timothy, to whom he entrusted the ministry and the message of that ministry, i.e., the gospel. The passage also reveals the *discipleship aspect* of the relationship. Timothy was a follower of Paul, as Paul followed Christ (1 Cor 11:1). Training and equipping today should be exercised in this atmosphere of a discipleship relationship, where the mentor not only teaches information, but passes on visually, through his or her lifestyle, *how* to do ministry and *how* to live. "Similarly, he [Timothy] doubtless began by watching the apostle's manner of life, but then he went on to imitate it. Because Paul knew himself as an apostle to be following Christ, he did not hesitate to invite others to follow himself . . ."[102]

A second observation in this passage is *the role of the Scriptures.* The relationship between mentor and disciple connects the dots, so to speak,

---

100. The perfect participle from eidon is causal. Guthrie, *Pastoral Epistles,* 174. "The character of teachers closely reflects the character of what is taught . . ."

101. Barclay, *Letters to Timothy, Titus, and Philemon,* 196 (emphasis original).

102. Stott, *Message of 2 Timothy,* 94.

to the Scriptures. Paul pointed Timothy back to the Scriptures because the Scriptures are foundational for the training. This is evident in Paul's last phrase in 3:16, "training in righteousness." Paul connected the Scriptures to the training. This reiterates a point made earlier that the basis of the training is the Word of God itself, i.e., the Scriptures. "The place of the Bible in the equipping of men for the ministry must always be recognized as the most powerful influence."[103]

A third observation is *the lifestyle integrity of the trainer*. There is a close relationship between the integrity of the trainer and the integrity of the lessons being taught. Thus, the whole gospel enterprise is contingent in some respects on the integrity of those who proclaim it. Christlikeness on the part of the trainer is an integral part of the trainer. Those trained need to see the life of their trainer. How a person lives is an essential aspect in the passing on of the truth.

Finally, the goal of training is that a disciple be *"thoroughly equipped for every good work"* (3:17, NIV). In the context, good works include all that Paul mentioned in 3:10ff. The goal is not just the acquisition of information about the Bible, but becoming more like Jesus Christ in lifestyle and in ministry. Training, thus, should be evaluated upon this goal; i.e., is it equipping trainees to be more like Jesus Christ and become "thoroughly equipped for every good work"?

Paul and Titus

Paul's work with Titus began at Antioch. In fact, Titus was Paul's test case during his second visit to Jerusalem (Gal 2:1–10). Titus was a Greek who had believed in the Lord Jesus Christ. As a result of a revelation (Gal 2:1), which was most likely the prophecy of a coming famine in Acts 11:27–30,[104] Paul and Barnabas hand carried the donation from the Antioch church. Titus, who was with them, refused to be circumcised when the attempt of persuasion was made (Gal 2:2). Paul took the opportunity to share his ministry with the pillars of Jerusalem, namely Peter, James (the half-brother of Jesus), and John. At the end of his visit, they came to a gentleman's agreement that Peter would continue to serve as the apostle to the Jews, while Paul served as the apostle to the gentiles (Gal 2:9–10). Paul's purpose in this meeting was to discuss his gospel message, not to

---

103. Guthrie, *Pastoral Epistles*, 177.
104. Bruce, *Epistles to the Colossians, Philemon, and Ephesians*, 244.

be encumbered by Jewish scruples, and ministry to the gentiles so that the church would be unified and there would not be a Jewish church and gentile church. Titus was a witness to this meeting. Not much more was said about Titus outside of the personal letter Paul sent to him while establishing the church at Crete. Titus is mentioned in 2 Corinthians 8 as the collector of the offering for the Judean believers who had suffered through a difficult famine. It can be gathered from the references about Titus that he and Paul were close associates and Paul spent considerable time with him. Paul's personal letter to Titus highlights his close personal relationship with Titus (e.g., Titus 3:12). Paul's concern in this letter included the training of faithful men who were to hold to sound teaching and that believers were to live out this sound teaching in their relationships with each other and the world (Titus 1:5, 9; 2:1–15; 3:1–11).

CONCLUSION

From the examples in the Old Testament and the New Testament, numerous principles have been drawn from the text of Scripture. This study has recognized that many examples studied are of the narrative genre. Didactic passages in Ephesians (4:11–16) and 2 Timothy (2:1–2; 3:10–17) were also cited that furnish exhortation to the church today. These passages are prescriptive for the life of the church. The principles derived from the examples of Old and New Testament biblical passages communicate the following principles. (1) Relational training is the catalyst and environment for effective training. (2) Life-on-life training, where the trainer's visible life is obvious, is a powerful tool in the hand of the trainer because the disciple can see in his or her mentor the lessons being lived out. The model of the mentor himself becomes a part of the training of the disciple. (3) Training in the context of ministry accentuates the training of the disciple. Actual ministry experience with an experienced role model will enable the disciple to gain valuable truths that are learned not only from study but also from experience. (4) Experience in a missional context with the broader scope of God's mission to the nations serves as a valuable context for the training.

(5) Local church-based training allows the disciple to grow in relationship with other believers and experience daily ministry contexts, and allows the mentor to guide the disciple's growth to maturity. (6) Ministry is to be entrusted as a disciple grows in his relationship to Christ and to

other believers, and in his understanding of Scripture and sound teaching. (7) Training bathed in worship and prayer allows for the development of the trainee's heart and character, guided by godly men. (8) Training that is organic (relational and natural) and structured (emphasis on the content) provides an excellent way for training. (9) Finally, personalization of these principles gives urgency to the importance of training and equipping leaders.

God expects pastors and church leaders to focus on the transferring of sound teaching and Christlikeness to the next generation. In addition, the church is growing faster than Bible colleges and seminaries can produce godly, competent leaders. While postmodern America is drifting more and more away from Scripture, the urgency of the present is all the more apparent. Malphurs and Mancini note that today's leadership crisis is "in reality a leadership development crisis."[105] Just as Paul expected Timothy personally to follow his injunctions, so should leaders today. Thus, a concerted effort on the part of present leaders to train and disciple "Timothies" is needed.

These principles can be followed by local churches as well as parachurch ministries, such as Bible schools and seminaries. These principles are not impossible to follow or beyond the capability of leaders to obey. The value of these principles has not been given sufficient weight. "Leadership training today has yet to become a priority for most Christian organizations . . ."[106] While the focus of many is on church growth and other issues, the focus of the examples of Scripture that have been purveyed in this book is on training the next generation of leaders. As Malphurs and Mancini succinctly state, "The ultimate test of a leader isn't the magnitude of his or her ministry but whether that leader trains other leaders who can sustain the church or parachurch organization when he or she is no longer present."[107]

This view of ministry, while it may seem tedious or cumbersome, will eventually yield the greatest impact, in the context of the local church and in any culture. Just as Jesus' training of the Twelve resulted in world impact, so is the church today poised to make a similar impact. God has virtually brought the world to America, and the prospect of a worshipping community in every culture and language is a possibility if leaders

---

105. Malphurs and Mancini, *Building Leaders*, 10.
106. Malphurs and Mancini, *Building Leaders*, 11.
107. Malphurs and Mancini, *Building Leaders*, 11.

will grab hold of the present opportunity. Stanley, Joiner, and Jones clearly enunciated the present situation with its urgency.

> Replacing yourself begins with a shift in your thinking as a leader. It demands that you face some personal tendencies that could be unhealthy for your organization. The signs are more obvious than you might think: the pastor insists on being the only speaker; administrators are easily frustrated by suggestions; progress is slow because only a few people are allowed to make decisions; the same singers or musicians are featured every week; staff members routinely stay late because they think they're the only ones who can do a job; raises and bonuses reflect only personal productivity.[108]

Thus, the situation is urgent but doable. As Elisha slaughtered the ox and followed Elijah, it is time for the church to leave cultural ideas of training and embrace the principles discovered throughout the examples in Scripture. God the Holy Spirit breathed these passages as examples to give us hope and warning (Rom 15:4; 1 Cor 10:6).

---

108. Stanley, Joiner, and Jones, *7 Practices of Effective Ministry*, 161.

DISCUSSION QUESTIONS

1. Of all the examples listed above, which is the greatest example of the discipleship relationship for you? Why?

2. What example is the most surprising to you?

3. How can you apply Ephesians 4:11–16 in your ministry context?

4. Which of Jesus' steps in training the Twelve is the most difficult to follow? Which do you think would be the most rewarding?

5. Write a short plan on how you could put this into action.

Conclusion

In this book, we have examined eight principles from Scripture for equipping leaders. First, we must be an example who will leave a mark on the people we are training. We must be a model for them to follow. Second, we must develop a close relationship with the people we are training. Effective training begins with our students. As we know them more closely, we will come to understand their strengths, weaknesses, abilities, and spiritual gifts. Third, we saw that we must entrust sound teaching. Our students must be able to defend the essential doctrines of the faith. They must be able to articulate our core beliefs and carefully and gently instruct those who oppose us (false teachers). Fourth, we must give our students guided opportunities. Giving them practical opportunities where they can practice what they have been learning is so essential to real learning. Jesus taught his disciples with piecemeal lessons that, when practiced, were learned and retained. Fifth, we must entrust authority and ministry to our disciples as they prove their faithfulness. As a person demonstrates faithfulness, more responsibility may be entrusted with the authority to carry out their ministry. Sixth, our training must be local church focused. Training can be local church based or even in institutional settings, but the local church should still be the focus of our disciples' service. Seventh, our training must focus on Christ's mission of making disciples of all nations. As we give our students exposure to cross-cultural opportunities, these opportunities expose a person's weaknesses, strengths, prejudice, and bias, and become opportunities for discipleship and personal growth. Eighth, our training must focus on the renewing and empowering work of the Holy Spirit in a person's life. Finally, we examined the examples of Scripture that teach these principles.

As you have read through this, I pray that God has brought to light areas in your life and ministry where you can apply these principles. My prayer is that the Word of God, through the Holy Spirit, will increase and multiply through your life and ministry. For more information on Crossing Cultures International's ministry, please visit our website at https://www.cciequip.org. God bless you and your work!

DISCUSSION QUESTIONS

1. List all your takeaways (principles) that you have learned in this book.

2. How will you apply this to your life and ministry?

Bibliography

Abbott, T. K. *A Critical and Exegetical Commentary on the Epistles to the Ephesians and to the Colossians*. Edinburgh: T. & T. Clark, 1979.

Alford, Henry. *The Greek Testament*. Rev. by Everett F. Harrison. Vol. 1, *The Four Gospels*. Chicago: Moody, 1968.

Anthony F. Casey, "Majority-World Theological Education in the Globalized Age." https://trainingleadersinternational.org/jgc/136/majority-world-theological-education-in-the-globalized-age.

Arndt, William, Frederick W. Danker, Walter Bauer, and F. Wilbur Gingrich. *A Greek-English Lexicon of the New Testament and Other Early Christian Literature*. 3rd ed. Chicago: University of Chicago Press, 2000.

Ashley, Timothy R. *The Book of Numbers*. The New International Commentary on the Old Testament. Grand Rapids: Eerdmans, 1993.

Barclay, William, trans. *The Letters to Timothy, Titus, and Philemon*. Rev. ed. Philadelphia: Westminster, 1975.

Barna Group. "Pastors Share Top Reasons They've Considered Quitting Ministry in the Past Year." April 27, 2022. https://www.barna.com/research/pastors-quitting-ministry/.

Barrett, C. K. *A Critical and Exegetical Commentary on the Acts of the Apostles*. International Critical Commentary. Edinburgh: T. & T. Clark, 2004.

The Bible and Money. Knoxville, TN: Crown Financial Ministries, 2012.

Black, Allen, and Mark C. Black. *1 & 2 Peter*. The College Press NIV Commentary. Joplin, MO: College Press, 1998.

Blair, P. A. "Increase." In *New Bible Dictionary*, edited by D. R. W. Wood et al. Downers Grove, IL: InterVarsity, 1996.

Bock, Darrell L. *Luke*. The NIV Application Commentary. Grand Rapids: Zondervan, 1996.

Brand, Chad, et al., eds. "Increase." In *Holman Illustrated Bible Dictionary*, 816. Nashville: Holman, 2003.

Breen, Mike, and the 3DM team. *Building a Discipling Culture*. Pawleys Island, SC: 3 Dimension Ministries, 2011.

Brown, Francis, Samuel Rolles Driver, and Charles Augustus Briggs. *Enhanced Brown-Driver-Briggs Hebrew and English Lexicon*. Oxford: Clarendon, 1977.

Bruce, Alexander B. *The Training of the Twelve*. Reprint. New York: Cosmio, 2007.

Bruce, F. F. *The Book of the Acts*. The New International Commentary on the New Testament. Grand Rapids: Eerdmans, 1988.

———. *Commentary on the Book of Acts*. Grand Rapids: Eerdmans, 1960.

———. *The Epistles to the Colossians, to Philemon, and to the Ephesians.* Grand Rapids: Eerdmans, 1984.

C., Rebecca. "10 Advantages of Taking Opportunities in Life and Business." *Basics By Becca* (blog), October 13, 2021. https://basicsbybecca.com/blog/taking-opportunities.

Chan, Francis, and Danae Yankoski. *Forgotten God: Reversing Our Tragic Neglect of the Holy Spirit.* Colorado Springs, CO: David C. Cook, 2009.

Cole, R. Alan. *Exodus: An Introduction and Commentary.* Downers Grove, IL: InterVarsity, 1973.

Coleman, Robert E. *The Master Plan of Evangelism and Discipleship.* Peabody, MA: Hendrickson, 1987.

Constable, Thomas L. "1 Kings." In *The Bible Knowledge Commentary: An Exposition of the Scriptures,* edited by J. F. Walvoord and R. B. Zuck, vol. 1. Wheaton, IL: Victor, 1985.

Danker, Frederick W., Walter Bauer, William F. Arndt, and F. Wilbur Gingrich. *Greek-English Lexicon of the New Testament and Other Early Christian Literature.* 3rd ed. Chicago: University of Chicago Press, 2000.

David Garrison. *Church Planting Movements: How God Is Redeeming a Lost World.* Midlothian, VA: WIGTake, 2004.

———. *Church Planting Movements.* Richmond, VA: International Mission Board, 1999.

Duarte, Fabio. "Average Screen Time for Teens" https://explodingtopics.com/blog/screen-time-for-teens.

Duffield, Guy P., and Nathaniel M. Van Cleave. *Foundations of Pentecostal Theology.* Los Angeles: L.I.F.E. Bible College, 1983.

Eims, LeRoy. *The Lost Art of Disciple Making.* Grand Rapids: Zondervan, 1978.

Erickson, Millard J. *Christian Theology.* Kindle locations 224–28. Grand Rapids: Baker, 2013.

Ferguson, Dave, and Warren Bird. *Hero Maker: Five Essential Practices for Leaders to Multiply Leaders.* Grand Rapids: Zondervan, 2018.

"5 Leadership Thoughts from John C. Maxwell." May 10, 2019. https://blog.leadr.com/5-leadership-thoughts-from-john-c-maxwell.

Forman, Rowland, Jeff Jones, and Bruce Miller. *The Leadership Baton: An Intentional Strategy for Developing Leaders in Your Church.* Grand Rapids: Zondervan, 2004.

Foulkes, Francis. *The Epistle of Paul to the Ephesians: An Introduction and Commentary. The Tyndale New Testament Commentary.* Grand Rapids: Eerdmans, 1989.

Friedrich, Gerhard. *Theological Dictionary of the New Testament.* Translated and edited by Geoffrey W. Bromiley. Vol. 8. Grand Rapids: Eerdmans, 1972.

Gaebelein, Frank E., ed. *The Expositor's Bible Commentary with the New International of the Holy Bible.* Vol. 2. Grand Rapids: Zondervan, 1990.

———, ed. *The Expositor's Bible Commentary with the New International Version of the Holy Bible.* Vol. 4. Grand Rapids: Zondervan, 1988.

———, ed. *The Expositor's Bible Commentary with the New International of the Holy Bible.* Vol. 11. Grand Rapids: Zondervan, 1978.

Goppelt, Leonhard "Τύπος, Ἀντίτυπος, Τυπικός, Ὑποτύπωσις." In *Theological Dictionary of the New Testament,* edited by Gerhard Kittel, Geoffrey W. Bromiley, and Gerhard Friedrich, vol. 8. Grand Rapids: Eerdmans, 1964–.

Gordon, T. Daid. "'Equipping' Ministry in Ephesians 4?" *Journal of the Evangelical Theological Society* 37:1 (March 1994) 69–78.

Grudem, Wayne A. *1 Peter: An Introduction and Commentary*. Tyndale New Testament Commentary 17. Downers Grove, IL: InterVarsity, 1988.

———. *Systematic Theology: An Introduction to Biblical Doctrine*. 2nd ed. Grand Rapids: Zondervan Academic, 2020.

Gupta, Paul R., and Sherwood G. Lingenfelter. *Breaking Tradition to Accomplish Vision: Training Leaders for A Church Planting Movement: A Case from India*. Winona Lake, IN: BMH, 2006.

Guthrie, Donald. *The Pastoral Epistles: An Introduction and Commentary*. Reprint. Grand Rapids: Eerdmans, 1996.

Hames, Daniel, and Michael Reeves. *What Fuels the Mission of the Church?* Wheaton, IL: Crossway, 2022.

Harris, R. Laird, Gleason L. Archer Jr., and Bruce K. Waltke, eds. *Theological Wordbook of the Old Testament*. Chicago: Moody Press, 1999.

Harrison, Everett F. *Interpreting Acts*. Grand Rapids: Zondervan, 1986.

Hauck, Friedrich. "Μένω, Ἐμ-, Παρα-, Περι-, Προσμένω, Μονή, Ὑπομένω, Ὑπομονή." In *Theological Dictionary of the New Testament*, edited by Gerhard Kittel, Geoffrey W. Bromiley, and Gerhard Friedrich, 4:581–82. Electronic ed. Grand Rapids: Eerdmans, 1964–.

Henry, Matthew. *Matthew Henry's Commentary on the Whole Bible*. Vol. 2, *Joshua to Esther*. New York: Revell, n.d.

Hoke, Steve, and Bill Taylor. *Global Mission Handbook: A Guide for Crosscultural Service*. Rev. ed. Downers Grove, IL: InterVarsity, 2009.

Hull, Bill. *Jesus Christ Disciplemaker*. Grand Rapids: Baker, 2004.

"The Importance of Opportunity." October 25, 2023. https://www.linkedin.com/pulse/importance-opportunity-quantum-research-grip-b7cjf/.

Jamison, Robert. *A Commentary: Critical, Experimental, and Practical on the Old and New Testaments*. Vol. 1, part 1, *Genesis–Deuteronomy*. Grand Rapids: Eerdmans, 1984.

Keil, C. F., and F. Delitzsch. *Biblical Commentary on the Old Testament*. Translated by James Martin. Grand Rapids: Eerdmans, 1950.

Kelly, J. N. D. *A Commentary on the Pastoral Epistles*. Reprint. Grand Rapids: Baker, 1981.

Kistemaker, Simon J. *New Testament Commentary: Exposition of the Acts of the Apostles*. Grand Rapids: Baker, 1990.

Kittel, Gerhard, ed. *Theological Dictionary of the New Testament*. Translated by Geoffrey W. Bromiley. Vol. 1. Grand Rapids: Eerdmans, 1968.

Knight, George W. *The Pastoral Epistles: A Commentary on the Greek Text*. New International Greek Testament Commentary. Grand Rapids: Eerdmans, 1992.

Kreider, Alan. *The Patient Ferment of the Early Church: The Improbable Rise of Christianity in the Roman Empire*. Grand Rapids: Baker Academic, 2016.

Laing, Mark. "Recovering Missional Ecclesiology in Theological Education." *International Review of Mission* 98:1 (2009) 11–24.

Langer, Richard, and Joanne J. Jung. *The Call to Follow: Hearing Jesus in a Culture Obsessed with Leadership*. Wheaton, IL: Crossway, 2022.

Larson, Craig Brian. "Introduction." In *Mastering Church Finances*, by Richard L. Bergstrom, Gary Fenton, and Wayne A. Pohl. Mastering Ministry. Portland, OR: Multnomah, Christianity Today, 1992.

Lenski, R. C. H. *The Interpretation of the Acts of the Apostles.* Minneapolis: Augsburg, 1961.

Lewis, Jack P. "The Schools of the Prophets." *Restoration Quarterly* 9:1 (1966) 1–10.

Lock, Walter. *A Critical and Exegetical Commentary on the Pastoral Epistles (I & II Timothy and Titus).* Reprint. International Critical Commentary. Edinburgh: T. & T. Clark, 1973.

Lockyer, Herbert. *All the Apostles of the Bible.* Grand Rapids: Zondervan, 1972.

Longenecker, Harold L. *Growing Leaders by Design.* Grand Rapids: Kregel, 1995.

MacArthur, John. *The MacArthur New Testament Commentary: 2 Timothy.* Chicago: Moody, 1995.

———. *Twelve Ordinary Men.* Nashville: Thomas Nelson, 2002.

Malphurs, Aubrey, and Will Mancini. *Building Leaders: Blueprints for Developing Leadership at Every Level of Your Church* Grand Rapids: Baker, 2004.

Marshall, I. Howard. *The Acts of the Apostles: An Introduction and Commentary.* Reprint. Grand Rapids: Eerdmans, 1994.

———. *New Testament Theology: Many Witnesses, One Gospel.* Downers Grove, IL: InterVarsity, 2004.

Maxwell, John C. *Life Wisdom: Quotes from John C. Maxwell, Insights from Leadership.* Nashville: B&H, 2014.

———. *The 21 Irrefutable Laws of Leadership.* Nashville: Thomas Nelson, 1998.

Mock, Dennis. *Program Summary Manual.* Atlanta: Bible Training Centre for Pastors, 2023.

Mohler, R. Albert, Jr. "The Scandal of Biblical Illiteracy: It's Our Problem." January 20, 2016. https://albertmohler.com/2016/01/20/the-scandal-of-biblical-illiteracy-its-our-problem-4/.

Moreau, A. Scott, Harold Netland, and Charles van Engen. *Evangelical Dictionary of World Missions.* Baker Reference Library. Grand Rapids: Baker, 2000.

Moulton, James Hope, and George Milligan. In *The Vocabulary of the Greek Testament.* London: Hodder and Stoughton, 1930.

Nicoll, W. Robertson. *The Expositor's Greek Testament: Commentary.* Vol. 2. New York: George H. Doran, n.d.

———. *The Expositor's Greek Testament.* Reprint. Grand Rapids: Eerdmans, 1990.

Peters, George W. *A Biblical Theology of Missions.* Chicago: Moody, 1972.

Pettegrew, Larry D. 2004. "The Perspicuity of Scripture." *Master's Seminary Journal* 15:2 (Fall 2004) 209–25.

Phillips, John. *Exploring Ephesians & Philippians: An Expository Commentary.* The John Phillips Commentary Series. Grand Rapids: Kregel, 1995.

Piper, John *Let the Nations Be Glad!: The Supremacy of God in Missions.* Grand Rapids: Baker, 1993.

Pohl, Wayne. "The Spiritual Side of Mammon." In *Mastering Church Finances,* by Richard L. Bergstrom, Gary Fenton, and Wayne A. Pohl. Mastering Ministry. Portland, OR: Multnomah, Christianity Today, 1992.

Polhill, John B. *Acts.* New American Commentary 26. Nashville: Broadman & Holman, 1992.

Qureshi, Nabeel. *Seeking Allah, Finding Jesus: A Devout Muslim Encounters Christianity.* Grand Rapids: Zondervan, 2016.

Ragan, Ben Laurence. *Help! We're Going on a Short-Term Trip! Team Leader's Manual.* Marietta, GA: n.p., 2015.

Rhodes, Matt. *No Shortcut to Success: A Manifesto for Modern Missions*. Wheaton, IL: Crossway, 2022.

Robertson, A. T. *Word Pictures in the New Testament*. Vol. 4, *The Epistles of Paul*. Grand Rapids: Baker, 1931.

Ryrie, Charles Caldwell. *Basic Theology: A Popular Systematic Guide to Understanding Biblical Truth*. Chicago: Moody, 1999.

Sailhamer, John H. "Genesis." In *The Expositor's Bible Commentary: Genesis, Exodus, Leviticus, Numbers*, edited by Frank E. Gaebelein, vol. 2. Grand Rapids: Zondervan, 1990.

Salmond, S. D. F. "The Epistle to the Ephesians." In *The Expositor's Greek Testament*, edited by W. Robertson Nicoll, vol. 3. Reprint. Grand Rapids: Eerdmans, 1990.

Schreiner, Patrick. *The Mission of the Triune God: A Theology of Acts*. Wheaton, IL: Crossway, 2022.

Schrenk, Gottlob. "Διαλέγομαι, Διαλογίζομαι, Διαλογισμός." In *Theological Dictionary of the New Testament*, edited by Gerhard Kittel, Geoffrey W. Bromiley, and Gerhard Friedrich, 2:93. Electronic ed. Grand Rapids: Eerdmans, 1964–.

"Shorter Catechism of the Assembly of Divines." https://www.apuritansmind.com/westminster-standards/shorter-catechism/.

Smietana, Bob. "Willow Creek Elders and Pastor Heather Larson Resign over Bill Hybels." https://www.christianitytoday.com/news/2018/august/willow-creek-bill-hybels-heather-larson-elders-resign-inves.html.

Stanley, Andy, Reggie Joiner, and Lane Jones. *7 Practices of Effective Ministry*. Colorado Springs: Multnomah, 2004.

Steffen, Tom. *Passing the Baton: Church Planting that Empowers*. La Habra, CA: Center for Organizational & Ministry Development, 1997.

Stott, John R. W. *The Message of 2 Timothy: Guard the Gospel*. Downers Grove, IL: Inter-Varsity, 1973.

"Take Opportunities While They Are There." *Morning Coach* blog, December 8, 2022. https://www.morningcoach.com/blog/take-opportunities-while-they-are-there.

Terry, John Mark, Ebbie Smith, and Justice Anderson. *Missiology: An Introduction to the Foundations, History, and Strategies of World Missions*. Nashville: Broadman & Holman, 1998.

Thiselton, Anthony C. *The First Epistle to the Corinthians: A Commentary on the Greek Text*. New International Greek Testament Commentary. Grand Rapids: Eerdmans, 2000.

Toussaint, Stanley D. "Acts." In *The Bible Knowledge Commentary: An Exposition of the Scriptures*, edited by J. F. Walvoord and R. B. Zuck, vol. 2. Wheaton, IL: Victor, 1985.

Wagner, Brian. "The Perspicuity of Scripture: Rehearsing the Testimony from Christian History of Those Who Consistently Held to the View as Foundational to Their Evangelical Hermeneutic." *Journal of Dispensational Theology* 12:17 (December 2008) 73–89.

Waltke, Bruce K., and Cathi J. Fredricks. *Genesis: A Commentary*. Grand Rapids: Zondervan, 2001.

Walton, John H. 2001. *Genesis*. The NIV Application Commentary. Grand Rapids: Zondervan.

Wanamaker, Charles A. *The Epistle to the Thessalonians: A Commentary on the Greek Text*. New International Greek Testament Commentary. Grand Rapid: Eerdmans, 1990.

Westcott, Brooke Foss. *Saint Paul's Epistle to the Ephesians*. Reprint. Grand Rapids: Baker, 1979.
Wilkins, Michael J. *Following the Master: Discipleship in the Steps of Jesus*. Grand Rapids: Zondervan, 1992.
Wiseman, Daniel J. *1 and 2 Kings: An Introduction and Commentary*. Downers Grove: InterVarsity, 1993.
Wood, Leon J. *The Prophets of Israel*. Grand Rapids: Baker, 1979.
Wright, Christopher J. H. *The Great Story and the Great Commission: Participating in the Biblical Drama of Mission*. Edited by H. Daniel Zacharias. Acadia Studies in Bible and Theology. Grand Rapids: Baker Academic, 2023.
Wyatt, Rocky. *Pastoral Training in the Church*. N.p., XL Ministries, 2021.
York, Hershael. "Why Seminary Can Never Qualify Anyone for Ministry." *Pastor Well* blog, February 13, 2014. http://www.pastorwell.com/blog/2014/2/13/t5c5n7ahmtsobew9oz7my2p865qurw.
Zurlo, Gina A. *Global Christianity: A Guide to the World's Largest Religion from Afghanistan to Zimbabwe*. Grand Rapids: Zondervan Academic, 2022.

www.ingramcontent.com/pod-product-compliance
Lightning Source LLC
Chambersburg PA
CBHW062039220426
43662CB00010B/1572